KENYA'S ROAD TO SUSTAINABLE DEVELOPMENT (1963 – 2050)

Looking Back to Look Forward

D R W A N Z A M B O L E

Printed in the United Kingdom

ISBN: 978-1-3999-1172-6

Published by Wanza Mbole

Editorial Production: The Editor's Chair

To my late parents, Anna and Mulandi Mbole,
who demonstrated to me the value of the common
good at an early age by giving out of their poverty.

TABLE OF CONTENTS

LIST OF FIGURES

LIST OF TABLES

TABLE OF ACRONYMS

ACRONYMS	DESCRIPTION
CIA	Central Intelligence Agency
COVID	Coronavirus Disease
DEMDIV	Demographic Dividend
DRFD	District Focus for Rural Development
EDPRISUR	Education Primary Survival Rate
EMRG	Economic Management for Renewed Growth
EPI	Environmental Performance Index
ERS	Economic Recovery Strategy
GDP	Gross Domestic Product
GDPPC	Gross Domestic Product Per Capita
GDPR	Gross Domestic Product Growth Rate
GEI	Green Economy Index
GEMA	Gikuyu, Embu and Meru Association
GINIDOM	Domestic Gini Index of Inequality
GNI	Gross National Income
HDI	Human Development Index
IDA	International Development Association
IMF	International Monetary Fund
KANU	Kenya African National Union

LIFEXP	Life Expectancy
LMCP	Last Mile Connectivity Programme
MDG	Millennium Development Goal
MFP	Multifactor Productivity
MFPHC	Human Capital Contribution to Multifactor Productivity Rate
MFPRATE	Multifactor Productivity Rate
NARC	National Rainbow Coalition
NESC	National Economic and Social Council
NPEP	National Poverty Eradication Plan
ODM	Orange Democratic Movement
OECD	Organisation for Economic Cooperation and Development
POVGAP	Poverty Gap
PPP	Purchasing Power Parity
PRSP	Poverty Reduction Strategy Paper
SDD	Social Dimensions of Development
SI	Sustainability Index
SSA	Sub-Saharan Africa
TFP	Total Factor of Productivity
TFR	Total Fertility Rate
TFRM	Total Fertility Rate Multiplier
UN	United Nations
UNDP	United Nations Development Programme
US	United States of America
USAID	United States Agency for International Development
VADD	Value Added

FOREWORD

I had the privilege of journeying with Dr. Wanza Mbole through the Doctor of Strategic Leadership Programme (with a focus on Strategic Foresight) at Regent University, Virginia Beach USA. We soon realised we had something in common: frustration with the state of things in Africa and a burning desire to make a difference. Dr. Mbole is a futurist and an economic inclusion enthusiast with over 20 years of experience in development work. She focuses on creating a more equitable and sustainable society with equitable access to opportunities and resources that enable one to contribute to and benefit from sustained development. She is a co-author of *Capital Transformed* in which she has written a chapter on how capitalism could be transformed to reduce inequality.

In this book, Dr. Mbole addresses very pertinent issues facing Kenya and most Sub-Saharan African countries: sub-optimal and inequitable growth. While there has been growth over the decades, it has been erratic, non-inclusive and the benefits disproportionately shared. Kenya and indeed many Sub-Saharan countries presently have an unprecedented opportunity to leverage their youth population bulge to realise inclusive and sustained growth. Forty-eight per cent of Kenya's population is in the age bracket of 14 – 29 years. This is a unique 'window of opportunity', which, if harnessed as China did, could propel growth and prosperity. On the other hand, if squandered, the consequences could be dire, ranging from mass unemployment to social unrest. One strategic way of harnessing this population bulge is by deliberately focusing on developing the youthful population through education.

Dr. Mbole demonstrates that education is a significant driver of equitable social change. It allows individuals to qualify for a greater range of job opportunities, contributes to an improved human development index (HDI), reduces maternal and infant mortality rates, and improves access to services. Studies point to the high productivity reward of education in low-income countries. Patrinos and

Psacharopoulos estimated the average social rate of return from completing primary education in low-income countries to be 21 per cent with lower figures for secondary (16 per cent) and tertiary education (11 per cent).

Pre-COVID-19, net primary education enrolment rates across the developing world were on the rise. However, to enrol does not assure completion. In many low-income countries, the quality of instruction is low, attendance rates of both children and teachers leave much to be desired and one-half of the entering cohorts may drop out before completing the primary cycle. Failure to complete the primary cycle is usually a harbinger of adult illiteracy, as it requires at least five to six years of schooling for children to achieve and retain basic literacy and numeracy. Literacy surveys conducted in African countries and elsewhere indicate that a high share of the adults who have completed less than five or six years of primary schooling remain functionally illiterate and innumerate for the rest of their lives. Especially striking in the data is the very limited impact on lifelong literacy from as many as three years of schooling. Although it is still an imperfect measure of whether the next generation achieves basic literacy and numeracy, primary school completion is a far better measure than enrolment in assessing overall education performance in low-income countries.

Basic education's most important goal is assuring that the next generation is not only able to read and write, but also that it has the essential skills to earn a living. Further, the foundation for a country's secondary and tertiary education sectors is a properly functioning primary sector. With few exceptions, literacy is a necessary condition for a country to escape poverty. However, governments in low-income countries are largely not focusing on creating effective primary school systems. Often, other powerful incentives in the context of poverty divert governments from assuring a reasonably efficient school system.

Improving primary school completion has long ranging benefits across the whole of society. It boosts several factors that lead to improved conditions for the population that ultimately improve the Gross Domestic Product per

Capita (GDPPC). The United Nations Sustainable Development Goal No. 4 is *'To ensure inclusive and quality education for all and promote lifelong learning'*. Few countries have risen out of extreme poverty with adult literacy below 80 per cent, and few countries have achieved respectable population health outcomes with female literacy below 80 per cent. However, achieving a high literacy rate requires effective governments that are able and willing to assure the supply of adequate education services at low cost to poor families. While a high adult literacy rate does not guarantee a country will overcome extreme poverty, its absence almost certainly guarantees poverty for the majority.

Enhancing human capital requires large long-term investment from the government, supplemented by investments from other institutions such as religious and other non-government organisations, as well as for-profit firms. It takes a reasonably effective government to produce effective faculty, supply quality education services at low cost to parents, and enable NGOs and private schools to flourish. There is also a pressing need for more expenditure on education and a better understanding of priorities to guide the flow of donor aid.

Though basic education is among the most expensive, complex and labour-intensive activities that governments undertake, its dividends are long lasting. Teaching is a professional activity that does not demand as high a level of professional expertise as healthcare. Effective teachers require a minimum of upper-secondary education, further training in education techniques, field support, decent school facilities and systems to measure learning outcomes. School administrators need to be competent and free from partisan political interference. A good education system also needs to involve parents in local school affairs. Reconciling these requirements and achieving progress is feasible, even on very modest budgets, but it is naïve to think that doing so is politically or administratively easy.

Dr. Mbole uses the International Futures (IFs) model, a highly sophisticated and comprehensive forecasting modelling system for this study. The model offers an integrated approach to exploring and understanding human development and the broad implications of policy choices (Window on the World, 2013). Dr. Mbole's research indicates that a focus on improving human capital would result in an improvement in the GDP per capita of the nation. The progress would be slow if based on these parameters alone. These changes would have a profound sustainable impact on the quality of life of all Kenyans and could happen with relatively little risk and fewer interventions compared to other policy interventions.

One challenge decision and policymakers face is that benefits from quality investments in education are realisable only after a lengthy time lag and yet both donors and aid recipient governments want quick results. It will often appear more attractive to ignore the problems of a weak school system and instead respond to poverty via policies that provide an immediate income transfer.

It is my hope that Dr. Mbole's work will help policy and decisionmakers in Africa to take the opportunity to create the future that we prefer by investing in education for inclusive and sustainable growth.

Dr. James Magara

Author of *Positioning Africa For the 21st Century: The Pivotal Role of Leadership and Think Tanks*

Notes

Bruns, B., Mingat, A. & Rakotomalala (2003). *A Chance for every child: Achieving universal primary education by 2015*. Washington: The World Bank.

Henderson, N. (2014). The new global professionals: Flexible and forward-thinking. *Foreign Policy*, (208), A2-A3, A5, A7, A9, A11.

Patrinos, H. & Psacharopoulos, G. (2011). Education: Past, Present and Future Global Challenges. *Working paper 5616*

Richards, J. (2012). What CIDA should do: The case for focusing aid on better schools. *Commentary - C.D.Howe Institute*, (349), 0_1,0_2,1-30.

United Nations (2010). *Millennium Development Goals Report*. 2010.

Window on the world. (2013). *Development, 56*(4), 536-540.

ACKNOWLEDGEMENTS

I am most grateful to all those who have walked with me and supported me in various ways while writing this book. I am particularly thankful to my husband, Francis Namboya, who has been a constant source of encouragement and a pillar of strength throughout this journey. Many thanks to Dr. Virginia Richardson of Regent University for her guidance, relentless nudges, and invaluable comments. My appreciation to Dr. James Magara and Dr. Kriz David, my co-sojourners in pursuit of knowledge in 'Foresight'. Finally, I appreciate Denise and Sophie of The Editor's Chair who have provided immeasurable support to get this book published. As evident in the myriad of references, I have drawn knowledge and wisdom from many experts on the economic and development history of Kenya, and sustainable and inclusive development. I express my gratitude to them all and absolve them of any errors and misrepresentations in this book. The views expressed in this book are mine and not necessarily theirs.

INTRODUCTION

The path to sustainable and inclusive development is not through redistribution of national resources but by providing most of the population with opportunities to actively participate in the economic development of their nation and to share in its economic growth. Whether or not Kenya has recognised this, its pursuit of sustainable and inclusive growth has been long and winding and its efforts have borne minimal fruit.

Following independence from the British government in 1963, the new African administration set out to deliver the populace from ignorance, disease, and poverty. In its endeavour to realise this noble mission, Kenya has in the last 50 years formulated and implemented many development strategies. Overall, Kenya's developmental results have been mixed and disappointing to many. While some level of economic growth has been realised, this has been minimal, erratic, and cyclical, and the benefits far from equitably spread. The economy's growth as shown by the gross domestic product growth has not surpassed two per cent per annum a third of the time since independence. Yet this is not due to lack of economic potential. The country has missed many opportunities for growth and development.

The means to realising its goal were clearly encapsulated in its first development blueprint, the *Sessional Paper No. 10 of 1965 on African Socialism and Its Application to Planning in Kenya*, which laid the foundation for the country's development. More than 40 years later, the current development roadmap, Vision 2030, was introduced to make Kenya a globally prosperous and competitive nation, providing a high quality of life to its citizens by the year 2030. After 10 years, the nation is no closer to realising the goal than it was in 2007 when the vision was launched. Based on the current trajectory, attaining an average annual economic growth rate of 10 per cent, the goal on which the vision is founded, is not feasible.

Despite the many challenges that Kenya faces in its search for sustainable and inclusive development, opportunities exist and key among these are its people. Kenya is a 'young' nation with a median age of 19.5 years and 60 per cent of its population below the age of 24 years (World Factbook). This youthful population is potentially a huge blessing to the nation, but it could turn out to be its curse in the future if not well managed. One way of benefitting from this youth bulge is by creating equal opportunities for the young to actively engage in economic development and ensuring that they, in turn, benefit from it.

Kenya is one of the countries where human capital has a significant contribution to multifactor productivity and hence economic growth. This situation is projected to continue in the future. Developing the capacity of Kenya's young population through education and training will, therefore, play a fundamental role in improving labour productivity and economic growth in turn. While the nation has largely attained universal primary education, this is no longer sufficient for the current marketplace and the society due to the fast evolving technologically driven change. As shown in this book, secondary school education for the masses is what will yield the desired sustainable and inclusive development.

Additionally, this book demonstrates that while Vision 2030 shows some prospects for improving the economic situation in future, its policy interventions and strategies will not enable the nation to achieve its goal of lasting prosperity and a high quality of life. However, driven by the current youth bulge and the declining fertility rates, Kenya is poised for a demographic dividend between 2040 and 2060. The demographic dividend is a window of opportunity for rapid economic growth and poverty reduction that if properly exploited would thrust the nation onto the path for sustainable and inclusive development.

Realising this demographic dividend will depend on Kenya's ability to harness its chief asset, the young population, and develop it to reap the anticipated economic gains. This book provides practical policy guidance that will enable Kenya to realise this benefit and subsequently sustainable development. By halving its total fertility rates and tripling the survival rates in upper secondary education, the country would ready itself to reap from this imminent demographic dividend in future.

The consequence of doing nothing or not doing the right things today would be a demographic bomb in the future in the form of a mass of economically disengaged and hence frustrated youths that could in turn lead to a social, economic or political crisis or a combination of these. Additionally, by failing to realise the demographic dividend, Kenya would have missed an economic opportunity for generations to come as the population bulge would gradually transition to a less productive age, increasing the economic burden of the country due to high dependency ratios. Using the guidance provided here, Kenya needs to ensure that the right policy interventions are formulated and effectively implemented to make the country ready to take advantage of this opportunity when the window opens.

Furthermore, this book looks at Kenya's past development journey and at Malaysia, which has been a development success story despite its 1960s historical and economic parallels to Kenya, with a view to understand the divergence and draw lessons for the future. The book is organised as follows. Chapter 1 reviews Kenya's development history and provides an understanding of the interventions and the factors that have bolstered or hindered the realisation of lasting and inclusive growth. Chapter 2 provides a comprehensive understanding of sustainable and inclusive development and its fundamental building blocks. It also presents indicators for measuring progress towards sustainable development.

Chapter 3 reviews Vision 2030, Kenya's current development roadmap, and assesses its ability to deliver inclusive and sustained development. Chapter 4 identifies the opportunities and conditions for Kenya to realise sustainable growth by emulating Malaysia, which was its peer in the early 1960s yet has been more successful in achieving this goal. It outlines the prerequisites for emulation and identifies the key success factors behind Malaysia's success. Chapter 5 provides an understanding of how human capital development can be used to realise lasting and inclusive growth and identifies where Kenya's opportunities for sustainable development lie.

Using scenario analysis, Chapter 6 uses the human capital model developed in Chapter 5 to identify high leverage points that would get Kenya onto the path of sustainable and inclusive development. Chapter 7 uses the model developed in Chapter 5 and the policy interventions that emerge from Chapter 6 to determine if Kenya is on the right path to sustainable and inclusive development. It also makes recommendations on practical policy interventions for attaining this goal based on the scenario analysis results from Chapter 6.

A high leverage point for Kenya as demonstrated later in this book is investing in girls' education. Keeping a girl in school even for one extra year equips her with skills for life and enhances her capacity to generate income. Often, it delays the time that she can give birth and empowers her to make decisions that relate to when to start a family and the number of children she can have. Ultimately, this impacts the national total fertility rate, that is the average number of children a woman gives birth to, and inclusive growth.

Finally, development cannot be sustainable unless it is inclusive—a term which will be defined in Chapter 2. While sustainable would imply inclusive, the phrase 'sustainable and inclusive development' rather than 'sustainable development' has been used throughout this book for emphasis. 'Growth' and 'development' have also been used interchangeably in the text.

Please note that the analysis and projections presented in this book do not take into consideration the impact of the COVID-19 pandemic on the Kenyan economy, which happened subsequently.

CHAPTER 1

The journey to the present

A journey of a thousand miles starts with one step.
— Japanese proverb

Kenya attained independence from the British in 1963. At independence, there was a marked difference between the economic status of its colonial masters and the majority black population. Frustrated by a situation where the resources of the country were mainly benefitting the colonial masters (non-Africans) as Kenyans remained uneducated, untrained, and inexperienced, the new African government set out to mobilise resources to attain rapid economic growth that would benefit its people. This desire for a prosperous and more equitable society was encapsulated in the *Sessional Paper No. 10 of 1965 on African Socialism and Its Application to Planning in Kenya* and has remained the development pursuit of the nation, with each subsequent strategy being focused on this goal.

Yet, a look at the outcomes from Kenya's past development blueprints leaves one wondering whether the goal is attainable. Today, this pursuit of rapid economic growth that benefits most Kenyans feels like a mirage, a chase after the wind. This chapter looks at Kenya's development history in light of the nation's ability to realise sustainable and inclusive development. It explores the various national development strategies that have been used thus far and their effectiveness in delivering sustainable and inclusive growth.

Past roadmaps

Since independence in 1963, various Kenyan governments have strived to rally the nation around a common agenda for development by formulating and leading the implementation of various development roadmaps. All these roadmaps have sought the same destination: a prosperous society built through economic growth and poverty reduction, which is tantamount to sustainable and inclusive development. While some of these strategies have deliberately endeavoured to build on previously successful ones, others have been disjointed and hence less impactful. Some have ended up taking the nation on costly detours from this development path.

Kenya's biggest challenge remains how to realise and sustain a high rate of economic growth at levels that can reduce poverty and deliver high standards of living and well-being to most Kenyans as promised at independence. The search for sustainable and inclusive development has been a challenging endeavour, as exemplified by the constant shifts in policy and strategy. In all these policy agendas, the persuasion, at least as stated, has been development for poverty reduction and sharing of the resultant economic benefits with most Kenyans.[1] The pursuit which started in 1963 is still on. Each of the consecutive development strategies merely marks yet another step in the journey.

Besides, the immediately after-independence efforts that were directly targeted at ensuring that the poor were economically engaged and hence poverty reduction, subsequent strategies which were focused on select key economic sectors, such as services and industry, and assumed an automatic trickle-down effect to the poor, were less effective. These programmes had little success in engaging the poor who are a significant proportion of the population and hence resulted in less economic growth and more inequality. Additionally, some of these policies only sought to address specific constraints to development without looking at the entire economy. Even where the stipulated policy interventions seemed to address broader economic issues, their effectiveness was compromised by the lack of coordination and collaboration in implementation.

Kenya's journey to sustainable and inclusive development has been long, yet the destination seems almost as distant in sight as when the journey first begun. Some of the development initiatives in this journey in addition to the Sessional Paper No. 10 of 1965, include the Economic Recovery Strategy for Wealth and Employment Creation, ERS, and the current Vision 2030. Outlined here are some of the strategies that the country has developed and implemented in the past decades, their goals, and a brief assessment of their achievements in relation to attaining sustainable and inclusive development.

Sessional Paper No. 10 of 1965 on African Socialism and Its Application to Planning in Kenya

Immediately after gaining self-independence from its colonial masters, the Kenyan leadership set out to free its citizenry from ignorance, disease, and poverty. The government envisaged fighting these three as the path to prosperity for the masses in this newly born republic. Several strategies have been developed and implemented to realise this noble mission starting with the Sessional Paper No. 10 of 1965. This first post-independence development blueprint sought to put in place the measures to ensure rapid economic development and social progress for all citizens.

The strategic areas emphasised in this paper were smallholder agricultural production and education (enrolment in primary and secondary schools), which were envisaged to present the greatest opportunity for the majority, who were rural-based, to participate in the development of the nation. Smallholder production and primary school enrolment had grown by 21 per cent and 15 per cent, respectively, in the one-and-a-half years since independence by the time Sessional Paper 10 was finalised.

The sessional paper embraced African socialism which its authors described as a deviation from Western capitalism and Eastern communism. African socialism meant creation and use of an economic system that was not imported from any country but would incorporate compatible and useful practices from other places. This Africanised system of development was to draw out the best of the African traditions for development, such as the highly collectivist nature of their society for harmony and development, and to rely less on relationships with other countries. The latter is not surprising given that the unpleasant memories of the nation's relationship with its colonial masters were still fresh.

The system also needed to be robust, adapting rapidly to the changing circumstances. The paper embraced the understanding that the prosperity of the nation demanded prosperity of its citizens. It summarised the essence of sustainable and inclusive development, as we know it today, in these words:

> It implies a mutual responsibility by society and its members to do their very best for each other with the full knowledge and understanding that if society prospers its members will share in that prosperity and that society cannot prosper without the full co-operation of its members.[2]

In Sessional Paper No. 10 of 1965, Kenya set out to attain five objectives: political equality, social justice, human dignity—including freedom of conscience, freedom from want, disease, and exploitations, equal opportunities, and high, growing and equitably distributed per capita incomes.[3] According to the authors, Kenya was to always serve the interests and needs of the majority and never to become an instrument for use by special interest groups to benefit themselves. The need and desire for sustainable and inclusive development were explicitly entrenched in the vision for this young nation, with universal education at its core.

The Africanised system of development envisaged in the sessional paper was to be adaptable—flexible enough to enable the country to make progress toward its ultimate development objectives, while at the same time solving its immediate problems with efficiency by adapting itself to the changing circumstances. The paper also encapsulated the value of relationships with other countries. Although the issue of Kenya's dependence on any nation was abhorred, the paper expressed Kenya's willingness and desire 'to borrow technological knowledge and proven economic methods from any country—without commitment',[4] to seek technical and financial assistance, and to participate in world trade.

The sessional paper laid out the mandate to stimulate accumulation of capital for development, while at the same time deterring individual wealth accumulation by putting in place measures such as capital gain, inheritance taxes and death duties. These disincentives were meant to make it hard for the wealthy to pass on their wealth perpetually across generations at the expense of other members of society. Even though the intentions of the paper were good, its implementation proved challenging. However, Sessional Paper No. 10 of 1965 is to this day one of the two most effective development strategies that Kenya has had since independence, as we will see later in this chapter when we look at the nation's economic performance over the decades.

Right after independence, the government identified three constraints to human development: poverty, disease and illiteracy. The paper set out the long-term vision and laid the groundwork for Kenya's development journey as reflected in its measures to fight against these. It provided guidelines to policy formulation for the economic future of the country and aimed to give long-term benefits to most Kenyans and the nation as a whole.[5] The effectiveness and success of the Sessional Paper No. 10 of 1965 are exemplified by the fact that Kenya attained substantial economic growth in the 1960s and 1970s, and its policies were emulated by many, including the East Asia Tigers.

The Sessional Paper No. 10 of 1965 marked the beginning of Kenya's quest for sustainable and inclusive development, with several development plans, strategies, and papers having been developed and implemented since then. These include: the 1994 Social Dimensions of Development (SDD) programme, the National Poverty Eradication Plan (1999 -2015), the Economic Recovery Strategy for Wealth and Employment Creation, ERS (2003 – 2007), and the current Vision 2030 (2008 – 2030). A summary of these development plans is presented below. As you will notice, besides Vision 2030, most of these development plans were short-term and failed to cast a long-term vision for the country's development.

District Focus for Rural Development (DRFD)

The District Focus for Rural Development strategy was launched in 1983 to stimulate broader participation in national development by shifting policy formulation and implementation to the districts.[6] The overarching aim of this decentralisation was to stimulate rural development through problem identification and prioritisation, resource mobilisation, implementation, and equitable allocation of resources.[7] Resources were to be allocated to the districts from the national kitty, with poorer districts getting more. The expectation was that this would result in a bottom-up kind of development.

Although the planning and implementation framework for district level development was created and provided at the national level, the DRFD failed to deliver the expected economic development results. This is because the process was patronised by the government district development officers who left no room for input by or collaboration with others.[8] Consequently, instead of stimulating economic growth, the strategy left the nation economically weaker than it was before.

Sessional Paper No. 1 of 1986 on Economic Management for Renewed Growth (EMRG)

The development of this sessional paper happened in the backdrop of a decade of poor economic performance and a worsening poverty situation in Kenya. The overarching goal of the EMRG was economic growth with a focus on addressing the issues around economic stagnation by managing high budget deficits, promoting the private sector, and correcting restrictive foreign trade policies.[9] The outcome of this concerted effort was that the government shifted its focus from rural development and poverty alleviation, and by extension, the populace. Government subsidies and basic social services were withdrawn. Unsurprisingly, like its preceding plan, it did not accomplish much growth.

Social Dimensions of Development (SDD) Programme

The Social Dimensions of Development programme was developed and launched in 1994 with an aim to cushion the poor against the adverse effects caused by the economic reforms of the 1980s.[10] As mentioned under the EMRG, these changes related to a reduction in the provision of basic services such as education and health for the poor and removal of crucial government subsidies such as those for rural agriculture, leading to a loss of jobs and erosion of the purchasing power of the rural poor, who comprised the majority of the population.

The design of the SDD programme was flawed—it was too focused on rural development without clear links to macroeconomic development, which was essential to realise the effects anticipated.[11] Additionally, it was largely dependent on donor funding for implementation, which did not materialise due to concerns related to the programme design, that is the objectives, scope, and implementation and other national issues.[12] The most significant of these funding gaps, both in terms of real monetary value and signalling, resulted from the International Monetary Fund's and the World Bank's suspension of their support to Kenya in 1997, citing widespread government corruption.[13]

Given these challenges in its implementation, the SDD programme had little impact on eradicating poverty and attaining development as summed up in United Nations Development Programme's (UNDP) *Kenya Human Development Report* of 1999: 'almost half the Kenyans are poor and their plight is not improving'.[14] The report outlined some of the persistent development issues, such as growing inequality and poverty, rapid population growth, and slow economic growth.[15] A common theme in this report was the need for gender mainstreaming for development. The UNDP report emphasised that the full participation and contribution of women was crucial for the achievement of sustainable development for Kenya.

National Poverty Eradication Plan (1999 -2015)

Following the failure to successfully implement the SDD programme, Kenya's National Poverty Eradication Plan (NPEP) was developed in 1999 with the support of UNDP. Building on the lessons from the SDD programme, the NPEP was driven by the need for a more comprehensive policy and planning framework for poverty eradication.[16] NPEP's objective was to alleviate poverty in line with the United Nations' Millennium Development Goals (MDGs). Its main aim was to halve Kenya's poverty level by 2015. The MDGs were eight development goals adopted by the 191 member nations of the United Nations in 1999 for attaining global peace, security, and development.

The NPEP was a 15-year development plan to 2015 that was intended to reduce poverty by 50 per cent (20 per cent by 2004 and a further 30 per cent by 2010)[17]; increase primary enrolment by 15 per cent by 2005; increase primary school completion rates (especially for girls) by 19 per cent in the first six years; to provide access to safe water for all by 2010, and to improve agriculture through technical assistance in the form of key messages[18] among other things. The plan, which was developed using a bottom-up participatory approach and through extensive consultations between the civil society, non-governmental organisations (NGOs), and government agencies, was to be implemented in three five-year phases starting from 2000.[19] The first of these five-year strategies was the Poverty Reduction Strategy Paper discussed below.

Poverty Reduction Strategy Paper, PRSP (2001 – 2003)

At the time of developing the Poverty Reduction Strategy Paper (PRSP), Kenya was going through the worst economic crisis since its independence.[20] By the year 2000, Kenya's GDP growth rate had fallen to less than 0.2 per cent, and nearly 60 per cent of Kenyans were living below the national poverty line.[21] Development partners funding support such as the IMF and World Bank had been withdrawn, crippling implementation of the government's development plans.

Following a largely failed SDD strategy and years of minimal economic activity, the leadership desperately needed to jumpstart Kenya's development. The PRSP was a short-term strategy launched in 2001 and the first of three phases of the 15-year long-term National Poverty Eradication Plan (NPEP) of 1999. As a sub-plan within NPEP, PRSP had multiple objectives aimed both at reducing poverty and increasing economic growth by providing the critical links between the government and its development partners such as the World Bank and the IMF to realise the MDGs.[22] The PRSP was envisaged as the right instrument for this.

At the time of its launch, the PRSP was described as the most focused and comprehensive policy in the fight against poverty since independence.[23] The paper was aimed at facilitating sustainable and rapid economic growth, improving governance and security, increasing the ability of the poor to raise their incomes, and enhancing the quality of life for all citizens, especially the poor. The formulation of the paper involved various stakeholders in addition to the government and an active effort to learn from past policy failures.[24]

The PRSP tried to rally donor support and to channel national action towards the MDGs. This was crucial given the dismal performance of the SDD programme due to lack of funding. The country had better luck in the implementation of the PRSP. In 1999, Moi, the president at that time, appointed a team of high-level technocrats headed by Richard Leakey, dubbed the 'dream team', to turn around the economy and create donor confidence in Kenya. This bore some immediate and much needed fruit. The resumption of funding support by both the World Bank and IMF after this show of commitment by the government to stump corruption helped overcome the funding constraint, which was the biggest hurdle encountered in the implementation of the prior strategies under Moi's tenure.

Economic Recovery Strategy for Wealth and Employment Creation, ERS (2003 – 2007)

Following the initial gains after independence, Kenya experienced a deterioration of economic growth in the 1980s and 1990s that led to increased poverty and a marked decline in the quality of life, as exemplified by declining enrolment in schools and poor health status.[25] The view of an economist in the Ministry of Planning and Devolution summarises Kenya's development progress in the first 40 years after independence in this area: '... the issues in 1963 were the same as the issues in 2003... in terms of poverty, literacy—four decades down the line, and the needs are essentially the same'.[26]

The National Rainbow Coalition (NARC) government that came to power in 2002 after almost a quarter century of Moi's rule thus sought to reverse these decades of weak governance and poor economic performance which had undermined the well-being of Kenyans. The key focus of the ERS was job creation through sound macroeconomic policies, efficient public service delivery, an enabling environment for the private sector, and improved governance, among others. The strategy sought to reduce inequalities in accessing essential goods and services and productive resources, a mission which had been abandoned in the 1980s.

The ERS chief means for reducing poverty and inequality was through universal primary education, improved access to basic health, and expanded productive capacity in agriculture. Regarding strengthening of governance, the strategy proposed extensive reforms to the judiciary and public administration. The formulation of the ERS coincided with the launch of the United Nations MDGs, one of which was universal primary education. This enhanced the commitment of the government to attain this goal, since Kenya is a member state of the United Nations.

The ERS envisaged rapid economic growth as the sure way to reduce poverty in the long run.[27] High economic growth was vital coming from a period of dismal economic development. In recognition that the poor were markedly less educated than the non-poor and with minimal employment opportunities, one of the ERS key strategies was education as a way of addressing the massive inequalities in the country.[28]

The NARC government perceived education as an enabler for people to participate more effectively in the economy and take advantage of opportunities to improve their well-being and exit from poverty. It thus set out to attain universal primary school enrolment by offering free primary education. The government was to cater for the tuition cost of primary education in public schools to reduce the financial burden on poor households. In addition, the education curriculum was to be reviewed to make it relevant to the changing socio-economic situation to enable graduates to fit better into the labour market.

The aim of the ERS was to realise quick wins through high-impact investments in areas such as education, health, and agriculture.[29] Its implementation marked Kenya's development turnaround, setting the country on the economic growth path once again. The economic results under the ERS were substantial. Economic growth rose from 0.6 per cent in 2002 to 6.4 per cent in 2006 as the percentage of people living in poverty dropped from 57 per cent in 2000 to 46 per cent in 2006.[30] Free primary education for all children of school age was also largely achieved.

Encouraged by this success, the NARC government developed Vision 2030 as a successive and longer-term national development strategy to transition Kenya into a middle-income country by 2030. The realisation of this vision was to be underpinned by achieving an average annual economic growth rate of 10 per cent in the 25-year period to 2030. Vision 2030 will be discussed in detail in Chapter 3.

Kenya's development track record

Kenya's development journey has been bumpy and minimally fruitful. While the country has made some strides toward economic development, the pace has been slow and inconsistent. Even more challenging has been Kenya's ability to ensure that the benefits of this economic growth are equally distributed across the various wealth quintiles. However, this challenge is not unique to Kenya but widespread across the continent since the economy is the fourth largest in Africa, one of the African lions, at an average annual economic growth rate of about 5 per cent before the onset of Coronavirus disease 2019 (COVID-19).

Whereas looking at the economic performance trend is useful, benchmarking with others helps to contextualise these achievements. The next section looks at Kenya's historical performance across time and space.

Various data sources have been used for this assessment, including the International Futures (IFs) model. IFs is a comprehensive futuristic forecasting model housed in the Pardee Centre at Denver University. It was developed nearly 40 years ago by a team led by Barry Hughes and continues to evolve for the better. The model uses rich data for 186 countries from credible global sources such as the World Bank, US Government's Central Intelligence Agency (CIA), and the United Nations, among others.

Performance across time

Figure 1.1 below shows how Kenya's economic development results have been mixed and erratic, and mostly disappointing.[31]

Figure 1.1: Kenya's GDP growth over time

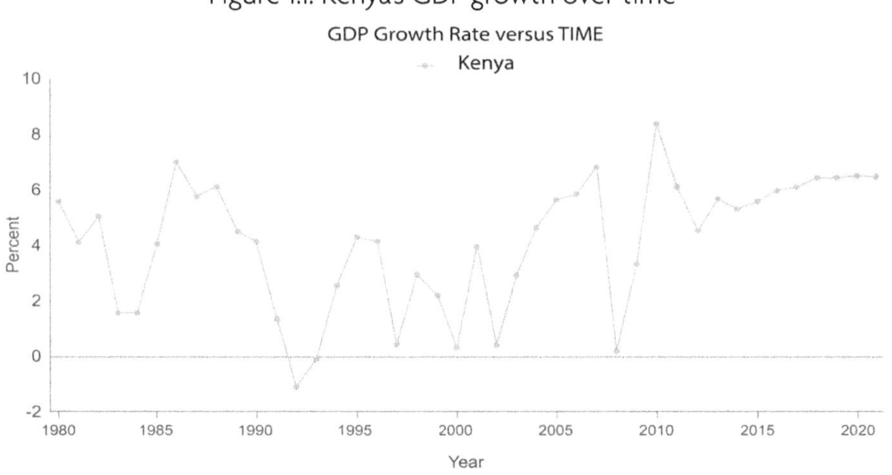

Source: Generated from International Futures Model [Computer Software, Version 7.00], 2017. Retrieved from http://www.ifs.du.edu/

Kenya's economic performance was particularly strong immediately after independence. This was underpinned by significant rural investment in smallholder agriculture which has substantively decreased over time.[32] The decrease has led to less productivity in agriculture and consequently an increased migration of people to urban areas in pursuit of the available limited economic opportunities. The cost of this has been a slackening of rural development and thus an enormous loss of economic growth opportunities for the country, and inequality. There has been a clear and consistent economic divide between the urban and rural populations for decades. Figures 1.2 and 1.3 below show a close correlation between the value added by agriculture to GDP and the economic growth rate in the 1970s.

Figure 1.2: Kenya's annual GDP growth rate - historical and forecasted at current trajectory

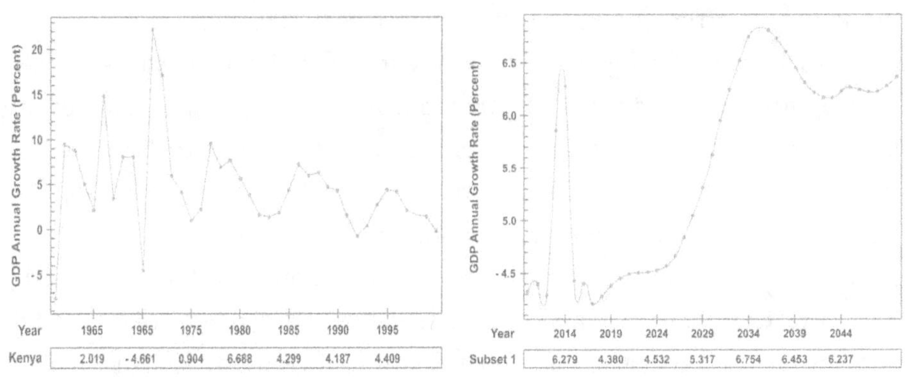

Source: Generated from International Futures Model [Computer Software, Version 7.00], 2017. Retrieved from http://www.ifs.du.edu/

Figure 1.3: Value added (VADD) to GDP by sectors

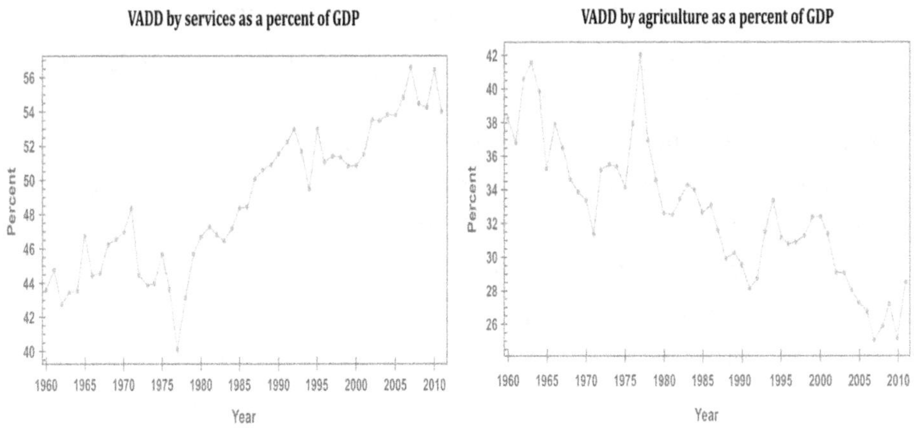

Source: Generated from International Futures Model [Computer Software, Version 7.00], 2017. Retrieved from http://www.ifs.du.edu/

The Kenyan economy has been agriculture based, with about 70 per cent of Kenyans deriving their livelihoods from the industry.[33] The figures above show a close positive correlation between value-added in agriculture as a percentage of GDP and GDP growth. There was a significant investment in smallholder agriculture especially in the rural areas following independence, which meant that most Kenyans were able to contribute to economic growth as reflected in the 1970s' performance. However, the level of investment in agriculture has been decreasing over the years, which is directly reflected in the sector's contribution to GDP that continues to dwindle.

As illustrated in figure 1.2 above, the lowest point in Kenya's economic development happened in the 1980s and 1990s during the Moi's era. Despite Moi's *Fuata Nyayo* slogan, which is Kiswahili translated to 'following in the footsteps of' the founding president under whose reign Kenya enjoyed significant economic growth, his tenure was everything but economically prospering and inclusive. Instead of at least maintaining the pace set by the Kenyatta administration after independence, Moi's regime managed the undoing of the economic gains that Kenya had realised in both absolute terms—in form of reduced economic growth—and by extending the degree of inequality as we shall shortly see.[34]

The cause of this slump in economic growth and the widening inequality was because growth was happening in the services sector such as communication and financial service industries—and not in agriculture, the livelihood of Kenya's poor.[35] By not investing sufficiently in agriculture and other rural-oriented economic activities, the poor were denied the power to participate in and contribute to Kenya's current economy growth. Consequently, they remained excluded and disadvantaged. Due to the lack of relevant knowledge and skills, even the vibrant rural youth were unable to keep pace with the drivers of change in the economy, and hence they could not transition to alternative employment.

Noteworthy is the fact that unlike many other developing countries in the region, Kenya has been a services economy right from the time of its independence. Kenya's service sector has continued to drive the economy as indicated by its much higher value added to GDP compared to agriculture.[36] As reflected in figure 1.3 above, the service sector seems to have an inverse relationship to the agricultural sector as far as value added to GDP is concerned. There appears to be a natural trade-off between these two sectors that can be theorised in the form of a direct or indirect shift of investment in agriculture to the service sector.

Kenya's economic growth performance has been particularly unsatisfactory when viewed through the lens of the economy's ability to provide economic opportunities for the masses and hence reduce poverty in line with the government's commitment at independence. As if in defiance of the wishes of the nation's founding fathers that were encapsulated in Sessional Paper No. 10 of 1965 and mimicked in subsequent development roadmaps, contrary to moving towards an equitable and prosperous society, the little economic gains seem to have benefitted only a few as the poverty gap has continued to widen.[37] Figure 1.4 below illustrates this sad reality.

Figure 1.4: Kenya's level of inequality -
Gini coefficient (historical and projected at current trajectory)

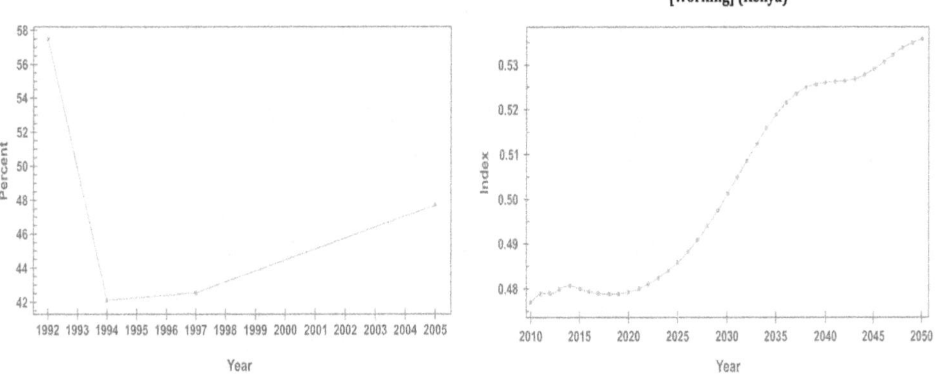

Source: Generated from International Futures Model [Computer Software, Version 7.00], 2017. Retrieved from http://www.ifs.du.edu/

The Gini coefficient measures the extent to which the economic distribution in a country deviates from an ideally equal distribution.[38] Lower values of the Gini coefficient index indicate greater equality. Kenya is among the world's nation with higher inequality as portrayed by the Gini index. The world Gini indices ranged between 30 per cent and 60 per cent in the period 1981 to 2013.[39]

Figure 1.4 above shows that while inequality dropped between 1991 and 1994 from a Gini coefficient of 57.5 per cent to 42 per cent respectively, based on available data, it had increased gradually to 47.9 per cent by 2016 and is forecasted to reach 50 per cent by 2030 and 54 per cent by 2050, going by the current trajectory. Although some progress was made in reducing poverty in the first three decades following independence, there was a significant deterioration in the 1980s and 1990s.[40] Lack of emphasis on inclusive growth and an acceptance of inequality underpinned by a significant deficiency of integrity in vital institutions has led to this sub-optimal economic performance which has had little impact on the well-being of most of Kenya's citizens.[41] On average, about half of the Kenyan population continues to live below the national poverty line.

Benchmarking Kenya's performance with others

Despite its sub-optimal economic performance, Kenya is a star and a peer-leader in the African continent. It is the ninth largest economy in Africa, the fourth largest in Sub-Saharan Africa (SSA), and the dominant economy in the East African Community[42] as shown in figure 1.5 below. Economically, Kenya has stayed ahead of its regional peers who were relatively at par in the early 1960s.

Figure 1.5: Gross domestic product (in 2005 constant dollars)

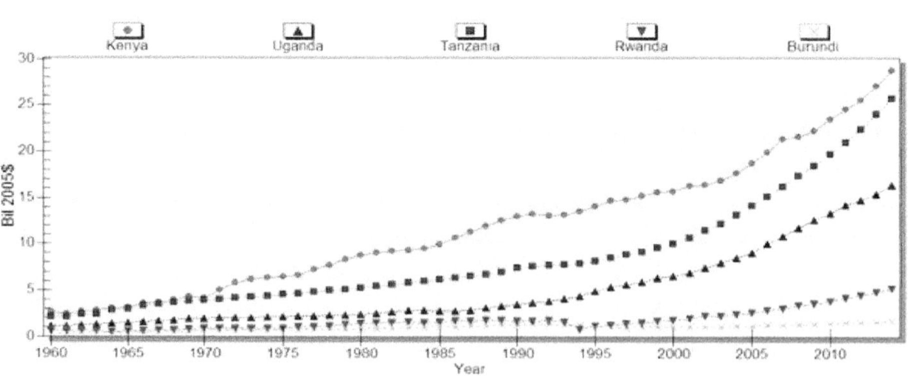

Source: Generated from International Futures Model [Computer Software, Version 7.00], 2017. Retrieved from http://www.ifs.du.edu/

Like the size of the economy (GDP), Kenya has maintained a lead in the region regarding GDP per capita, which can be construed to portray the quality of life of its citizens, as illustrated in figure 1.6 below.

Figure 1.6: Gross domestic product per capita (in current dollars)

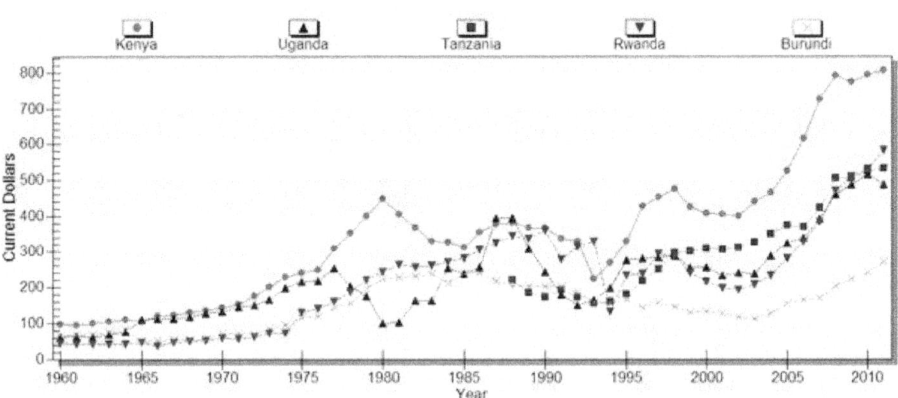

Source: Generated from International Futures Model [Computer Software, Version 7.00], 2017. Retrieved from http://www.ifs.du.edu/

This means that given the common challenges that bethrong the continent, Kenya has performed relatively well developmentally compared to most of its African peers, although far from satisfactorily in comparison with other nations such as the East Asian Tigers that were also its peers in the 1960s. For instance, the economy has performed sub-optimally when compared with Malaysia, which was at a similar economic level in the early 1960s soon after both nations gained independence from the British, as shown in figure 1.7 below.

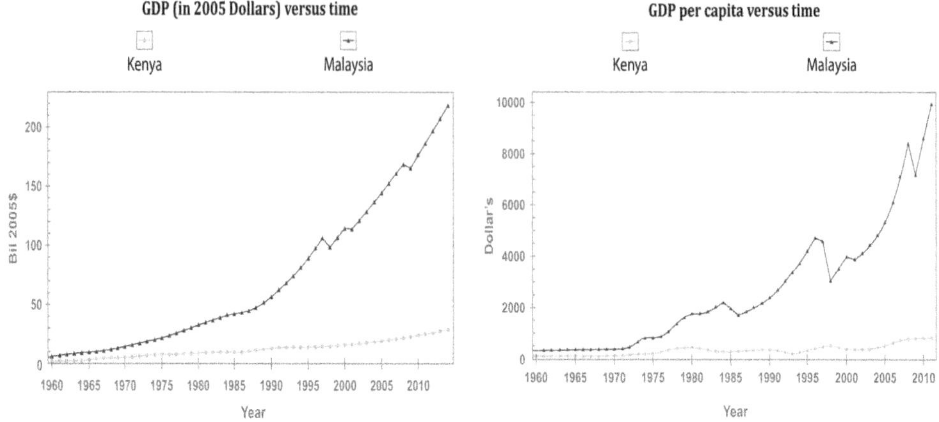

Figure 1.7: Kenya and Malaysia's economic performance over time

Source: Generated from International Futures Model [Computer Software, Version 7.00], 2017. Retrieved from http://www.ifs.du.edu/

Ironically, at that time, Kenya was more advanced than most of its peers in areas such as agriculture, infrastructure, and construction yet the country's GDP per capita is now just about a tenth that of Malaysia (IFs model, 2017). This economic divergence between Kenya and Malaysia will be examined in more detail in Chapter 4.

Barriers to inclusive and sustainable growth

Kenya's poor track record in attaining sustainable and inclusive development points to significant challenges in realising this goal. Yet, the nation has not suffered from a lack of credible policies for making this happen. If anything, the opposite is true. As seen earlier in this chapter, its development roadmaps, particularly the 1965 Sessional paper No. 10, had well thought-out development policies and strategies. Kenya was a role model to its peers, including some of the East Asian Tigers, in the early 1960s. Its rural and agricultural policies were widely copied.

Many policy ideas were borrowed from its 1965 Sessional Paper No. 10 to inform these countries' development strategies, such as the use of technocrats to govern nations and social re-engineering.[43] Kenya's development challenge relates to policy implementation. As shown in Chapter 1, many of the development and reform strategies were never fully implemented.[44] There seems to have been a lack of political will and commitment for inclusive and sustained development.

Moreover, Kenya has struggled to grow its human capital stock for development. After attaining independence, education was perceived as a crucial instrument for realising both rapid development and promoting unity and nationhood.[45] Fuelled by an understanding of the importance of education and the optimism that prevailed around independence, like other nations in Africa, Kenya invested in education and experienced a dramatic increase in the quantity of education in the 1960s and 1970s.[46]

However, like other aspects of its development, these gains were reversed in the 1980s and 1990s due to poor economic performance and accompanying high population growth rates, which substantively reduced the level of GDP per capita investment in education.[47] For instance, the gross enrolment rate declined from 92.1 percent in 1990 to 86.9 percent in 1993.[48] Consequently, general enrolment rates for primary schooling dramatically decreased despite the increase in the population of potential school going age as shown in figure 1.8 below.

Figure 1.8: Kenya's basic education enrolment rate (% per cent)

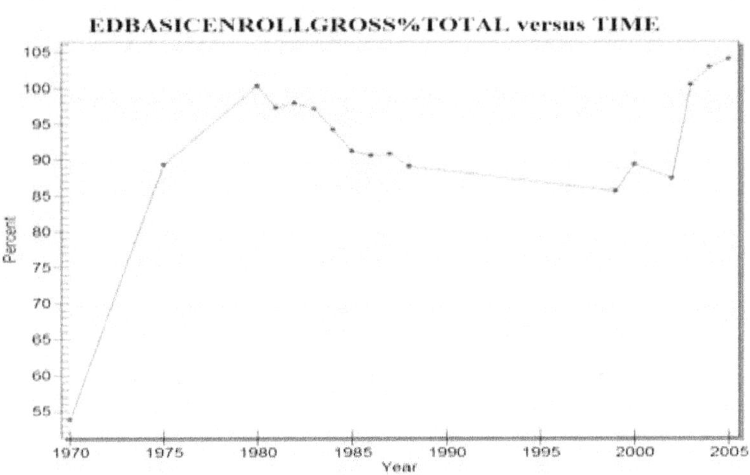

Source: Generated from International Futures Model [Computer Software, Version 7.00], 2017. Retrieved from http://www.ifs.du.edu/

In an attempt to salvage the situation, Kenya introduced the current 8-4-4 system of education (eight years in primary school, four at secondary level, and four in university) in the 1980s. In addition to adjusting the years spent at each educational level, this policy altered the terms of access to education and changed the curricula assumedly to meet the requirements for the nation's socio-economic development.[49]

Contrary to the expectations, the quality of education deteriorated even further (as indicated by the pupil to teacher ratio in figure 1.9 below) because the public expenditure on education had decreased due to poor economic performance. While the expenditure on education improved from 2003 when Kibaki's government came to power, the promotion of universal primary education by making it free led to a further increase in the pupil to teacher ratio. A substantive investment in education is still needed to ensure the quality of education.

Figure 1.9: Kenya's primary school pupil to teacher ratio over time

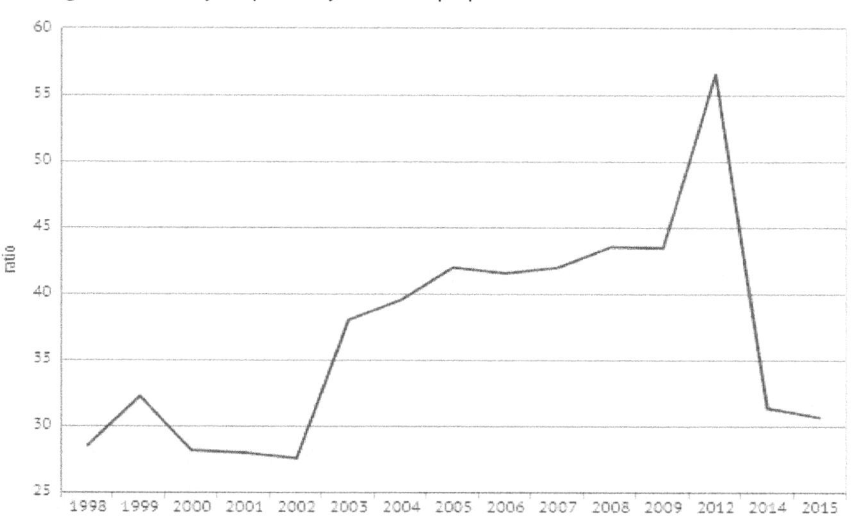

Source: Knoema.com. Accessible at https://bit.ly/2TiyBih.
Retrieved 17 Nov 2020

Kenya's single biggest constraint to attaining sustainable and inclusive development has been its poor political governance as exemplified by weak public institutions.[50] Societal governance has been shown to be vital for development.[51] This governance challenge has been compounded by the nation's multi-ethnicity.

The nation emerged from colonialism highly ethnically polarised as its masters used the divide-and-rule strategy to accentuate ethnic differences to widen the rifts between the various people groups. Some of the larger ethnic communities in Kenya today, such as the Kalenjin, Mijikenda, and Luhya, arose from an active effort by the colonial government to form coalitions of several small groups for ease of governance in the twentieth century.[52] This deep-rooted ethnicity was accompanied by differential development as rewards by the colonial government to its 'faithfuls', which has been perpetuated until now.[53]

With more than 40 ethnic groups, Kenya remains highly polarised along ethnic lines. This has frustrated efforts at rallying the country around a shared development agenda. Instead of genuinely mobilising the nation's resources—particularly the people—for development, Kenya's political leaders, like their colonial predecessors, have tended to practise divisive politics along ethnic lines, which has led to differentiated development. This fact has manifested in the weak governance of public institutions, most of which are led not by technocrats appointed based on their technical capabilities, but by appointees of the political leadership in office and drawn from their ethnic groups. The various administrations have consistently failed to develop an inclusive policy agenda to address these ethnic divides.[54]

The appreciation of the need for an efficient government that would engender a culture of delivering quality services to all its citizenry across the nation goes back to 1965 when the Sessional Paper No. 10 set out a framework for institutional reforms.[55] The second economic medium-term plan (MTP2) of Kenya's current development roadmap, Vision 2030, especially appreciated the need for an efficient and effective public service in creating an enabling environment for the private sector, which is its engine for growth.[56] Kenya started off well in this area—with its civil service reported as efficient and one of the best in Sub-Saharan Africa—but decline set in during the late 1970s.[57]

National leadership tenures have been viewed as opportunities for the ethnic groups in office to enrich themselves, a mentality of 'it is our turn to eat'. Some regions of the country have consequently remained economically marginalised and lacking in infrastructure for delivering essential services such as roads, water, electricity, and even healthcare and education, simply because their ethnic chieftains have not had a chance to get into national leadership offices. National resources have been viewed as means for those in office to strengthen their networks of influence and positions of power rather than communal possessions, a situation that continues to worry Kenya's private sector and development partners.[58]

Kenya's governments have tended to be merely ethnic coalitions that generate short-term gains for themselves at the expense of long-term and inclusive national development. The short spans of growth such as 2003 to 2007 have been typified by an improvement in this core aspect. However, these incidences of success have been isolated. Even the recent efforts underpinned by the new constitution have not yielded much of the needed change. The quest for good governance should thus be sustained as governance will remain a critical pillar to Kenya's development. In full concurrence with Robert Hope in his book *The Political Economy of Development of Kenya*,[59] an effective public governance would be the rising tide that lifts all boats for national development.

Conclusion

In sum, Kenya's development road thus far has been rugged with minimal, sporadic, and exclusive economic growth and it is likely to remain so unless deliberate policy measures are taken to shift this trajectory. This calls for effort in the search for appropriate policy solutions to promote inclusive growth in the country. The real challenge relates to identifying and implementing practical policy interventions which can foster economic growth while at the same time enabling the poor to participate fully in the opportunities this growth presents, to further contribute to the growth. For growth to be sustainable, it would need to be inclusive.

Kenya's pursuit of sustainable and inclusive development that started immediately after independence continues. Sessional Paper No. 10 of 1965 marked that first step in the right direction. Many strides have since been made, some of which have taken the country off the path to this noble mission. The journey is far from over and the end is almost as far as when the journey first started. However, John F. Kennedy, the former American president once cautioned, 'those who look only to the past or the present are certain to miss the future'. The aim should always be to look back to look forward. The next chapters will draw lessons from the past, both locally and globally, and look at what the future portends in order to identify what Kenya needs to do today to realise its desired prosperous and inclusive society in the future.

References

[1] Alila, P. & Njeru, E. (2005). 'Policy-based approaches to poverty reduction in Kenya: Strategies and civil society engagement'.

[2] Sessional Paper No.10 (1965). 'African Socialism and its Application to Planning in Kenya'. The World Bank, Washington, DC.

[3] Ibid p. 2

[4] Ibid p. 8

[5] Mule, H. (2004). 'Mboya as a Minister'. Tom Mboya Foundation.

[6] Nyamboga, T., Nyamweya, B., Sisia, A. & Gongera, E. (2014). 'The effectiveness of poverty reduction efforts in Kenya: An evaluation of Kenyan government's policy initiatives on poverty alleviation'. *International Affairs and Global Strategy. 2014, Vol.23*, pp. 31-40.

[7] Ibid

[8] Ibid

[9] Ibid

[10] Alila, P. & Njeru, E. (2005). 'Policy-based approaches to poverty reduction in Kenya: Strategies and civil society engagement'.

[11] Ibid; UNDP (1999). 'Kenya human development report 1999'. United Nations Development Programme.

12   UNDP (1999). 'Kenya human development report 1999'. United Nations Development Programme.

13   Ibid

14   Ibid p. iii

15   Ibid

16   Ibid

17   United Nations (2012). 'Sustainable Development in Kenya: Stocktaking in the run up to Rio+20'.

18   UNDP (1999). 'Kenya human development report 1999'. United Nations Development Programme.

19   Ibid; Alila, P. & Njeru, E. (2005). 'Policy-based approaches to poverty reduction in Kenya: Strategies and civil society engagement'.

20   BBC (2000, Jul 28). 'Kenya welcomes IMF decision'. BBC News.

21   United Nations (2012). 'Sustainable Development in Kenya: Stocktaking in the run up to Rio+20'.

22   Ibid

23   Alila, P. & Njeru, E. (2005). 'Policy-based approaches to poverty reduction in Kenya: Strategies and civil society engagement'.

24   Ibid

25   World Bank (2003). 'Kenya: Economic recovery strategy for wealth and employment creation 2003 – 2007'.

26   Gainer, M. (2015). 'Planning transformation in a divided nation: Creating Kenya Vision 2030, 2005–2009'. Innovation for Successful Societies. Princeton University.

27   World Bank (2003). 'Kenya: Economic recovery strategy for wealth and employment creation 2003 – 2007'.

28   Ibid

29   Gainer, M. (2015). 'Planning transformation in a divided nation: Creating Kenya Vision 2030, 2005–2009'. Innovation for Successful Societies. Princeton University.

30   Kimenyi, M., Mwega, F. & Ndung'u, N. (2016). 'The African Lions: Kenya country case study'. Brookings Institute; Thugge, K., Ndung'u, N. & Otieno, O. (2009). *Unlocking the Future Potential for Kenya: The Vision 2030.*

31   Kimenyi, M., Mwega, F. & Ndung'u, N. (2016). 'The African Lions: Kenya country case study'. Brookings Institute; Nyanjom, O. & Ong'olo, D. (2012). 'Erratic development in Kenya: Questions from the East Asian miracle'. *Development Policy Review, 2012, Vol. 30 Issue 1,* p73-99.

32 Nyanjom, O. & Ong'olo, D. (2012). 'Erratic development in Kenya: Questions from the East Asian miracle'. *Development Policy Review, 2012, Vol. 30 Issue 1*, p73-99.

33 FinAccess (2019, Apr). 'The 2019 FinAccess Household Survey. Central Bank of Kenya, Kenya National Bureau of Statistics, and FSD Kenya'; Kimenyi, M., Mwega, F. & Ndung'u, N. (2016). 'The African Lions: Kenya country case study'. Brookings Institute.

34 Nyanjom, O. & Ong'olo, D. (2012). 'Erratic development in Kenya: Questions from the East Asian miracle'. *Development Policy Review, 2012, Vol. 30 Issue 1*, p73-99.

35 World Bank (2016). 'Kenya Country Economic Memorandum: From Economic Growth to Jobs and Shared Prosperity'. The World Bank, Washington, DC.

36 Ibid; International Futures Model [Computer Software, Version 7.00], 2017.

37 International Futures Model [Computer Software, Version 7.00], 2017; Nyanjom, O. & Ong'olo, D. (2012). 'Erratic development in Kenya: Questions from the East Asian miracle'. *Development Policy Review, 2012, Vol. 30 Issue 1*, p73-99.

38 United Nations (2015, Oct 21). 'Inequality measurement. Department of Economic and Social Affairs'. *Development Issues No. 2*. United Nations.

39 Ibid

40 Nyanjom, O. & Ong'olo, D. (2012). 'Erratic development in Kenya: Questions from the East Asian miracle'. *Development Policy Review, 2012, Vol. 30 Issue 1*, p73-99.

41 Ibid

42 Kimenyi, M., Mwega, F. & Ndung'u, N. (2016). 'The African Lions: Kenya country case study'. Brookings Institute.

43 Nyanjom, O. & Ong'olo, D. (2012). 'Erratic development in Kenya: Questions from the East Asian miracle'. *Development Policy Review, 2012, Vol. 30 Issue 1*, p73-99; Fourie, E. (2014). 'Model students: Policy emulation, modernization, and Kenya's Vision 2030'. *African Affairs (London). 2014, Vol. 113 Issue 453*, p540-562; Nyamboga, T., Nyamweya, B., Sisia, A. & Gongera, E. (2014). 'The effectiveness of Poverty Reduction efforts in Kenya: An evaluation of Kenyan government's policy initiatives on poverty alleviation'. *International Affairs and Global Strategy. 2014, Vol.23*, p31-40.

44 World Bank (2016). 'Kenya Country Economic Memorandum: From Economic Growth to Jobs and Shared Prosperity'. The World Bank, Washington, DC.

45 Eshiwani, G. (1990). 'Implementing educational policies in Kenya'. *World Bank Discussion Papers Africa Technical Department Series*. The World Bank, Washington, DC.

46 Ibid

47 Ibid; International Futures Model [Computer Software, Version 7.00], 2017.

48 Bold, S., Sanderfur, J., Kimenyi, M. S. & Mwabu, G. (2010). Education for Prosperity: Improving Access and Quality. Adam, C., Collier, C. & Ndung'u, N. *Kenya Policies for Prosperity: Africa Policies for Prosperity* (pp293-308)

49   Eshiwani, G. (1990). 'Implementing educational policies in Kenya'. *World Bank Discussion Papers Africa Technical Department Series*. The World Bank, Washington, DC.

50   Nyanjom, O. & Ong'olo, D. (2012). 'Erratic development in Kenya: Questions from the East Asian miracle'. *Development Policy Review, 2012, Vol. 30 Issue 1*, p73-99; Vlasblom, D. (2013). 'The richer harvest: Economic development in Africa and Southeast Asia compared'. *African Studies Centre*, Leiden; Donge, J. (2012). 'Governance and access to finance for development: An explanation of divergent development trajectories in Kenya and Malaysia'. *Commonwealth and Comparative Politics. Feb 2012, Vol. 50 Issue 1*, p53-74; Hope, K. R. (2011). *The Political Economy of Development in Kenya*. Continuum, NY.

51   Nyanjom, O. & Ong'olo, D. (2012). 'Erratic development in Kenya: Questions from the East Asian miracle'. *Development Policy Review, 2012, Vol. 30 Issue 1*, p73-99.

52   Chilungu, S. (1985, Sep). 'Kenya: Recent developments and challenges'. *Cultural Survival Quarterly Magazine*.

53   Ibid

54   World Bank (2016). *'Kenya Country Economic Memorandum: From Economic Growth to Jobs and Shared Prosperity'*. The World Bank, Washington, DC.

55   Hope, K. R. (2011). The Political Economy of Development in Kenya. Continuum, NY.

56   Ibid; Vision 2030 (2007). Vision 2030 Brochure. Republic of Kenya.

57   Hope, K. R. (2011). *The Political Economy of Development in Kenya*. Continuum, NY.

58   Vlasblom, D. (2013). 'The richer harvest: Economic development in Africa and Southeast Asia compared'. *African Studies Centre*, Leiden.

59   Hope, K. R. (2011). *The Political Economy of Development in Kenya*. Continuum, NY.

Building blocks for sustainable development

*Prefer knowledge to wealth, for the one is transitory,
the other perpetual.—Socrates*

This chapter provides a comprehensive understanding of sustainable and inclusive development and outlines the fundamentals to achieve it. The chapter also presents ways of measuring progress towards sustainable development.

Inclusive growth

Inclusive growth, which is also referred to as shared or broad-based growth, is focused on increasing growth opportunities for every member of society.[1] It is concerned with the pattern and pace of economic growth and entails giving all citizens equal opportunities. In principle this means that circumstances surrounding people's births should not determine their outcomes in life. Inclusive growth has also been termed pro-poor growth, which is economic growth characterised by a significant share going to the poor.[1] One thing that these descriptions all have in common is that inclusive growth benefits everyone—households, both wealthy and poor, and organisations in the economy.

Sustained poverty reduction necessitates inclusive growth that enables the citizens of a nation to both contribute to and benefit from its economic growth. As the authors of the World Development Report 2007, *Development and the Next Generation,* argue: 'because labour is the main asset of the poor, making it more productive is the best way to reduce poverty'.[2] Enhancing the productivity of the poor's labour can be accomplished by increasing the opportunities accorded to them to earn money by developing their capacities to take advantage of these opportunities.[3] This should be accompanied by broad-based economic growth.

The inclusive growth path focuses on productive employment rather than on a direct redistribution of income to the disadvantaged members of the society and hence is a longer-term approach to sustainable development.[4] By contrast, anti-poverty programmes that promote redistribution of income and other resources have been shown to be less equalising in the long run.[5] Shared growth is about indiscriminately teaching the members of the society to fish instead of giving them fish to eat.

Inclusive growth increases the incomes of excluded groups through three main ways: (1) focusing on productive employment instead of income redistribution; (2) using a broad-based approach that is spread across sectors; and (3) including the large part of the country's labour force by ensuring equality of opportunity in terms of access to markets, resources and an unbiased regulatory environment for businesses and individuals.[6] In other words, it is labour-intensive growth fuelled by interventions that increase opportunities for employment and the quality of labour or human capital.

According to the World Bank[7], the prerequisites for inclusive growth are improved productivity and the creation of new employment opportunities. That is, the size of the economy must be increased by accelerating the pace of economic growth while at the same time levelling the playing field for investment and increasing opportunities for productive employment. Sustained high economic growth rates and poverty reduction are only realisable through an expansion in the sources of growth and an increase in and efficient involvement of the labour force in the growth process.[8]

Evidence shows that when it comes to opportunities, inequality is often directly related to insufficient investment in people in the form of unequal access to basic social services, such as education and health.[9] Consequently, improved education has been identified as one of the top three solutions to income inequalities globally.[10] Usually, inequality manifests in social and economic institutions that favour the interests of the influential within the society at the expense of the poor.

As a result, the talent of poorer groups of the population is left undeveloped and unexploited, disenfranchising them further and robbing the nation of an opportunity for shared national development. To realise sustainable development, every citizen needs to do their part and, in turn, benefit from this joint effort in nation-building. As per the old African adage, 'if you want to go fast, go alone but if you want to go far, go together'. Sustainable and inclusive development is a long-term pursuit that can only be realised through collective effort.

An individual's ability to be productively employed depends not only on the available employment opportunities but also on his or her own ability to take advantage of these opportunities as the economy grows.[11] This ability is subject to the individuals' health, education, and the other productivity attributes relevant to the job. Policy interventions related to education for the majority have thus been shown to have a positive effect on both economic growth and inequality reduction, as they enhance the nation's human capital.[12]

As seen in Chapter 1, despite a good post-independence start, Kenya did not realise sustained economic growth because it lacked some of the pre-conditions to make this happen. Donge, Henley, and Lewis,[13] in their effort to understand the significant divergences in development outcomes that have happened between Sub-Saharan Africa and South-East Asia in the last fifty years, identified three key pre-conditions for sustained economic growth, namely, macroeconomic stability, pro-poor public spending, and economic freedom. Their views are closely concordant with Justin Lin's, the former World Bank's Vice President and Chief Economist, who outlined the essentials of robust and inclusive growth as sound macroeconomic policies, a conducive private investment climate, access to vital infrastructure, and good governance.[14] Following is a brief description of these factors and their implications on Kenya's lasting growth.

Macroeconomic stability: Macroeconomic stability is crucial for developmental take-off. It helps to attract foreign investment[15] although stability without pro-poor policies does not attain much for general development and particularly sustainable and inclusive growth.[16] Macroeconomic stability has not been a problem in Kenya. Despite the typical challenges faced in the governance of public institutions, the Central Bank of Kenya has done a relatively good job at this throughout the decades.[17] It has been one of the few public institutions that have suffered least from political patronage over the decades, having had the luck of being led by technocrats in most of Kenya's history.

Pro-poor public spending: Pro-poor public spending is a government expenditure that is targeted at sectors of the economy that involve a significant proportion of the nation's poor. For Kenya, such expenditure should be on agriculture, which supports the livelihood of about 70 per cent of Kenyans, and other rural spending given that most of the nation's population is rural.[18] Going by the sustained decline in value added in agriculture to GDP, the government should diversify into other broad-base sectors that can absorb most of the country's productive labour. The focus on enhancing manufacturing, one of the four pillars of Uhuru Kenyatta's current 'Big 4' development agenda—rest, food security and nutrition, universal health coverage, and affordable housing—seems to be driven by this need for diversification. Sustained high growth rates and poverty reduction will only be realised by expanding the sources of growth and increasing the proportion of the workforce that is included in the growth process.[19]

Economic freedom: This entails giving freedom to market players while at the same time exercising the right level of oversight. Economic freedom alone cannot deliver sustainable and inclusive development; it must be combined with pro-poor economic policy.[20] While various levels of government participation have happened in the successful East Asian economies over the decades, these governments have deliberately avoided having state monopolies, which would smother development of the affected sectors of the economy.[21] Lamentably, this has not been the case in Kenya where state monopolies or near-monopolies, such as the National Cereals and Produce Board and the Kenya Power and Lighting Company, still exist. As the 2014 World Economic Forum[22] exploring the *New Growth Models: Challenges and steps to achieving patterns of more equitable, inclusive and sustainable growth* concluded, it is only through private sector engagement that the long-term orderly and efficient allocation of resources can be assured. This engagement is necessary for creation of a thriving entrepreneurial environment. The direct involvement of government in markets disincentivises the private sector from taking its rightful place in the development omnibus.

Based on this understanding and looking at Kenya's isolated spurts of relatively high growth in the last fifty years, rapid growth is not necessarily sustainable let alone inclusive. However, it is possible to realise this twin developmental objective by meeting the pre-conditions for take-off. Sustainable development involves investment on two fronts: human capital development and physical capital growth for improved productivity to absorb the resultant higher quality of labour.

One of Kenya's challenges to attaining rapid and subsequently sustainable growth has been the inability to invest optimally in its human capital through education and training.[23] Sustainable and inclusive development is distinguished by three key attributes: rapid and sustained economic growth, reduced inequality, and enhanced societal quality of life. The next two sections focus on inequality and quality of life.

Equality

A lot has been said about addressing inequality and the need for inclusiveness in attaining sustained development. The pertinent question is, why bother about inequality? The UNDP identifies inequality as the global root cause of poverty.[24] Dabla-Norris and colleagues,[25] in their exploration of the causes and consequences of inequality, arrived at the conclusion that 'irrespective of ideology, culture, and religion, people care about inequality'.

Adjacent to each of the upper-class residential areas in Nairobi, the capital city of Kenya, is an informal settlement. Yet, the existence of these informal settlements and their physical location and proximity to the more affluent residential areas is not by design. This shows the reality of the interdependence between the various wealth quintiles—the better off economically need the less economically endowed and *vice versa*. One would imagine that this physical proximity would heighten the awareness of the better off in society about the plight of the less economically advantaged. Unfortunately, this large economic differential and the status quo seems to be firmly entrenched in the societal values and norms.

Throughout history, social unrest and conflict have been initiated by youth who have ended up on the streets instead of channelling their energy into productive economic activities. As Inayatullah[26] observes, revolutions often tend to occur in societies with disproportionately large populations of youth, that is, youth bulge. When such youth feel alienated from the society, they start to demonstrate against these perceived injustices by others.[27] When inequality is allowed to go on for long, it can result in political instability. The 2010s Arab uprising is a case in point.

Widening inequality can have far-reaching impact on economic growth such as sub-optimal use of human capital, political and economic instability, and concentration of decision-making power in the hands of a few people.[28] Research has shown that income inequality, as measured by the Gini coefficient and the poverty gap, has an adverse effect on the ability to realise sustainable growth.[29]

Inequality of opportunities, on the other hand, denies the disadvantaged members of the society a chance to participate in growing the economy of their nation. For instance, a lack of education denies the uneducated and the country an opportunity to improve their productivity. Increasing inequality could also lead to a lower aggregate demand as higher income households ordinarily spend a smaller proportion of their incomes on basic commodities and services such as food and education.[30]

Empirical evidence also shows that inequality stops economic growth by fuelling economic and political instability, hence dampening prospects for growth.[31] Ironically as Martin[32] argues, 'if the proceeds of growth are not shared, the pie stops growing'. This means that the pursuit of wealth by the rich at the expense of the poor is short-lived. Demonstrably, the prolonged period of relative inequality in Western economies that intensified leverage, over-extension of credit, and relaxed mortgage underwriting regulation led to the 2007-2008 global financial crisis.[33] Inequality weakens social cohesion as people across the economic divide lose the sense of belonging together.[34]

Mohammed, UN's Secretary-General's Special Adviser on Post-2015 Development Planning, declared inequality as one of the key challenges of our times. The result of inequality is therefore either economic, political, or social crisis, and at times a combination of these, none of which is desirable or beneficial to society.

Quality of life

An essential aspect of sustainable and inclusive development is that it delivers an improved quality of life or well-being to the people in the long-term. For many decades, the gross domestic product as used as a gauge of the quality of life or societal well-being, and it is only recently that economists have started to explore alternative ways of measuring well-being.[35] As Simon Kuznets, the US Nobel Laurette, observed, 'the welfare of a nation can scarcely be inferred from a measurement of national income'.[36] A major weakness of using GDP alone as a measure of the economic well-being of a nation is that GDP does not factor in the population that produces the output or depends on it.[37] For instance, an increase in GDP accompanied by an equal increase in the population would be inconsequential in improving the well-being of its citizens.

The GDP is a way of estimating economic activity by gauging the value of all the country's transactions for goods and services.[38] Additionally, whereas GDP covers a nation's production in general—the product of both firms and households—as the Stiglitz Commission pointed out, well-being only relates to households and not institutions, hence there is need to focus on what is happening at the household level as opposed to looking at GDP collectively.[39] The Stiglitz Commission, named after one of its co-chairs, Nobel laureate Joseph Stiglitz, was set up by the French government in 2008 to take a global look at the measurement of economic performance and social progress with a core aim of improving France's quality of life.[40] The commission also pointed out that a society's quality of life depends on people's conditions and capabilities.

Another fundamental limitation of GDP as a measure of well-being is that it does not show the incomes from resources in a country that is owned by nationals of another country. Gross national income (GNI), which measures not only production in an economy but also how much of that production, together with incomes from abroad are available to citizens of that country, is thus a better measure of economic well-being than GDP.[41] To illustrate the arguments here, the global economy and GDP of many nations have grown consistently for years without an equivalent improvement in the well-being of the majority.

GDP is much more inadequate as a measure of prosperity when the growth is not sustainable, that is, where rapid growth today means a depletion of the resources that would be needed for well-being tomorrow. The assumption that an increase in GDP is equivalent to economic progress needs to be put to rest.[42] GDP only measures societal prosperity in monetary terms that does not reflect the real state of life and particularly so for the majority. As Robert F. Kennedy, a former American Attorney General and politician, frustratingly opined, 'GDP measures everything, in short, except that which makes life worthwhile.'[43] It does not measure people's level of happiness or state of health.

The well-being or quality of life of a society or individual is multi-dimensional but can be defined as satisfaction with life, as subjectively measured by access to food, housing, healthcare, quality education, and other aspects such as political stability, job security, environmental quality, and individual freedom.[44] The concept that 'societal progress occurs when there is an improvement in the sustainable and equitable well-being of a society' is broadly accepted by the Organisation for Economic Cooperation and Development (OECD) and is gaining traction globally.[45] The OECD is a group of 34 member countries that work together and with over 70 other non-member economies to promote sustainable development in the form of economic growth and prosperity.[46] OECD provides a forum for the member governments to compare policy experiences, identify good practices, seek answers to common problems, and coordinate both domestic and global policies.[47]

According to the UNDP, human development is about improving the level of people's well-being and widening their choices in life.[48] These choices change across time and space. That is, societies are at different stages of development and are faced, therefore, with different choices. However, regardless of their location, people have three essential choices to make as identified by the UNDP, namely: the choice (i) to lead a long and healthy life; (ii) to acquire knowledge; and (iii) to have access to the resources needed for a decent standard of living.[49]

Informed by this conviction, UNDP's human development index (HDI) seeks to gauge people's ability to exercise these choices based on three indicators: (a) longevity as measured by life expectancy at birth; (b) educational attainment as measured by a combination of adult literacy (two-thirds weight) and combined primary, secondary and tertiary gross enrolment ratios (one-third weight); and (c) standard of living, which is measured by real GDP per capita expressed in purchasing power parity.[50]

Borrowing heavily from the UNDP's HDI indicators, the World Bank's *Kenya Country Economic Memorandum*[51] identifies life expectancy, poverty headcount ratio at $1.25 a day (purchasing power parity), school enrolment (per cent gross), and the percentage of the population with access to electricity as some of the indicators of quality of life. Life expectancy at birth in total years is the average number of years one is expected to live at the point he or she is born.[52] The poverty headcount ratio at $1.25 a day of purchasing power parity is the proportion of the population or society that is living below $1.25 a day.

School enrolment is the number of students enrolled at each level of education—primary, secondary, tertiary—a proportion of those that should be enrolled (a percentage of the gross). An improvement on this indicator would be the education attainment—the average years of schooling attained by the whole population—or graduation rate at each of these levels, with higher rates presumably representing a better quality of life. The final indicator is the proportion of the societal population with access to electricity.

Although education attainment is undisputedly a better measure of quality of life and human capital stock than enrolment, enrolment rates have at times been considered acceptable, especially in the early stages of education-related interventions, because the time lag between investments in education and the ultimate expected outcome can be significant.[53] For instance, Kenya's primary school education takes at least eight years and waiting for this duration to determine progress would be ineffective. Providing basic healthcare and education to children lays the foundation for their well-being.[54]

UN's sustainable development goals (SDGs)

On the eve of the new century, the United Nations member countries adopted the eight MDGs in pursuit of global peace, security, and development by 2015. The MDGs were intended to capture and advance common global goals. While good progress was made in some goals, such as reducing extreme poverty, little was realised in others like health and education.[55] Although

Sub-Saharan Africa, and Kenya in particular, made some progress, given its relatively diminished circumstances compared with the more developed countries, they did not attain most of the MDGs. This global effort at attaining sustainable development was aimed at focusing the globe on the most important issues to pursue.

Following the lapse of the MDGs timeline, the UNDP came up with 17 sustainable development goals (SDGs), which have similarly been adopted as the global development targets under *The 2030 Agenda for Sustainable Development* (commonly referred to as *Agenda 2030*).

The essence of the SDGs and *The 2030 Agenda* is that sustainable development is much more than just economic prosperity—it is the economy, environment and society working together in a sustainable manner. People's quality of life cannot improve infinitely without regard for the environment given the existing planetary boundaries. SDGs are at the nexus of society, economy and environment as shown in figure 2.1.

Figure 2.1: The essence of sustainable development

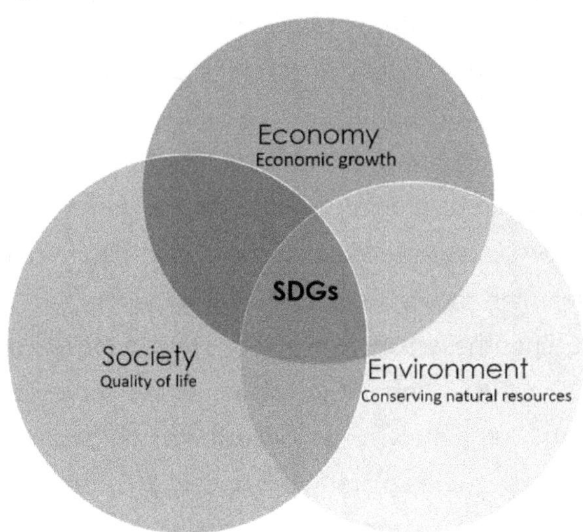

Appreciating the interconnectedness between the environment, economy and people (society) will be crucial in realising the SDGs. SDG 4, ensuring equal access to quality education, is a key pillar to attaining sustainable development. Achieving this goal would mean that by 2030 all boys and girls complete secondary education. Quality education underpins all the other SDGs.

Based on country reviews of their performance, success in realising the MDGs was attributed to their application to build national consensus for progressive change; enable poor and marginalised communities to be heard; attract international support and build partnerships for change; highlight inequalities and other constraints to development; learn from practice and refine initiatives; and finance and develop catalytic initiatives to advance multiple goals.[56]

Informed by the global lessons from the MDGs implementation, the UNDP in its *From the MDGs to Sustainable Development for All* 2016' report makes the following recommendations (among others) to governments on implementation of the ambitious Agenda 2030: (a) use an inclusive process, that is, leave no one behind; (b) set targets that reflect national priorities for the future; (c) ensure broad public engagement—listen to stakeholders and consider their views; (d) identify big picture opportunities with regards to an appreciation of the integration and indivisibility of the SDGs; (e) prioritise policy accelerators—identify entry points for the transformational change that is needed for sustainable development; and (f) strengthen adaptive capacity using learning-through-practice environments.[57]

The list outlines the lessons from nations that made real developmental progress in 2000 to 2015 under the MDGs. These serve as guidelines as each government is ultimately responsible for its own development. Each government's ownership and commitment to the SDGs through ensuring that the necessary institutional structures and national policies are developed and implemented will determine its ability to realise the desired outcomes.[58]

Measuring sustainable and inclusive growth

The only way to attain anything is by measuring progress towards it. However uncertain the measurement is, it still provides more knowledge than one would have without measuring.[59] The gross domestic product has for decades been used as a measure of the economic well-being of nations. However, driven by the debate over ways to measure true wealth and well-being, several indicators have been developed, some of which are outlined here.

Sustainability of growth: The economic growth of a nation is considered unsustainable if it is realised at the expense of future generations by depleting the country's wealth, that is, its physical, human and natural capital.[60] The World Bank has come up with the gross national savings and natural capital accounting as indicators of sustainable growth. Other indicators in this space include the environmental performance index (EPI), the green economy index (GEI), and the sustainability index (SI).[61]

Inclusiveness of growth/inequality: Ensuring inclusiveness of growth can be viewed from two angles: addressing income inequalities and opportunities inequalities.[62] A commonly used indicator for income inequalities is the poverty gap index (based on $1.25 a day), which 'measures the extent to which individuals fall below the poverty line (the poverty gaps) as a proportion of the poverty line'.[63] Another measure of income inequality is the Gini coefficient which looks at domestic income distribution and compares inequality across nations (GINIDOM). Inequality of opportunities, on the other hand, is often measured by tracking access to basic services such as health and education, and other opportunities.[64]

Human well-being (quality of life): The 2014 World Economic Forum report identifies the following indicators of human well-being: 'health, education, employment, political freedom, social relationships, and environmental quality and security'.[65] Others include the average years of schooling, life expectancy, and the percentage of the population with access to electricity.[66]

These indicators will be used in reviewing the achievement of Kenya's Vision 2030 in the next chapter and in Chapter 5 to develop a Kenyan model for sustainable and inclusive development.

References

[1] World Bank (2009, Feb 10). 'What is inclusive development?' World Bank, Washington, DC.

[2] World Bank (2007). 'World Development Report 2007: Development and the next generation'. World Bank, Washington, DC., p.2.

[3] Ibid

[4] World Bank (2009, Feb 10). 'What is inclusive development?' World Bank, Washington, DC.

[5] McKay, A. (2002). 'Defining and measuring inequality'. *Overseas Development Institute, Briefing Paper No 1 (1 of 3), March 2002.*

[6] World Bank (2009, Feb 10). 'What is inclusive development?' World Bank, Washington, DC.

[7] Ibid

[8] Ibid

[9] World Bank (2011). *Reducing Inequality for Shared Growth in China: Strategy and Policy Options for Guangdong Province.* World Bank, Washington, DC.

[10] Mohammed, A. (2015). 'Deepening income inequality'. World Economic Forum. Global Agenda 2015.

[11] World Bank (2009, Feb 10). 'What is inclusive development?' World Bank, Washington, DC.

[12] Ibid; Hull, K. (2009). 'Understanding the relationship between economic growth, employment and poverty reduction'. Organisation for Economic Co-operation and Development.

[13] Donge, J., Henley, D. & Lewis, P. (2012). 'Tracking development in South-East Asia and sub-Saharan Africa: The primacy of policy'. *Development Policy Review. February 2012, Vol. 30 Issue 1,* p5–24.

[14] United Nations (2015, Oct 21). 'Inequality measurement'. Department of Economic and Social Affairs. Development Issues No. 2. United Nations., p. 51.

[15] Hammond, A. (2013). *Which World? Scenarios for 21st Century.* Earthscan Publications Ltd. Kindle Edition.

16   Donge, J., Henley, D. & Lewis, P. (2012). 'Tracking development in South-East Asia and sub-Saharan Africa: The primacy of policy'. *Development Policy Review. February 2012, Vol. 30 Issue 1*, p5–24.

17   Ibid; Nyanjom, O. & Ong'olo, D. (2012). 'Erratic development in Kenya: Questions from the East Asian miracle'. *Development Policy Review, 2012, Vol. 30 Issue 1*, p73-99.

18   Donge, J., Henley, D. & Lewis, P. (2012). 'Tracking development in South-East Asia and sub-Saharan Africa: The primacy of policy'. *Development Policy Review. February 2012, Vol. 30 Issue 1*, p5–24.

19   World Bank (2009, Feb 10). 'What is inclusive development?' World Bank, Washington, DC.

20   Donge, J., Henley, D. & Lewis, P. (2012). 'Tracking development in South-East Asia and sub-Saharan Africa: The primacy of policy'. *Development Policy Review. February 2012, Vol. 30 Issue 1*, p5–24.

21   Ibid

22   WEF (2014). 'New growth models: Challenges and steps to achieving patterns of more equitable, inclusive and sustainable growth'. World Economic Forum.

23   Kimenyi, M., Mwega, F. & Ndung'u, N. (2016). 'The African lions: Kenya country case study'. Brookings Institute.

24   UNDP (1999). 'Kenya human development report 1999'. United Nations Development Programme.

25   Dabla-Norris, E., Kochhar, K., Ricka, F., Suphaphiphat, N. & Tsounta, E. (2015). *Causes and Consequences of Income Inequality: A Global Perspective.* International Monetary Fund, p.5.

26   Inayatullah, S. (2016). 'Youth bulge: Demographic dividend, time bomb, and other futures'. *Journal of Future Studies. 2016, Vol. 21 Issue 2*, p21-34.

27   Ibid

28   Dabla-Norris, E., Kochhar, K., Ricka, F., Suphaphiphat, N. & Tsounta, E. (2015). *Causes and Consequences of Income Inequality: A Global Perspective.* International Monetary Fund.

29   Ibid

30   Ibid

31   Ibid; Martin, A. (2014, Dec 18). 'Why inequality is an economic problem'. New Economics Foundation.

32   Martin, A. (2014, Dec 18). 'Why inequality is an economic problem'. New Economics Foundation.

33   Dabla-Norris, E., Kochhar, K., Ricka, F., Suphaphiphat, N. & Tsounta, E. (2015). *Causes and Consequences of Income Inequality: A Global Perspective.* International Monetary Fund.

34   Mohammed, A. (2015). 'Deepening income inequality'. World Economic Forum. Global Agenda 2015.

35   New York Times (2008, Sep 1). 'Economists look to expand GDP to count 'quality of life''. The New York Times.

36   Casse (n.d.). 'GDP and indicators of economic well-being'. Center for Advancement of the Steady State Economy.

37   Khan, J. & Calver, J. (2014). 'Measuring national well-being: Economic well-being'. Office for National Statistics.

38   Suzuki, D. (2014, Feb 28). 'How the GDP measures everything 'except that which makes life worthwhile''. EcoWatch.

39   Khan, J. & Calver, J. (2014). 'Measuring national well-being: Economic well-being'. Office for National Statistics.

40   European Union (2010). 'GDP and beyond'. The European Union; New York Times (2008, Sep 1). 'Economists look to expand GDP to count 'quality of life''. The New York Times.

41   ONS (2014). 'Measures of economic well-being'. Office for National Statistics, UK

42   Casse (n.d.). 'GDP and indicators of economic well-being'. Center for Advancement of the Steady State Economy.

43   Uchitelle, L. (2008, Sep 1). 'Economists look to expand GDP to count "quality of life"'. The New York Times.

44   IESE Business School (2013, Sep 4). 'Quality of Life: Everyone Wants It, But What Is It?'. Forbes.

45   European Union (2010). 'GDP and beyond'. The European Union, p. 9

46   OECD (n.d.). What is OECD? The Organization for Economic Cooperation and Development.

47   Ibid

48   UNDP (1999). 'Kenya human development report 1999'. United Nations Development Programme.

49   Ibid, p. xi

50   Ibid

51   World Bank (2016). 'Kenya Country Economic Memorandum: From Economic Growth to Jobs and Shared Prosperity'. The World Bank, Washington, DC.

52   Hughes, B. B. & Hillebrand, E. E. (2016). *Exploring and Shaping International Futures*. Routledge Taylor and Francis Group, NY. Kindle Edition.

53   Fuente, A. (2011). 'Human capital and productivity'. *Barcelona Economics Working Paper Series, Working Paper Nº 530*; World Bank (2009, Feb 10). 'What is inclusive development?' World Bank, Washington, DC.

54   World Bank (2007). 'World Development Report 2007: Development and the next generation'. World Bank, Washington, DC.

55   World Bank & UNDP (2016). 'Transitioning from the MDGs to the SDGs'. United Nations Development Programme.

56   UNDP (2016). 'From the MDGs to sustainable development for all: Lessons from 15 years of practice'. United Nations Development Programme, p. v-vi.

57   Ibid, p. 67-73

58   World Bank & UNDP (2016). 'Transitioning from the MDGs to the SDGs. United Nations Development Programme'.

59   Hubbard, D. W. (2010). *How to Measure Anything: Finding the Value of Intangibles in Business*. Wiley. Kindle Edition.

60   WEF (2014). 'New growth models: Challenges and steps to achieving patterns of more equitable, inclusive and sustainable growth'. World Economic Forum.

61   Ibid

62   Ibid; Dabla-Norris, E., Kochhar, K., Ricka, F., Suphaphiphat, N. & Tsounta, E. (2015). *Causes and Consequences of Income Inequality: A Global Perspective*. International Monetary Fund.

63   World Bank (2005). 'Poverty Manual Chapter 4. Measures of Poverty'. The World Bank, Washington, DC., p. 69.

64   Dabla-Norris, E., Kochhar, K., Ricka, F., Suphaphiphat, N. & Tsounta, E. (2015). *Causes and Consequences of Income Inequality: A Global Perspective*. International Monetary Fund.

65   WEF (2014). 'New growth models: Challenges and steps to achieving patterns of more equitable, inclusive and sustainable growth'. World Economic Forum, p. 6.

66   World Bank & UNDP (2016). 'Transitioning from the MDGs to the SDGs'. United Nations Development Programme.

CHAPTER 3

Vision 2030: Kenya's current roadmap

*If one advances confidently in the direction of his
dreams, and endeavours to live the life which he
has imagined, he will meet with success unexpected
in common hours. — Henry David Thoreau*

This chapter looks at the ability of Vision 2030, Kenya's current development roadmap, to deliver sustainable and inclusive growth by assessing its progress to date. The key aspects of interest in this review include the vision's origin, development process, and implementation. All these have a direct bearing on the prospects of realising the set goals.

What is Vision 2030?

In June 2008, the Kenya government launched Vision 2030 whose goal is to make Kenya 'a globally competitive and prosperous nation with a high quality of life by the year 2030'. The aim is to transform Kenya into a 'newly industrialising, middle-income country'.[1] Vision 2030, Kenya's national development blueprint for the period 2008 to 2030, is touted as the most comprehensive since independence.[2]

The genesis of Vision 2030

Vision 2030 was developed at a time when Kenya was in a state of optimism following the transition in political leadership from the Kenya African National Union (KANU) single-party regime, which had been in office since independence, to a multi-party leadership under the new National Alliance Rainbow Coalition (NARC), at the close of 2002. Results of the Gallup International Annual End of Year Survey undertaken in 65 countries just before NARC assumed leadership showed that Kenya was the most optimistic country on earth.[3] As Wolf and colleagues reported, the shift in power from KANU to NARC was welcomed with 'an outpouring of optimism and euphoria, as the vast majority of Kenyans clearly hoped that... NARC's promises to reform and revitalize the government would lead them to prosperity and a fully realised democracy'.[4]

The optimism that emanated from this change in political leadership was reflected in other spheres of the nation, including the economy. Kenyans had come to believe in the possibility of change and more so positive change as manifested in NARC's campaign Kiswahili mantra, '*Yote yawezekana bila KANU (Moi)*', meaning 'All is possible without KANU and Moi'—the ruling party and president before Kibaki's NARC party came into power. The results of Wolf and colleagues' *Afrobarometer* national survey undertaken in August 2003 showed that about three quarters of Kenyans expected an improvement in the national economy (79 per cent) and their personal well-being (77 per cent) by the end of 2003, a year after NARC came into power.

NARC did not disappoint. The economy's 2.9 per cent growth in 2003 (from 0.6 per cent in 2002) within the first year of Kibaki's NARC government furthered this optimism. While opinions differ depending on which side of the political divide one stands, it seems that having a technocrat executive leading national economic reforms paid off. Kibaki is praised as a top-notch economist, having graduated top of his class from the London School of Economics with an MSc in Public Finance following a first-class Bachelor's degree in Economics, History, and Political Science.[5] It seems his understanding of what this entailed ensured that the job was done well.

Vision 2030 was developed in the backdrop of NARC's successful Economic Recovery Strategy for Wealth and Employment Creation (ERS) of 2003 to 2007, which got Kenya's economy back to rapid growth. The ERS aimed at restoring high economic growth, reducing poverty, and improving equity and governance.[6] The annual GDP growth rate rose from 0.6 per cent to 7.1 per cent during this period, reversing the poor economic performance of the 1980s and 1990s.[7] This exemplary performance under NARC's first development strategy fostered Kenyans' faith in the impossible.

Moreover, the UN vision, Transforming our world: The 2030 agenda for sustainable development, is described as a 'supremely ambitious and transformational vision'.[8] In the agenda, the UN encourages its member states to similarly develop practical and ambitious national agendas to implement this global *Agenda 2030*. Although this UN call came during the Vision 2030 implementation, it appears that Kenya was driven by the same sense of ambition, urgency, and desperation in realising tangible and lasting development. A dream driven by a spirit of playing catch-up with its 1960s peers like the Asian Tigers, which it looked to for the Vision 2030 development and sought to emulate.

Developing the vision

In 2006, Mwai Kibaki, who had successfully championed the formulation and implementation of the ERS which had gotten Kenya back on its economic development path after the rough 1980s and 1990s, launched the Vision 2030 development process. Vision 2030 was developed through a highly consultative process involving a varied range of key stakeholders, such as the government, industry leaders, and ordinary Kenyans. The National Economic and Social Council (NESC), a group of technocrats composed of senior technical government officers, industry leaders, and researchers, was constituted to steer the vision's formulation process.

The vision was to have realistic and concrete plans for implementation starting from 2008 after the expiry of the ERS. In developing the vision, the

NESC drew inspiration and lessons from East Asia's 'newly industrialising nations' such as Malaysia and Singapore, which had realised continuous rapid growth and a significant improvement in the lives of their citizens for nearly three decades by that time.[9] The Vision 2030 authors sought to copy these nations both in terms of the standards they had achieved and the strategies they had used. In developing the vision, the technical expertise in several key areas was drawn from nations of East Asia that had done well in these particular sectors.[10] The NESC envisaged that Kenya would continue to make use of such technical support in the implementation of the vision.

With inputs from government ministries, the private sector, wide public consultations, and guidance from the technical experts, the National Economic and Social Council identified priority sectors, selected high-impact projects, and mobilised support for the vision across political, ethnic, and geographical divides.[11] The identification of economic sectors that had the biggest potential in driving the development of the country by 2030 was based on two key criteria: the potential for economic impact, and the likelihood of unlocking the sector's potential for economic growth and poverty reduction.[12]

Kenya's future as per Vision 2030

As said above, Vision 2030 aims to focus the country's development effort on making Kenya 'a newly industrialising, middle-income country providing a high quality of life to all its citizens in a clean and secure environment country by 2030'.[13] The vision comprises three core pillars: the economic pillar, the social pillar, and the political pillar. The economic pillar was designed to accelerate economic growth; the social pillar to achieve just, equitable and cohesive social development; and the political pillar to reinforce an accountable democratic political system.

The economic pillar's goal is to provide prosperity for all Kenyans through an economic development programme by achieving an average gross domestic product (GDP) growth rate of 10 per cent per annum up to the year 2030. In Vision 2030, Kenya set itself an ambitious and inspirational goal—a huge endeavour that had only been achieved by four other countries (Oman, Equatorial Guinea, Botswana, and China) before then.[14] The challenge was particularly huge considering the nation's context—the economy was just recovering from nearly two-and-a-half decades of dismal economic performance.

The target of 10 per cent per annum was meant to accentuate the economic performance realised under the ERS, which was a significant and consistent improvement from 0.6 per cent in 2002 to 7.1 per cent in 2007, an average growth of about 5.5 per cent per annum during this period.[15] This envisaged improvement to economic growth was to be attained by mitigating the constraints to growth and using the nation's resources more efficiently. Some of the immediate actions identified in the vision were to grow the national savings from 17 per cent in 2006 to 30 per cent by 2012, and to deal with the 75 per cent informal employment issue.[16] This growth in the national savings was to provide the much-needed capital for investment and hence increase employment opportunities.

Under the social pillar, Kenya seeks to build 'a just and cohesive society, enjoying equitable social development'.[17] One of the strategies to get to this equitable society is through education and training. Kenya plans to provide globally competitive education, training, and research for development. The overall goal for 2012 was to reduce illiteracy by increasing access to education, improving the transition rate from primary to secondary schools, and raising the quality and relevance of education.

Other social goals in the vision include the integration of all special needs education into learning and training institutions, achieving an 80 per cent adult literacy rate, increasing the net enrolment rate to 95 per cent and transition rates to technical institutions and universities from 3 per cent to 8 per cent, and expanding access to university education from 4.6 per cent to 20 per cent.[18] The government is to partner with the private sector to increase the level of investment to achieve these goals.

Besides education, some of the other strategies outlined under social pillar are to: (a) reduce the number of people living in poverty and guarantee equality regarding access to public services and income generation; (b) improve the livelihoods of vulnerable groups; (c) have a prosperous, responsible, and globally competitive youth, and (d) increase access to services such as health and education, business opportunities, housing, and justice for all disadvantaged groups.[19] The Vision places emphasis on increasing school enrolment for girls and children from the economically marginalised poor, rural and slum communities. Under the political pillar, in recognition of the essential role governance plays in development, Kenya's national governance system is to be reformed to the high capability typical of rapidly industrialising nations to enable the country to meet the objectives of the economic and social pillars.

Looking at these select goals of Vision 2030, the core building blocks for sustainable and inclusive development seem to be in place. The vision touches on all the right things. Actually, as typical of prior Kenyan development strategies, the issue is not about lack of policy ideas, but more about the ability to implement these policies, as we shall shortly see.

Implementing the vision

Vision 2030 is being implemented through five-year medium-term plans (MTPs), with the first two (MTP1 and MTP2) having been concluded and that of the third one (MTP3) currently underway. This third medium-term plan (2018-2022) is aligned to the SDGs and is expected to fast-track progress towards them. In formulating the vision, concrete flagship projects were identified under each pillar whose implementation is prioritised under the medium-term planning. The focus of the first medium term plan was envisaged as the first step in this long journey. Its aim was to lay the groundwork in each of the three spheres—economic, social, and political—for attaining the vision.

The actual implementation of Vision 2030 is undertaken by the various government ministries and departments in collaboration with the private sector, civil society, and other stakeholders. The relevant government ministries are charged with developing and implementing the medium-term plans in collaboration with the market players and other stakeholders. The overall implementation responsibility of the vision rests with the Vision 2030 Delivery Secretariat, currently under the Ministry of Planning and Devolution. The Secretariat is headed by a director-general who receives overall guidance from the Vision 2030 Delivery Board, which plays a policy-making and advisory role. The Board draws its membership from both the government and other stakeholders and is currently chaired by one of Kenya's market leaders.

To give the implementation of the vision the support it required, the Delivery Secretariat was envisaged to be under the Office of the President in the formulation stage. However, it ended up being established under the Ministry of Planning. This change was to accommodate the necessary power-sharing between the NARC and Orange Democratic Movement (ODM) parties following the brokering of a peace deal and formation of a coalition government after the 2007-2008 post-election violence.

As identified in the vision, its successful implementation would require a new style of management; a shift to 'business unusual', which would entail having a centralised implementation process, changing the management philosophy to 'a sense of urgency and relentless follow-up', fast and proactive legislating, high and ring-fenced investments, and management of top talent that uses a 'war for talent' tactic.[20]

Noteworthy is that while Vision 2030 was developed in a resemblance of oneness in 2006-2007 under the NARC government, its implementation did not start until 2008 after the 2007 elections. The 2007 elections ended up in post-election violence that left the nation more ethnically fragmented than ever before and in a situation of national administrative power-sharing between the main two political parties. At the start of 2008, the nation was at almost the other extreme of the enthusiasm and optimism of 2003, only five years later.

The national unity and commitment that was crucial for pursuing the vision waned in the aftermath of the 2007 elections. Individual party interests impacted several aspects of the vision's implementation such as where to house the Vision's Delivery Secretariat and recruitment of its

Director-General.[21] Although some progress has been attained since its inception, housing the Vision 2030 Secretariat outside the Office of the President denied it the president's steer and signal of commitment that was critical for its successful implementation.

Policy experts identify inclusive planning, robust prioritisation, adaptability, and effective monitoring as key criteria in evaluating development strategies.[22] While Vision 2030 has performed well in many of these aspects, it has faced challenges in some areas, key among them national governance. The Vision 2030 Delivery Secretariat was resourced with the right talent to drive the vision; the success in accomplishing the milestones set under MTP1 is largely attributable to having the right leadership in place. Both the Vision 2030 Director-General and the Board Chair were allied to the president. As a technocrat and industry leader, the first Director-General was able to mobilise both the government ministries and departments (with the political good will rendered by the presidency), and the market (based on his understanding of what needs to be done to align government and market incentives) for delivery.

In 2015, after seven years of implementation, more than a hundred projects were underway, and the vision was generally accepted as the roadmap to Kenya's future.[23] However, the implementation of Vision 2030 would have been more effective if the political climate and governance in Kenya were better. One cannot help wondering if Kenya might have realised the ambitious economic growth goal if the post-election, which accentuated the political and ethnic differences dividing the nation and undoing the little gains that had been made since independence, had not happened.

It is highly possible that if the economic momentum that started under Kibaki's NARC government had been sustained into the future, fostered by the national unity under the 2003 NARC government, Vision 2030 would seem less aspirational than it does today. In the words of Henry Adams, the American historian, 'unity is vision; it must have been part of the process of learning to see'. The important thing though is not to dwell on the past but to learn from it and stay focused on the future.

Looking back to look forward

This section analyses Kenya's progress towards realising sustainable and inclusive development under Vision 2030. I have used the IFs model to generate forecasts of the journey ahead to determine if Kenya will achieve the set goals by 2030 based on the current trajectory. Instead of focusing on attainment of the specific targets outlined in Vision 2030, this section looks at progress with regards to the parameters identified in Chapter 2 as indicators of sustainable and inclusive development. This review of achievement under Vision 2030 is categorised into three main areas: driving sustainable economic growth, addressing inequality and enhancing the quality of life.

Driving economic growth

Despite the dismal economic performance in 2008 following the 2007-2008 post-election violence, Kenya's economic growth picked up again from 2009. Following a rebasing of its national accounts (including GDP) in 2014, Kenya has joined the league of low-middle income countries.[24] However, despite this rebasing, which led to revising the GDP growth rate for 2013 from 4.7 per cent to 5.7 per cent, the economic growth remains well below the goal set in Vision 2030. The nation has struggled to attain the 10 per cent average annual growth envisioned in 2007.

The average annual economic (GDP) growth rate for the period 2000 to 2014 was only 4.4 per cent and not significantly above its population growth rate of 2.7 per cent, which effectively means that its GDP per capita has remained relatively stagnant.[25] An important point to note is that the historical data used by the Ifs model is based on the 2005 dollars and not this recent rebasing, but it is still a good indication of the growth trajectory.

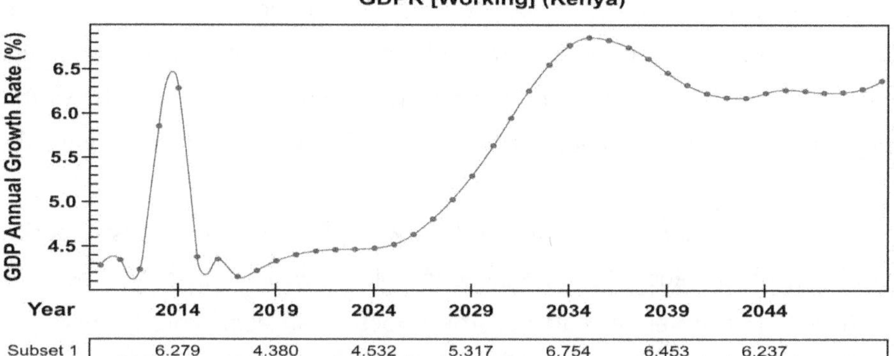

Figure 3.1: Kenya's projected annual GDP growth rate (at current trajectory)

Subset 1	6.279	4.380	4.532	5.317	6.754	6.453	6.237

Source: Generated from International Futures Model [Computer Software, Version 7.00], 2017. Retrieved from http://www.ifs.du.edu/

As shown in figure 3.1 above, not much improvement to Kenya's GDP is anticipated in the remaining period to 2030 based on the current trajectory—that is, implementation of the planned development policies and strategies. We are way past the initial or take-off stage, usually characterised by high levels of investment and well-developed political and societal institutions, which is the most important in making economic growth self-sustaining.[26]

In sum, Kenya's chances of realising the economic growth targets as encapsulated in Vision 2030 within the stipulated timeframe are very slim. The impressive economic growth under ERS, which informed the aspirational goal of an average of 10 per cent per annum for the period 2008-2030, was not sustained. Under ERS, Kenya had realised a high economic growth of about 7 per cent in 2007. This was probably the first time Kenya had effectively designed and implemented a policy and achieved the desired results.[27] However, the nation has struggled to maintain the economic momentum gained through the ERS after the 2007-2008 post-election violence.

The vision's economic goal on which all the other goals are anchored seems to have been based on fantasy and not reality. Franklin Roosevelt once said it is wise to 'keep your eyes on the stars and your feet on the ground' when planning. Rather than take proper stock of its strengths and resources, the vision authors appear to have been enticed by the living standards of the highly-developed nations—wanting to be like other countries—and downplayed what it would take to make this happen. For instance, one thing that appears to have been missed out in this planning was the cyclical nature of Kenya's economic development, which is exemplified by dismal performance in election years due to the political risk associated with the event.

Political risk soon manifested following the 2007-2008 post-election violence, which caused the annual economic growth to dip to 0.23 per cent in 2008.[28] The violence shattered the hopes of an economic take-off and pushed the development curve back to the pre-Kibaki era. However, the incidence was a wake-up call to Kenya and instilled a sense of caution in the leadership. The latter was evidenced in the 2013 elections in the form of a cautiousness by the political leadership to avoid a repeat of 2008.

Addressing inequality

Addressing inequality in Kenya remains a challenge even under Vision 2030. As shown in figure 3.2 below, while there has been consistent growth in GDP per capita since 2010, it is minimal compared to the achievements of the middle-income nations that Kenya yearns to emulate. Also, an improvement in GDP per capita simply indicates a faster rate of economic growth compared with its population growth and does not necessarily show shared or inclusive growth.

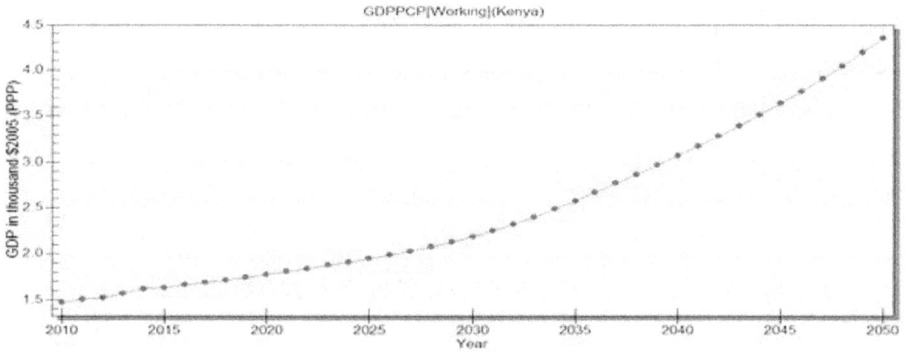

Figure 3.2: Kenya's GDP per capita at $ 2005 (PPP) over time

Source: Generated from International Futures Model [Computer Software, Version 7.00], 2017. Retrieved from http://www.ifs.du.edu/

As seen earlier, a better measure of inequality is the poverty gap. The IFs model defines the poverty gap as 'the mean shortfall from the poverty line, expressed as a percentage of the poverty line'. The poverty gap (POVGAP) is used to measure the depth of poverty. The non-poor are considered to have a zero shortfall thus, the bigger the number, the worse the poverty gap.

Figure 3.3: Kenya's projected poverty gap
(based on $1.25 a day income)

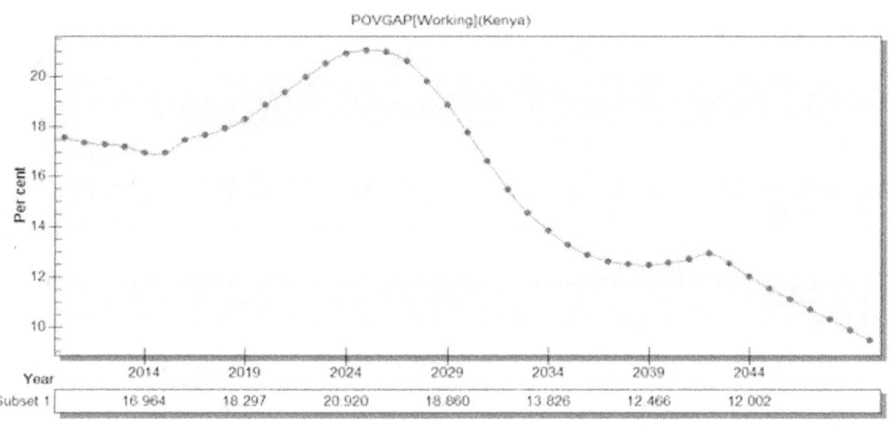

Source: Generated from International Futures Model [Computer Software, Version 7.00], 2017. Retrieved from http://www.ifs.du.edu/

As shown in figure 3.3 above, Kenya experienced a slight drop in the poverty gap from 17.6 per cent in 2010 to 16.9 per cent in 2016. However, this achievement towards equality was short-lived as the poverty gap started widening again from 2017 and this is to continue up to the year 2025, when it will peak at around 21 per cent based on the current development trajectory.

Figure 3.4: Kenya's projected inequality (GINIDOM)over time

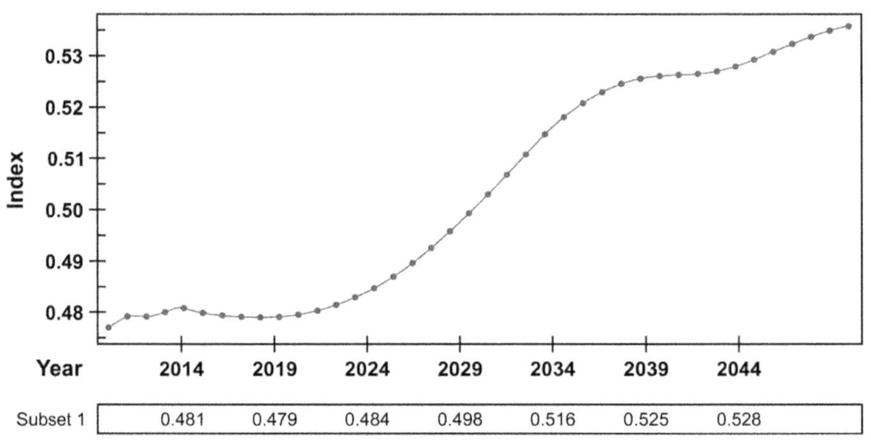

	2014	2019	2024	2029	2034	2039	2044
Subset 1	0.481	0.479	0.484	0.498	0.516	0.525	0.528

Source: Generated from International Futures Model [Computer Software, Version 7.00], 2017. Retrieved from http://www.ifs.du.edu/

The other measure of inequality is the domestic Gini index of inequality (GINIDOM). Figure 3.4 shows a continued increase in this index—larger means more unequal incomes. Both these trends imply that the poor are expected to become poorer as the rich become richer in the future. Although there will be some gains in the economy as reflected in GDP growth, these will continue to benefit only a small segment of the population, a situation which James Mwangi, a Kenyan market leader and the current Chair of the Vision 2030 Delivery Secretariat, refers to as a 'dual economy'. This scenario is typical of Kenya's past and the situation in most African countries where poverty levels have continued to rise even during periods of economic growth.[29]

Enhancing Kenyans' quality of life

Attaining rapid economic development for Kenya as per Vision 2030 is not meant to be an end in itself. Strongly embedded in the Vision is an aspiration to provide Kenyans with a high quality of life, that is, to enhance the well-being of its citizens. Anticipating an average annual growth rate of 10 per cent per annum for Kenya is a positive and ambitious goal, but it means little in light of the majority's well-being because it ignores the aspect of the distribution of wealth.

This section uses the 2016 World Bank's quality of life or societal well-being indicators outlined in Chapter 2 (with slight modifications to each indicator where necessary based on available data) to gauge Kenya's progress and prospects for realising this goal as per Vision 2030. These indicators are life expectancy, poverty headcount ratio at $1.25 a day (purchasing power parity), school enrolment (per cent gross), and the percentage of the population with access to electricity.

a) Life expectancy

Figure 3.5: Kenya's life expectancy

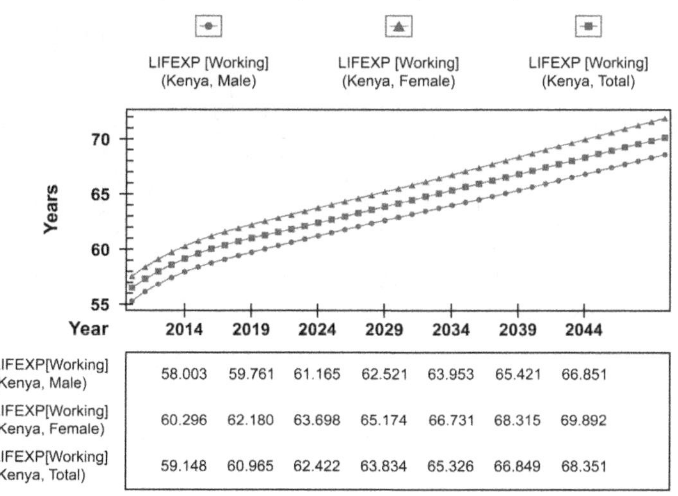

	2014	2019	2024	2029	2034	2039	2044
LIFEXP[Working] (Kenya, Male)	58.003	59.761	61.165	62.521	63.953	65.421	66.851
LIFEXP[Working] (Kenya, Female)	60.296	62.180	63.698	65.174	66.731	68.315	69.892
LIFEXP[Working] (Kenya, Total)	59.148	60.965	62.422	63.834	65.326	66.849	68.351

Source: Generated from International Futures Model [Computer Software, Version 7.00], 2017. Retrieved from http://www.ifs.du.edu/

Based on figure 3.5 above, Kenya has experienced an improvement in the average total number of years one is expected to live at birth since the inception of Vision 2030, and this is forecasted to continue into the future—to reach an average of 64.1 years in 2030 from 60 years currently.

b) Poverty headcount

Kenya's poverty headcount (at $1.25 per day) has been growing and is forecasted to continually increase up to around the year 2035 when it will peak at about 23.5 million people as shown in figure 3.6 below. However, the growth in absolute numbers living in poverty will mainly be driven by an increase in the gross population as shown. By 2035, the poverty headcount ratio at $1.25 per day will drop to nearly 33 per cent (the gross population is forecasted to be about 72 million) from 37 per cent currently.

Figure 3.6: Kenya's poverty headcount 1.25 a day
versus population (in millions)

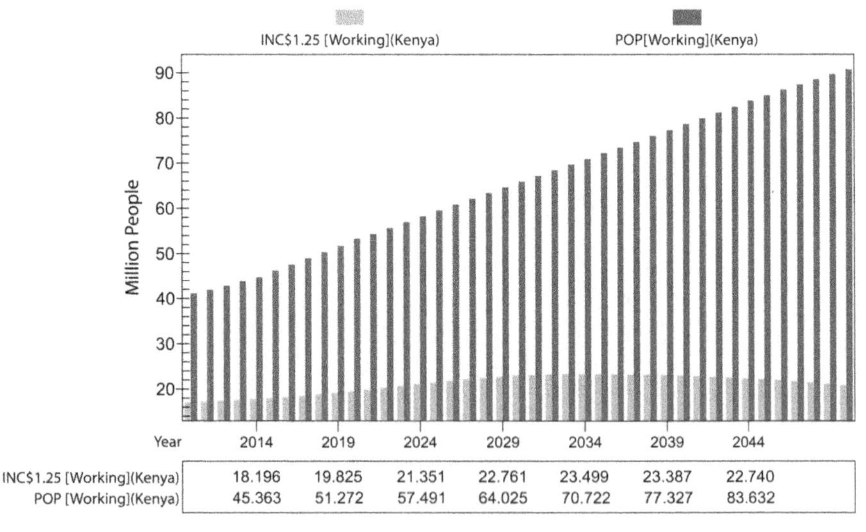

Year	2014	2019	2024	2029	2034	2039	2044
INC$1.25 [Working](Kenya)	18.196	19.825	21.351	22.761	23.499	23.387	22.740
POP [Working](Kenya)	45.363	51.272	57.491	64.025	70.722	77.327	83.632

Source: Generated from International Futures Model [Computer Software, Version 7.00], 2017. Retrieved from http://www.ifs.du.edu/

c) Education attainment

As illustrated in figure 3.7 below, Kenya has experienced an overall improvement in the general human capital stock but more so in the level of education attained since the start of this decade. There has been a near universal attainment of primary education (currently at about 87 per cent) and improvements in both the proportions of those with secondary and tertiary education from 3.9 per cent and 1.5 per cent in 2010 to about 6.5 per cent and 2.0 per cent in 2016, respectively.

Figure 3.7: Education attainment (% per cent of gross population)

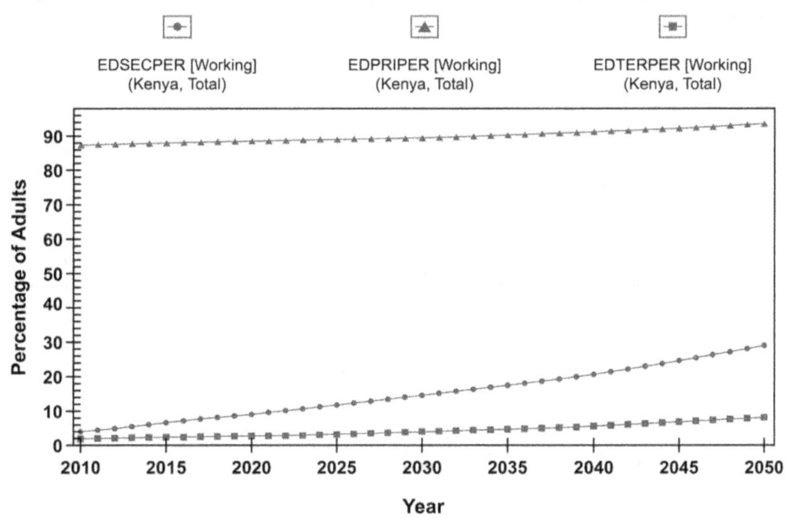

Source: Generated from International Futures Model [Computer Software, Version 7.00], 2017. Retrieved from http://www.ifs.du.edu/

At its current trajectory, this trend is forecasted to continue to reach 88.4 per cent (primary education), 13.9 per cent (secondary education), and 3.4 per cent (tertiary level) by 2030. While these trends are positive, they are way below Vision 2030's target of 95 per cent enrolment for primary school and 8 per cent transition to tertiary education, and a far cry from Malaysia's education attainment levels which Kenya seeks to emulate, as shown in figure 3.8 below.

Figure 3.8: Comparison of Kenya and Malaysia's education attainment levels

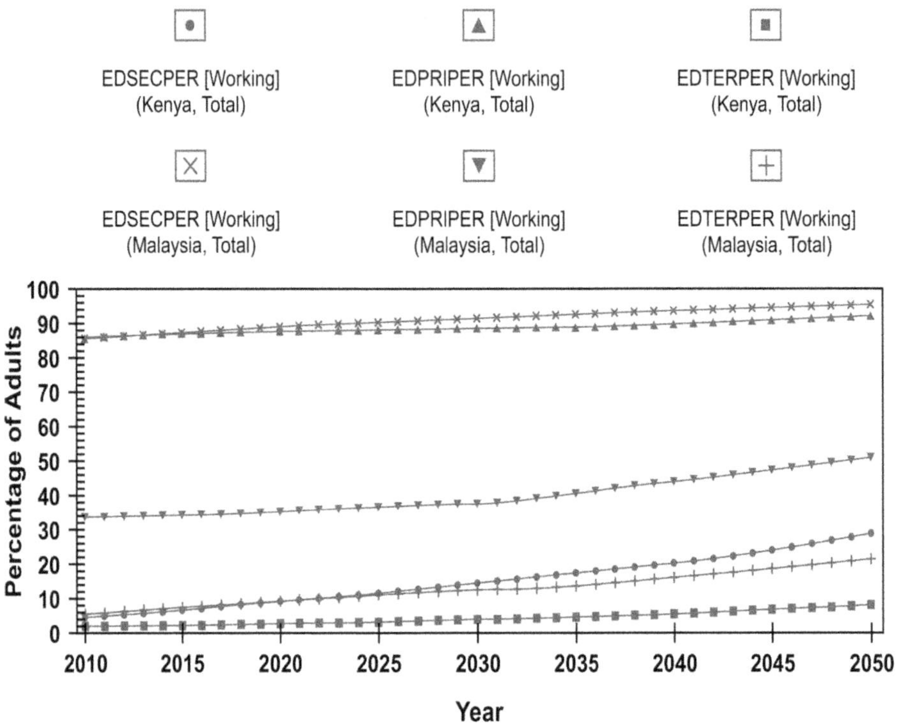

Source: Generated from International Futures Model [Computer Software, Version 7.00], 2017. Retrieved from http://www.ifs.du.edu/

For instance, at 7.3 per cent of the population, Malaysia's current tertiary level education attainment is slightly higher than Kenya's secondary school attainment, which is estimated at 6.5 per cent. Furthermore, these figures are purely for the time spent in school and say nothing about the quality of the education. Research done on the high performing East Asia economies (HPEAs) at the close of the twentieth century praised the quality of their education system, as detailed in the next chapter.

d) Access to electricity

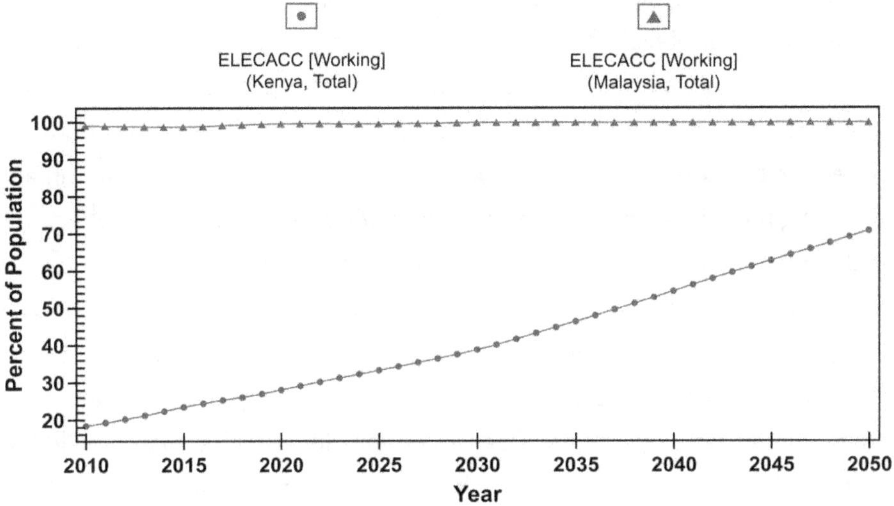

Source: Generated from International Futures Model [Computer Software, Version 7.00], 2017. Retrieved from http://www.ifs.du.edu/

Based on figure 3.9 above, the Kenyan government has made marked progress in availing electricity to rural households through the rural electrification programme. About 25 per cent of the population now has access to electricity compared with 18 per cent in 2010. This proportion is expected to reach 40 per cent by 2030 at the current trajectory. The Last Mile Connectivity Program (LMCP), whose aim was to ensure every Kenyan household had access to electricity by 2020, can significantly boost access especially in rural areas.

Overall, Kenya has made progress in improving the quality of life of its citizens but at a much slower pace than envisaged under Vision 2030. Based on the illustrations and discussions here, it is evident that Kenya will not realise the Vision 2030 goal based on the current trajectory. Furthermore, there is no guarantee that the current pace of progress will be sustained. The next section looks at some of the challenges that have hindered progress.

Challenges in realising the vision

Instead of simply looking at the progress attained through Vision 2030 towards sustainable and inclusive development, it is important to review the fundamentals on which the goals are anchored, such as governance, which is classified under legal and institutional reforms in the political pillar. A key milestone in Kenya's national governance was the promulgation of a new constitution in 2010, which enshrined basic human rights such as equality. Moreover, the constitution empowered core public institutions with an aim of making them function more effectively. For instance, it gave independence to the judiciary and removed it from political patronage.

Another major win from the new constitution has been the two-tier government or devolved government system. This has enabled better distribution of national resources through the county governments, although challenges of poor governance at the county level still prevail. While the new constitution has been a key achievement in improving the institutions of governance, a lot remains to be done to ensure its full implementation. Based on the experience thus far, the quality of Kenya's public institutions will continue to pose a significant barrier in the journey to realising sustainable and inclusive growth.[30]

One of the reasons given for the sub-optimal economic performance under Vision 2030 is *a lack of prioritisation* despite the level of effort that was deployed into its development. There are numerous strategies outlined in Vision 2030 which would be hard for any government to implement at once, and more so Kenya given its budgetary and technical capacity limitations. This lack of prioritisation has led to the partial and poor implementation of the identified interventions with the outcome being minimal economic impact. It is important for the government to determine the high-leverage points—those that would have the greatest and most widespread impact on the whole economy—and focus on these. Having a few reforms that are optimally sequenced to surmount the binding constraints can generate big positive economic impacts.[31]

The lack of concreteness and prioritisation in Vision 2030 has not been lost on the part of Kenya's development partners, who consequently have not given its implementation as much support as would have been expected.[32] For instance, Michael Ranneberger, the former US Ambassador to Kenya, was reported in the *Wikileaks* as saying that 'Vision 2030 often reads like a naïve call for a perfect society'.[33] The same applies to the markets which still await a demonstration of seriousness and commitment by the government by way of providing the right environment and incentives through policy. Although the private sector wants to be involved, some entrepreneurs have been in a state of cautious optimism regarding the government's efforts and its ability to implement this ambitious vision successfully.[34] If the leaders themselves have little conviction about their vision, it is hard for their followers to believe in it and rally behind them.

Understandably, some of the interventions will not immediately bear results. The current chair of the Vision 2030 Delivery Secretariat Board, James Mwangi, argues that the impact of the development interventions under the Vision are yet to be felt by the ordinary Kenyan because most of the emphasis has been put on infrastructure and institution building.[35] This prioritisation is evidenced in the new roads around the capital city and the standard gauge railway line which connects Mombasa, the main seaport into Kenya, and Nairobi, the capital city. This railway will be extended to link Kenya with other nations in the East African Community.

While longer-term infrastructural investments are necessary, they cannot be undertaken at the expense of the more important and deeper reaching human capital investments in basic services such as education that will yield the highest returns to the country in the long run. As shown above, human capital is increasingly becoming the most important factor of production generally and more so for service economies such as Kenya— services currently contribute about 47.9 per cent of the country's GDP.[36] Consequently, there is a need to employ an integrated effort in development, typified by a clear prioritisation of interventions.

Understandably, the nation needed to transform itself into the 'new Kenya' described in the vision, but this should have been grounded in reality and pursued in manageable bits. Small wins always encourage the heart, which is crucial for long and gruelling journeys such as attaining sustainable and inclusive development. A shorter-term government policy like the 2003–2007 ERS had the benefit of rallying effort and realising results within one administrative government and was better grounded in terms of what was achievable. Its effective implementation and positive results, the first since independence as Kimenyi and colleagues[37] point out, had the effect of making people believe in the impossible, and hence the creation of Vision 2030. This demonstrates the power of small and quick wins.

Another reason for the sub-optimal performance has been *weak governance*. One strong indication of the quality of governance is the presence or absence of corruption (as measured by Transparency International's Corruption Perceptions Index). While there has been some improvement, Kenya's government is almost as corrupt as it was before Vision 2030 (ranked 137/198 in 2019 compared to 150/179 in 2007—lower ranking signifies more corruption). The government needs to demonstrate its commitment to fighting corruption and stop paying it lip service if it hopes to effectively realise Vision 2030.[38] Corruption is a tax on the poor which deepens inequality. It erodes the incentives for foreign investments by markets and development partners, both of which are crucial for successful implementation of Vision 2030 given Kenya's low level of national savings. By the end of 2016, Kenya's gross national savings were only 10.6 per cent of GDP compared to its 2012 target of 30 per cent.[39]

Kenya is yet to build strong institutions of governance to make Vision 2030 happen.[40] To echo Fourie[41], the implementation of Vision 2030 has lacked 'technocratic insulation', with those in the essential government institutions being appointees of the political leadership. Although the recruitment process for these executive positions is open to the public, the presidency has an ultimate say as per the constitution. Top public office holders thus end up being the appointees of the political leadership to whom they owe full allegiance and thus lack the space to apply their expertise to drive development.

Overall, Vision 2030 seems overly ambitious and unrealistic given its breadth of strategy and policy interventions. To concur with the views of the International Development Association (IDA) and the International Monetary Fund, the vision lacks a clear sense of prioritisation as exemplified by the 28 priority sectors and 120 flagship projects.[42] It fails to answer the question; what is the one thing or the small combination of policy interventions that Kenya must immediately implement to make tangible developmental progress? Reading the vision gives one a sense of playing catch-up with other nations—wanting to be like the economically successful East Asia economies. Kenya seems to be waking up to its developmental reality decades late and desperately wanting to make up the time lost. However, the vision's implementation has been organised into the Medium-Term Plans (MTPs), which gives room for further prioritisation and more detailed planning for each of these five-year periods.

Nevertheless, sustainable and inclusive growth takes a long-term perspective, and hence it might be premature to expect to see real impacts. The adopted mid-term planning approach presents an opportunity for the vision implementation steering team to identify, prioritise, and implement sequenced interventions that could lead the nation towards the desired goals, even if they are attained after year 2030. Additionally, it is also important to appreciate the time lag of outcomes from the initiated reforms.[43] For instance, the universal primary education, which was instituted in 2003, is only starting to bear results now in the form of better-skilled labour and lower fertility rates. This calls for sustained implementation of the policy interventions beyond political administration tenures to yield positive results.

National governance is a critical input for development. The new constitution was promulgated in 2010 and building the institutions of public governance stipulated in its underway. Politics pose the biggest risk to successful implementation of the vision. Therefore, inclusion of the political pillar was crucial. The cyclical five-year electoral votes will, therefore, continue to be 'a barometer measuring Vision 2030's ability to create a genuinely democratic political system respecting the rule of law and protecting the rights and freedoms of all Kenyans,' as envisaged under the political pillar.[44]

Yet, amidst these negative developments, Kenya has one thing in its favour; due to the highly participatory and far-reaching process adopted in developing the vision, the national leadership across all political divides still has faith in the vision. For instance, despite their political rivalry, NARC and ODM adopted the vision as a common development agenda in 2008, a position that was retained when Uhuru Kenyatta's Jubilee government came into power in 2013. Kenya is, therefore, unlikely to face a situation where future governments develop new development plans before the full term of Vision 2030, as happened to the NPEP. The broad-based engagement and support attained in its development will help the vision transcend future transitions in government.[45]

It is evident though that unless there is a total change of strategy, Kenya is not likely to realise this ambitious development goal by 2030. The predisposition of the vision developers towards urgency, ambition, and catch-up may have obscured them from the economic realities facing the country. Without a review of the current policies and reprioritisation, Vision 2030 is likely to remain aspirational and unrealistic, a goal not meant to be attained but merely something to aim towards, to use Bruce Lee's description of aspirational visions.

References

[1]   Vision 2030 (2007). *Vision 2030 Brochure*. Republic of Kenya.

[2]   Gainer, M. (2015). 'Planning transformation in a divided nation: Creating Kenya Vision 2030, 2005–2009'. *Innovation for Successful Societies*. Princeton University.

[3]   The Standard (2003, Jan 21). 'Kenyans most optimistic people on earth, says survey'. *The Standard*.

[4]   Wolf, P., Logan, C. & Owiti, J. (2004). 'A new dawn? Popular optimism in Kenya after the transition'. *Afrobarometer working papers No. 33, p. ix*.

[5]   Aron, M. & Machi, T. (2012, Jun 26). 'The making of 'Kibakinomics''. Standard Digital.

[6]   Thugge, K., Ndung'u, N. & Otieno, O. (2009). 'Unlocking the Future Potential for Kenya: The Vision 2030'.

7   Vision 2030 (2007). Vision 2030 Brochure. Republic of Kenya.

8   United Nations (n.d.(b)). 'Transforming our world: The 2030 Agenda for Sustainable Development'. United Nations Sustainable Development Knowledge Platform.

9   Vision 2030 (2007). Vision 2030 Brochure. Republic of Kenya, p. 3.

10   Fourie, E. (2014). 'Model students: Policy emulation, modernization, and Kenya's Vision 2030'. *African Affairs (London). 2014, Vol. 113 Issue 453*, p540-562.

11   Gainer, M. (2015). 'Planning transformation in a divided nation: Creating Kenya Vision 2030, 2005–2009'. *Innovation for Successful Societies*. Princeton University.

12   Vision 2030 (2007). Vision 2030 Brochure. Republic of Kenya, p. 3.

13   Ibid

14   Fourie, E. (2014). 'Model students: Policy emulation, modernization, and Kenya's Vision 2030'. *African Affairs (London). 2014, Vol. 113 Issue 453*, p540-562.

15   Kimenyi, M., Mwega, F. & Ndung'u, N. (2016). 'The African lions: Kenya country case study'. Brookings Institute.

16   Vision 2030 (2007). Vision 2030 Brochure. Republic of Kenya.

17   Ibid, p. 11

18   Ibid

19   Ibid

20   Ibid, p. 26

21   Gainer, M. (2015). 'Planning transformation in a divided nation: Creating Kenya Vision 2030, 2005–2009'. Innovation for Successful Societies. Princeton University.

22   Ibid; UNDP (2016). 'From the MDGs to sustainable development for all: Lessons from 15 years of practice'. United Nations Development Programme.

23   Gainer, M. (2015). 'Planning transformation in a divided nation: Creating Kenya Vision 2030, 2005–2009'. Innovation for Successful Societies. Princeton University.

24   World Bank (2014, Sep 30). Kenya: A bigger, better economy. The world Bank.

25   Kimenyi, M., Mwega, F. & Ndung'u, N. (2016). 'The African lions: Kenya country case study'. Brookings Institute.

26   Fourie, E. (2014). 'Model students: Policy emulation, modernization, and Kenya's Vision 2030'. *African Affairs (London). 2014, Vol. 113 Issue 453*, p540-562.

27   Thugge, K., Ndung'u, N. & Otieno, O. (2009). 'Unlocking the Future Potential for Kenya: The Vision 2030'.

28   Kimenyi, M., Mwega, F. & Ndung'u, N. (2016). 'The African lions: Kenya country case study'. Brookings Institute.

29   Donge, J., Henley, D. & Lewis, P. (2012). 'Tracking development in South-East Asia and sub-Saharan Africa: The primacy of policy'. *Development Policy Review. February 2012, Vol. 30 Issue 1*, p5–24.

30   Nyanjom, O. & Ong'olo, D. (2012). 'Erratic development in Kenya: Questions from the East Asian miracle'. *Development Policy Review, 2012, Vol. 30 Issue 1*, p73-99.

31   World Bank (2009, Feb 10). 'What is inclusive development?' World Bank, Washington, DC.

32   Fourie, E. (2014). 'Model students: Policy emulation, modernization, and Kenya's Vision 2030'. *African Affairs (London). 2014, Vol. 113 Issue 453*, p540-562.

33   Ibid p. 550.

34   The Economist (2014, Sep 17). 'The Kenyan state of innovation: Will the Kenyan government's mainstreaming of the innovation sector foster growth?' The Economist, GE Look ahead.

35   Shikwati, J. (2012, Oct 18). 'Viewpoint: Will corruption kill off Kenya's Vision 2030 plans?' BBC News Africa.

36   World Factbook (2018, Oct 10). Kenya. Central Intelligence Agency.

37   Kimenyi, M., Mwega, F. & Ndung'u, N. (2016). 'The African lions: Kenya country case study'. Brookings Institute.

38   The Economist (2014, Sep 17). 'The Kenyan state of innovation: Will the Kenyan government's mainstreaming of the innovation sector foster growth?' The Economist, GE Look ahead.

39   World Factbook (2018, Oct 10). Kenya. Central Intelligence Agency.

40   Donge, J., Henley, D. & Lewis, P. (2012). 'Tracking development in South-East Asia and sub-Saharan Africa: The primacy of policy'. *Development Policy Review. February 2012, Vol. 30 Issue 1*, p5–24; Nyanjom, O. & Ong'olo, D. (2012). 'Erratic development in Kenya: Questions from the East Asian miracle'. *Development Policy Review, 2012, Vol. 30 Issue 1*, p73-99.

41   Fourie, E. (2014). 'Model students: Policy emulation, modernization, and Kenya's Vision 2030'. *African Affairs (London). 2014, Vol. 113 Issue 453*, p540-562.

42   Gainer, M. (2015). 'Planning transformation in a divided nation: Creating Kenya Vision 2030, 2005–2009'. Innovation for Successful Societies. Princeton University.

43   World Bank (2009, Feb 10). 'What is inclusive development?' World Bank, Washington, DC.

44   Shikwati, J. (2012, Oct 18). 'Viewpoint: Will corruption kill off Kenya's Vision 2030 plans?' BBC News Africa.

45   Gainer, M. (2015). 'Planning transformation in a divided nation: Creating Kenya Vision 2030, 2005–2009'. Innovation for Successful Societies. Princeton University.

CHAPTER 4

Following in the footsteps of Malaysia

*Do not seek to follow in the footsteps of the men
of old; seek what they sought. —Matsuo Basho*

This chapter identifies the opportunities and conditions for Kenya to realise sustainable and inclusive development by emulating other countries that have been more successful in this endeavour. The Asian Tigers have undisputedly done this in realising inclusive development. Out of these, I zero in on Malaysia because of its close historical parallels with Kenya. This chapter outlines its key success factors and lays the ground for Kenya's emulation of Malaysia.

Need for emulation

In this chapter, emulation is used to mean actively learning from others. Fourie[1] describes emulation as the voluntary utilisation of programme or policy evidence, or lessons from an overseas programme. In emulation, one size does not fit all. To be successful, the consideration of the application of evidence should be informed by an objective evaluation and a strong conviction of the value these policies portend, but not the promise of funding, as is at times the case. A demonstration of utilisation of knowledge and experience from a particular context is always evident in emulations.[2] In other words, emulation is everything, but a blind imitation of what others have done to succeed. The process should be based on similarity of end goals, that is, 'seeking what they sought' as Matsuo Basho, the ancient Japanese poet, advised.

The fact that African governments have not readily welcomed lessons from others is an open secret. Often, good policy proposals are rejected purely on the grounds of being perceived as an imposition of a foreign agenda, without exploring their potential benefits to the country. This is especially true when those behind them are foreigners. At times, the reason for this is the absence of a clear demonstration of where the policies have worked and the ability to draw a close parallel between the two nations to provide some level of assurance that they could succeed. This calls for deliberateness and caution in selecting those to emulate.

The intention of Kenya's founding fathers was to emulate positive lessons from others as embodied in Sessional Paper No. 10 of 1965, which explicitly expressed Kenya's willingness and desire 'to borrow technological knowledge and proven economic methods from any country'.[3] Kenya's political economy, which affects international relationships, has morphed over the decades, but there is still an openness to learning from others.

However, the ability to emulate the success of other nations may have been hampered by the impression that policy interventions are being imposed on the country by its funding partners. This is particularly the case when these examples are offered as part of the funding package, even when at times they are not closely aligned with the government's development agenda and priorities. While development partners can guide and point policymakers to places to learn from, they cannot afford to appear to be pushing them to blindly follow the steps of others. For Kenya, the latter would seem contrary to Sessional Paper No. 10 of 1965 which laid out the broad development agenda for the nation.

Informed by the colonial experience which was still fresh in the minds of the policymakers, the Sessional Paper No. 10 stated that the country was to owe no allegiance or commitment to any nation. Kenya has many times been left with little choice but to adhere to the prescriptions of its partners, especially the West, to finance its development. However, a significant degree of 'looking East' for funding is emerging as the government reaches out to countries like China for infrastructural support, both in terms of technology and cash, and to other newly industrialised Asian economies.

Conditions for successful emulation

Kenya has tended to benchmark itself against equally stunted economies in the African region, which has given it a level of comfort. For instance, as mentioned in Chapter 2, Kenya has been the biggest economy in the Eastern Africa region since independence and is currently the fourth largest in Sub-Saharan Africa. On the other extreme, it has wanted to be like the developed West and other developed nations—aspiring to be where others seem to be without taking stock of its own context and what it would take to get there. This is exemplified in Vision 2030 in Chapter 3 in the form of the lack of a sense of prioritisation of interventions, proper appreciation of the country's current development status, what it has taken the East Asian countries that the vision looks up to, to get where they are, and what it would take Kenya to realise the goals in the vision.[4]

A lot has been written about the success of the East Asian Tigers and the historical similarities between them and a select African countries, the African lions, among them Kenya.[5] The World Bank, in its book *The Asian Miracle: Economic Growth and Public Policy,*[6] sought to understand what was driving the success of these nations in attaining rapid and equitable growth, given that the policy guidance they used was also availed to other developing countries without the same degree of success.

Subsequent related work that is of relevance to Kenya includes Donge and colleagues' *Tracking Development in South-East Asia and Sub-Saharan Africa: The Primacy of Policy;*[7] Nyanjom and Ong'olo's *Erratic Development in Kenya: Questions from the East Asian Miracle;*[8] Fourie's *Model Students:*

Policy Emulation; Modernization, and Kenya's Vision 2030;[9] and more recently Kimenyi and colleagues' *The African Lions: Kenya country case study*.[10]

From a broad look, Kenya seems to have what is required to emulate the policies and assume the economic growth trajectory outlined in the for sustainable and inclusive development, yet this has not been the case.[11] Fourie[12] identifies four key things to look out for in successful emulation: (a) similarity of policy and institutional design; (b) conscious awareness of drawing evidence and lessons from others; (c) clear mechanisms for transfer of evidence and knowledge; and (d) adherence to conditionalities to guard against voluntarism or selection of what to transfer—the need to ensure that every bit that is crucial for success is emulated.

In sum, effective emulation takes active and intentional effort. It is much more than having knowledge about other nations that have succeeded and wanting to be like them. As the authors of the World Bank report conclude, 'there is nothing "miraculous" about the East Asian economies' success; each has performed these essential functions of growth better than most other economies'.[13] Noted in the *East Asian Miracle* is that there seemed to be many similarities in the economies of the East Asian and other developing nations like Kenya, so one would have thought that the policy interventions that worked for them would have worked for others too, yet this did not happen. Additionally, Kenya was even ahead of some of these success story nations, and hence a role model in a few aspects such as agriculture. The next section looks deeper into this East Asian success with a view to identify lessons for Kenya.

Learning from Malaysia

While most of the policy interventions deployed in realising the East Asian Miracle hold promise for Kenya and other developing countries, there is a need for a careful selection of who to emulate. Following are some key considerations in selecting Malaysia as an example for Kenya.

Firstly, **Malaysia is a success story**. Malaysia is one of the eight East Asian economies that overcame significant barriers to attain rapid growth, twice that of most other countries, between 1965 and 1990.[14] Even more impressive is that this growth was widely shared, resulting in a significant reduction in poverty and inequality during this period.[15] These results have been sustained since then. Although we are still far from declaring victory, Malaysia is clearly a development success and is probably the only nation which 50 years ago, was unambiguously classified as a 'third world' country that has almost entirely succeeded in eradicating acute poverty.[16]

Secondly, **Kenya and Malaysia have close historical parallels**. Both nations were colonised by the British and gained self-independence around 1960. The British government left behind similar socio-legal structures and institutions which formed the basis of these states' future development initiatives. The structure and governance of social institutions strongly determine its developmental performance. Until 2010, Kenya used the constitution that was developed immediately after independence to govern its social and economic affairs. That constitution had significant inputs from and was heavily borrowed from the British. Kenya's constitution at independence in 1963 was based on the 'Lancaster House template', which was used by all former British colonies.[17] Although minor amendments to the constitution happened along the way such as in 1964 and 1969, it largely remained the same until 2010 when the new constitution was promulgated.

Thirdly, **both Kenya and Malaysia have consistently followed the capitalist route**, relying on privately owned capital for development.[18] Although state corporations (parastatals) were established, the successful East Asian governments followed the capitalist route, promoting free enterprises and markets.[19] Similarly, unlike its neighbour, Tanzania, Kenya has consistently used markets as an engine for its development as spelled out in Sessional Paper 10 of 1965. The ideology of capitalism is continually gaining acceptance as more efficient and inclusive markets are perceived to be the way to bring prosperity and positive social change to the large number of the world's poor.[20] Businesses have massive resources which, if deployed effectively and sensitively, can bring collective prosperity to the nation.

A sustainable economic system is one that caters for the weakest and the poorest and allows for widespread prosperity instead of concentrating the wealth of the nations in the hands of a few capitalists.[21] Malaysia used elaborate regulation to further the economic interests of the majority Malay population while Kenya promoted the establishment of an African, mainly Kikuyu, class of entrepreneurs alongside the Asians through the Gikuyu, Embu and Meru Association (GEMA), until the early 1980s, when these ethnic coalitions were banned by the Moi regime.[22]

Fourthly, **the two countries were at relatively the same stage in many aspects of development in the 1960s,** as will be illustrated later in the book, and had similar economic profiles. Agriculture played a significant role, with a value addition in the agricultural sector of about 37 per cent of GDP in both economies in 1961.[23] Another common factor between them was that the manufacturing and industry sectors made very small contributions to their economies, with the value added in manufacturing being about 12 per cent of their GDP in 1969 and, industry about 20 per cent in 1960.[24] Additionally, both nations had a population of about 8 million in the 1960s.

Fifthly, **like Kenya's Vision 2030, Malaysia's development has been guided by a concerted national effort and clear vision**, for example Vision 2020. There was an active effort in the formulation of Vision 2030 to involve a broad range of stakeholders—similar to the approach seen in the development of Malaysia's long-term development plans. In both nations, this effort was led by a group of societal elites or technocrats. In the development and subsequent implementation of Vision 2030, the Kenyan technocrats deliberately endeavoured to emulate successful East Asian economies including Malaysia.[25] A noticeable similarity in both Vision 2020 (Malaysia's) and Vision 2030 (Kenya's) is the highly consultative development process and rallying of national effort toward successful implementation.

Sixthly, **both Malaysia and Kenya are highly multi-ethnic** which can be a big challenge in development. Establishing the sense of a shared national destiny was one of the first things that Malaysia needed to do, just like Kenya would need to overcome ethnic rifts to forge forward as one united nation focused on one goal. The 'peace, love, and unity' campaign during Moi's reign failed to address the issue of ethnicity and so has the idea of enrolling children into secondary schools in different ethnic locations from their own after the 2007-2008 post-election violence. Yet, instead of weakening, the storm of ethnicity in Kenya seems to be gaining momentum.

Finally, there was ***an active effort to emulate Malaysia in the formulation of Kenya's current development roadmap, Vision 2030***. There is a direct reference to the newly industrialising East Asian countries in Vision 2030[26] which is evidence of this intentional emulation. In coming up with Vision 2030, Kenya particularly sought to emulate both Singapore and Malaysia and has used technocrats from East Asia (including both countries) to support its implementation and optimise the learning and knowledge transfer.[27] Additionally, the name and aim of Kenya's current development roadmap, Vision 2030, closely mimics Malaysia's Vision 2020 which was put in place in 1990 to transform Malaysia into a fully developed and industrialised nation by 2020.[28] Moreover, in Vision 2030, Kenya explicitly seeks to attain the living standards of the newly industrialised East Asian countries, particularly Malaysia.

In choosing to learn from Malaysia and other East Asian countries, Kenya seems to have been driven by a conviction that the development policies that these nations used would work, and not by other considerations such as funding. The next section looks at the development divergence between Kenya and Malaysia which is crucial for learning.

The divergence between Kenya and Malaysia

Kenya and Malaysia were at relatively the same stage of development in the early 1960s and reasonably kept pace until the 1970s when a total divergence happened.[29] While Malaysia managed to attain and maintain rapid and shared growth, Kenya, on the other hand, experienced substantial growth in the 1960s and 1970s and a reversal of these gains in the 1980s and 1990s. Kenya's economic performance then remained low and sporadic until around 2003. This section explores this developmental divergence with a view to understand the reasons for it and suggest what Kenya can learn from Malaysia's path. A comprehension of what caused this divergence is useful in determining if the policy interventions that have worked for Malaysia can be emulated in Kenya, and in coming up with policy recommendations to help Kenya realise sustainable and inclusive growth.

The main reason identified for the divergence in the developmental paths of Kenya and Malaysia was governance.[30] Being nations that relied on the private sector or markets for development, the criticality of governance is summed up in Donge's view that 'governance is widely credited as the source of Malaysia's development success and as the explanation for Kenya's stagnating performance'.[31] For instance, up to around 2000, Kenya scored much lower than Malaysia on the economic freedom index, as shown in figure 4.1 below (index ranges from 0 to 10 with 10 being most free).

Figure 4.1: Economic freedom index

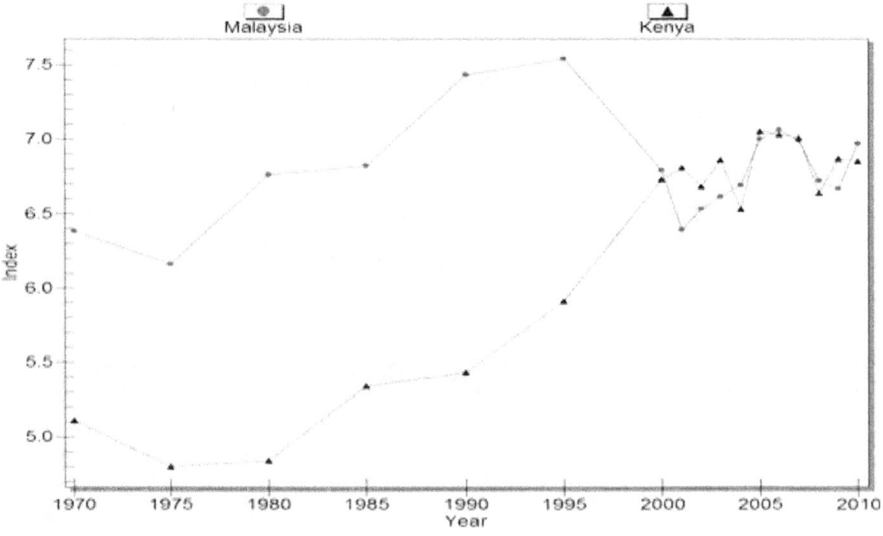

Source: Generated from International Futures Model [Computer Software, Version 7.00], 2017. Retrieved from http://www.ifs.du.edu/

Kenya also ranked poorly on Transparency International's Corruption Perceptions Index. It was in position 145 out of 176 countries compared to

Malaysia in position 55, with the first being the least corrupt.[32] The difference between both countries is even starker when one looks at government effectiveness as measured by the World Bank, as illustrated in figure 4.2 below (index ranges from 0 to 5 with 5 being most effective).

Figure 4.2: Government effectiveness

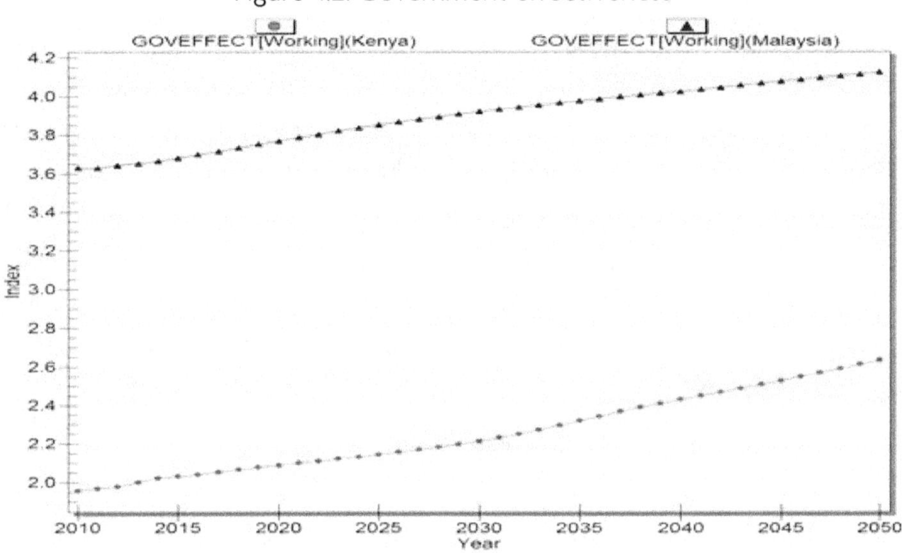

Source: Generated from International Futures Model [Computer Software, Version 7.00], 2017. Retrieved from http://www.ifs.du.edu/

Another reason for this divergence is that *Kenya did not take advantage of the growing rate of globalisation to increase export of manufactured goods despite its market orientation and the presence of cheap labour*. Unlike East Asian countries such as China and Malaysia which highly benefitted from outsourcing due to their ability to provide much cheaper labour compared to the West, Kenya has been less successful.[33] This is because labour costs in Kenya have remained relatively high compared to East Asia, as they are mainly legally imposed on markets due to the pressure imparted by the labour unions. In contrast, labour unions do not exist in the high performing East Asian economies.[34] For example, Kenya's 2007 labour law revisions have particularly elicited many industrial disputes between employers and employees, resulting in an increased cost of doing business as many man-hours are lost.[35] This labour cost differential meant that while Malaysia's attractiveness to foreign investors grew, enhancing its manufacturing and industrial sectors, Kenya's remained poorly developed, as we will see shortly.

The other key difference is that Kenya had fewer natural resources than Malaysia in the early 1960s. For instance, Kenya had little high-potential land for agriculture and no known deposits of fossils fuels in the first decade after independence.[36] Consequently, Kenya has struggled to finance its development agenda over the decades due to this natural resource limitation, a situation which has been compounded by its governance challenge.[37] To date, Kenya continues to subsist while Malaysia thrives in the abundance of its natural riches.[38] Unlike most other resource-rich developing countries, Malaysia escaped the 'resource curse'—a situation where the natural resources of richly endowed nations end up only benefiting the elites as the poor become poorer.[39] Through sound governance, Malaysia's natural resources benefited the everyone.

Over the years, governance related issues have posed significant constraints to growth, especially by hindering access to sufficient development aids. Given its persistent budget deficit, Kenya has had to rely on foreign aid for development, which has not been consistently assured as shown in figure 4.3. This over-reliance on foreign aid has made the nation vulnerable and affected implementation of its development strategies. Frequently, Kenya's development partners have terminated funding support mid-way the implementation of development programmes due to malfeasances within the government. For instance, the British Department for International Development, which had committed significant support for Kenya's free primary education programme under the NARC government, withdrew their funding in 2011 due to corruption. Access to development funds also depends on sound policy which is reliant on credible governance. In sum, Kenya's access to development aid has not been consistent.

Figure 4.3: Kenya's foreign aid compared to GDP

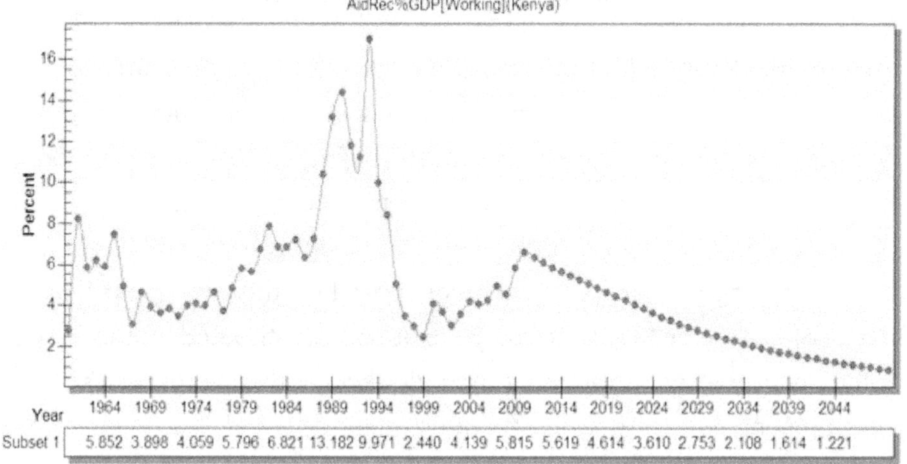

Source: Generated from International Futures Model [Computer Software, Version 7.00], 2017. Retrieved from http://www.ifs.du.edu/

Without the assurance of development aid, Kenya has had to rely on investment capital. This has been an important factor in economic growth in Kenya, with a close positive correlation between investment capital and growth.[40] Although there was an increase in investment ratio in the period 2000 to 2014 (from 17.4 per cent to 21.3 per cent), the levels of investment capital remain low due to low domestic savings (was about 16 per cent in 2016), and equally low foreign domestic investments.[41] Vision 2030's goal of growing domestic savings from 17 per cent in 2006 to 30 per cent by 2012 proved overly ambitious.

The stunning success of the HPEAs is usually attributed to the adoption of a combination of appropriate economic policies by these countries. Noteworthy is that these policies were availed to all developing countries, yet substantial success was only registered among the HPEAs.[42] For the policies to work in these East Asia economies, it was crucial for each nation's populace to believe that the proposed policies could sustainably deliver tangible benefits that would be available to all.[43]

While the Malaysia leadership committed themselves to sustainable and shared growth that would improve the lives of the populace, Kenya's leadership seems to have resigned to its economic fate. The biggest difference between the HPEAs' and Kenya's experiences was Kenya's 'acceptance—and even exacerbation—of socio-economic inequality as an immutable reality of development, plus the weak belief in the integrity of Kenyan institutions'.[44] Kenya's poor development track record seems to confirm this view.

Moreover, it is worth exploring if Kenya's post-independence stance to resist having development policies imposed on them (as spelled out in the Sessional Paper No. 10 of 1965), might have contributed to this lack of commitment by the government in implementing the World Bank's set of development policies that led to the success of the HPEAs. For instance, there have been several incidences of conflict between Kenya and its bilateral and multilateral partners such as the United Kingdom, United States of America, the World Bank, and the International Monetary Fund, over its rejection of their economic and political conditionalities, prescriptions, and ideologies for development.[45]

One would assume that the intention of these development partners is to provide a policy framework to guide governments in formulating country-specific policies and strategies that are tailored to their own needs and unique contexts, such as their cultural heritage and natural resources, and not to serve as blueprints for implementation.[46] This aside, Vision 2030 demonstrates some intentionality in seeking to learn from others.

As seen in Chapter 1, Kenya's development has been minimal. Figures 4.4 and 4.5 below show that the economic growth has been suboptimal compared with Malaysia's. Kenya's performance is particularly dismal when assessed in terms of its ability to benefit the populace.

Figure 4.4: Kenya's and Malaysia's historical and forecasted economic growth rates

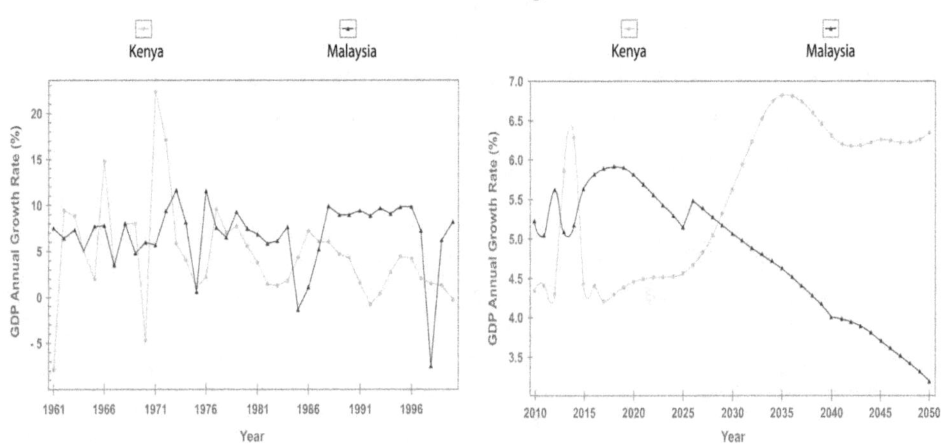

Source: Generated from International Futures Model [Computer Software, Version 7.00], 2017. Retrieved from http://www.ifs.du.edu/

The economic gains made in the first 50 years of self-independence have only benefitted a few, effectively widening the gap between the poor and the rich instead of closing it as shown by the GDP per capita growth, which has grown less proportionately and consistently compared to GDP growth.

Figure 4.5: Kenya and Malaysia's economic performance over time

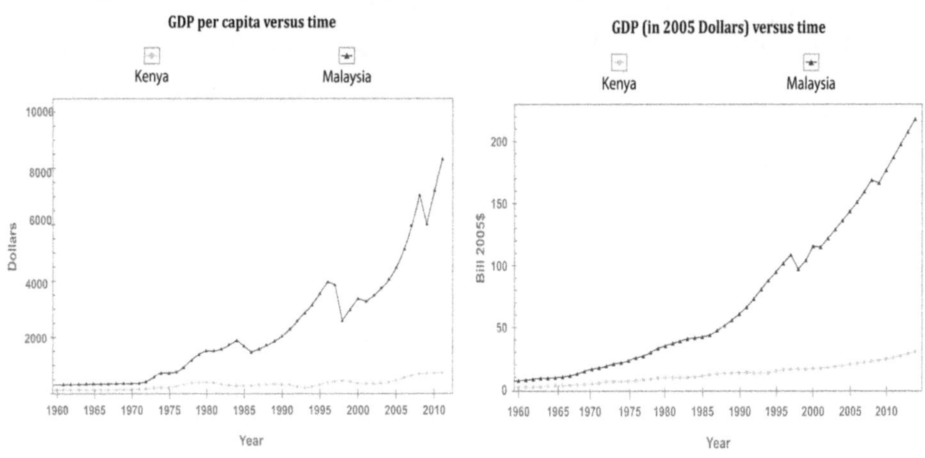

Source: Generated from International Futures Model [Computer Software, Version 7.00], 2017. Retrieved from http://www.ifs.du.edu/

The divergence between the economic performance of these two nations is projected to further widen in the future. There is minimal improvement forecasted in Kenya's performance between now and 2050 while Malaysia's will grow further based on the current trajectory as shown in figure 4.5 above and figure 4.6 below.

Figure 4.6: Kenya's and Malaysia's historical and forecasted GDP (as per current trajectory)

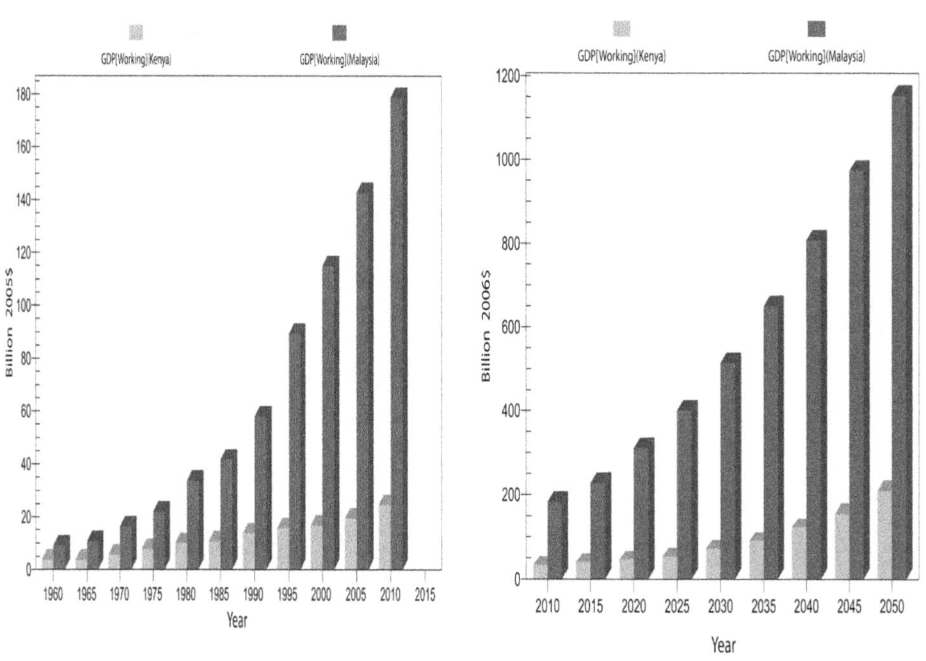

Source: Generated from International Futures Model [Computer Software, Version 7.00], 2017. Retrieved from http://www.ifs.du.edu/

A relatively good measure of inclusive growth is GDP per capita. In relation to this, Kenya kept pace with Malaysia up until around 1972, then experienced a stagnation. Kenya's GDP per capita grew rapidly, more than doubling between 1965 and 1975 from $105 to $242 (at current dollar rates) as shown in figure 4.7 below, before hitting a relative stagnation.[47]

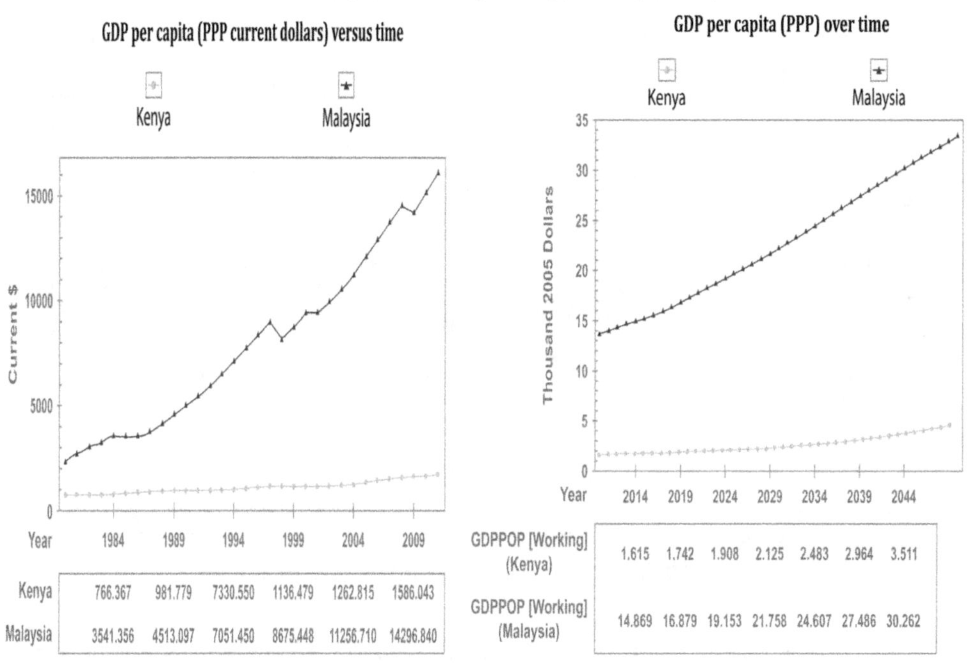

Figure 4.7: Kenya's and Malaysia's historical and forecasted (current trajectory) GDP per capita

Source: Generated from International Futures Model [Computer Software, Version 7.00], 2017. Retrieved from http://www.ifs.du.edu/

As discussed earlier, macroeconomic stability is a key condition for sustainable and inclusive development. Malaysia's macroeconomy has been relatively stable throughout the last half-century as shown in figure 4.8 below. Like in most other aspects of development, Kenya has done better than its Sub-Saharan peers in maintaining macroeconomic stability—gauged by the rate of inflation of consumer prices. However, its performance has not been as impressive when compared with Malaysia's. There have been a few instances that have threatened to substantively perturb the macroeconomic stability of Kenya's economy, such as the Goldenberg scam of the early 1990s.[48]

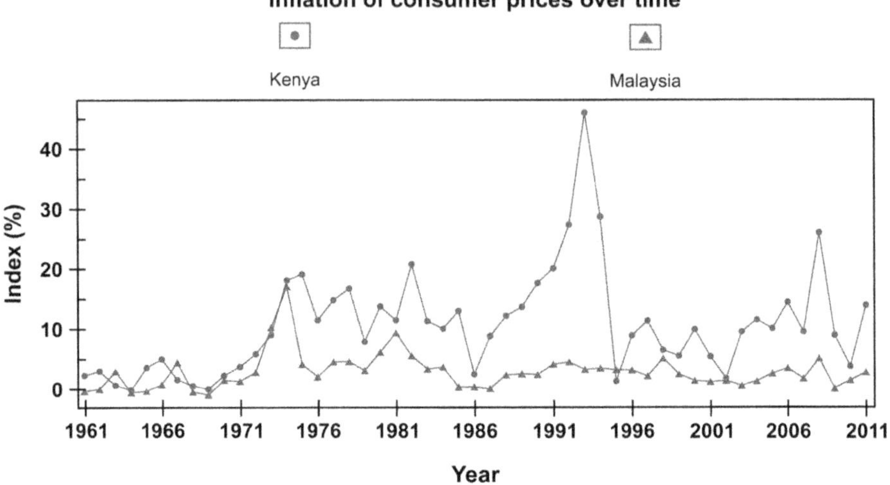

Figure 4.8: Kenya and Malaysia's macroeconomic stability
- Inflation of consumer prices over time

Source: Generated from International Futures Model [Computer Software, Version 7.00], 2017. Retrieved from http://www.ifs.du.edu/

However, the government has continually managed to put in measures to rein in inflation following each of these incidences, preventing hyper-inflation. This has mainly been due to strong institutional structures of the related government departments, particularly the Central Bank of Kenya.[49] Kenya has continually managed macroeconomic stability using technocrats in the Central Bank who have been comparatively well insulated from politics.

Tables 1 and 2 show a comparison of the current and forecasted (2030) human capital related development profiles between both countries. Based on the indices, Malaysia is way ahead of Kenya in the development of its human capital. Noteworthy, however, is Kenya's significantly higher human capital contribution to annual groups compared with Malaysia's—at 1.093 versus 0.3012. This implies that Kenya stands to gain much greater returns than Malaysia from its investments in human capital development.

Table 1: Comparison of current development profiles (human capital) between Kenya and Malaysia

☐ Development Profile

Continue   Using Countries/Regions   Comparison Option

Countries or Regions   Kenya   Select Year   2016   Click on variable description to get graph,
or click on computed value to show over time

Select File: O-Working File, based on IFSBASE.RUN

Compare Countries or Regions   Malaysia   Compare year   2016

GDP Per Capita (Thou. Real PPP$) Kenya (2016); 1,659 Malaysia (2016); 15,619	Computed Value	Expected Value Predicted from GDP per Capita at PPP	Standard Error (SE) of Estimate	Standard Errors of Value from Prediction	Contribution to Annual Growth (Percent)	Parameter Contribution of Factor
Human Capital – Kenya - 2016					1.093	
Human Capital – Malaysia - 2016					0.3012	
Years of Education – Kenya - 2016	7.484	5.847	1.629	1.005		0.2
Years of Education – Malaysia - 2016	10.4	9.319	1.629	0.6651		0.2
Education Expenditure (Log) - Kenya - 2016	6.302	3.711	1.847	1.403		0.2
Education Expenditure (Log) - Malaysia - 2016	5.725	4.995	1.847	0.3948		0.2
Life Expectancy – Kenya - 2016	59.99	56.5	7.633	0.4583		0.007
Life Expectancy – Malaysia - 2016	74.79	75.55	7.633	-0.0988		0.007
Stunting (Log) – Kenya - 2016	17.51	35.44	9.738	-1.041		-0.025
Health Expenditure (Log) -Malaysia - 2016	15.37	12.84	9.738	0.2597		-0.025
Disability – Kenya - 2016	0.0661	0.0583	0	0.0003		-0.5
Disability – Malaysia - 2016	0.0543	0.0583	0	-0.0037		-0.5

Source: Generated from International Futures Model

[Computer Software, Version 7.00], 2017. Retrieved from http://www.ifs.du.edu/

Table 2: Comparison of current development profiles (human capital) between Kenya and Malaysia by 2030

GDP Per Capita (Thou. Real PPP$) Kenya (2030); 2,183 Malaysia (2030); 22,316	Computed Value	Expected Value Predicted from GDP per Capita at PPP	Standard Error (SE) of Estimate	Standard Errors of Value from Prediction	Contribution to Annual Growth (Percent)	Parameter Contribution of Factor
Human Capital – Kenya - 2030					1.122	
Human Capital – Malaysia - 2030					0.2222	
Years of Education – Kenya - 2030	7.94	6.272	1.629	1.024		0.2
Years of Education – Malaysia - 2030	11.11	9.872	1.629	0.7577		0.2
Education Expenditure (Log) - Kenya - 2030	6.088	3.868	1.847	1.202		0.2
Education Expenditure (Log) - Malaysia - 2030	5.813	5.2	1.847	0.3318		0.2
Life Expectancy – Kenya - 2030	64.12	58.83	7.633	0.6939		0.007
Life Expectancy – Malaysia - 2030	76.98	78.58	7.633	-0.2094		0.007
Stunting (Log) – Kenya - 2030	15.37	32.68	9.738	-1.778		-0.025
Health Expenditure (Log) -Malaysia - 2030	13.61	9.246	9.738	0.4485		-0.025
Disability – Kenya - 2030	0.0587	0.0531	0	0.0001		-0.5
Disability – Malaysia - 2030	0.0502	0.0531	0	-0.0024		-0.5

Source: Generated from International Futures Model

[Computer Software, Version 7.00], 2017. Retrieved from http://www.ifs.du.edu/

Overall, Kenya's economic performance will remain relatively constant based on the current trajectory as that of Malaysia continues to accelerate. It seems like Malaysia laid the right foundation for sustained development and took off while Kenya's economy continued to sit on the runway, awaiting its time for take-off.

Key success factors for Malaysia's development

The fact that Malaysia has succeeded where Kenya has failed in the last half-decade is evident from the analysis of their economic performance and other aspects of development, as seen above. Some of the key success factors behind Malaysia's sustained and inclusive development were strong leadership, rural investment, governance of markets, and human capital investments.

Demonstrated strong leadership

As the common adage goes, 'everything stands and falls on leadership'. Leadership was the anchor for Malaysia's success and underpinned all the other factors. Like the other eight economies of the East Asian Miracle, the Malaysian government fostered and demonstrated strong dictatorial leadership, for development. There is a clear link between developmentalism and authoritarianism in Malaysia's approach, as exemplified in the ability to push for implementation of the national developmental vision (Fourie, 2014). This is evident in Malaysia's Prime Minister, Mahathir's, Vision 2020 foreword.[50]

The East Asian developmental-authoritarian kind of leadership was characterised by: (a) wealth-sharing programmes which were designed to include all citizens in economic growth; (b) a cadre of economic technocrats (bureaucrats) who were insulated from political pressures; and (c) institutions and mechanisms for sharing information and winning the support of business elites.[51]

Malaysia's political leadership had to contend with two main forces: ethnic diversity-related difficulties and internal communist insurgencies.[52] The leadership thus had to justify its legitimacy to remain in office. This legitimacy was attained through the promise of shared economic growth for all their subjects, including the non-elites.[53] They identified shared growth with the success of their regimes and devised rules which aligned their bureaucracies to this goal.[54] The ability to broker effective bureaucracy systems and know which incentives to use to get the right types of results, was a key distinguishing factor between the highly successful East Asian economies and their African and Latin American counterparts.[55]

In addition, the leadership signalled their commitment to shared growth for the whole population, which persuaded the bureaucrats to pursue the envisaged long-term collective gains at the expense of short-term personal gains.[56] Thirdly, strong oversight and monitoring mechanisms were put in place to ensure performance accountability of the bureaucrats to the national leaders.[57] This kind of leadership contrasted starkly with the Kenyan political leadership in terms of its lack of commitment, as exemplified by the series of development strategic plans which say the right things but are followed by little practical action to make them happen.

The shared growth strategy had two main components: (a) it fostered growth by encouraging the private sector to make long-term investments such as organisational development and building the capacity of their management teams as a way of growing the nation's economy; and (b) the non-elites (lower income groups) were encouraged to make short-term sacrifices for long-term benefits.[58]

Tangible wealth-sharing measures with long-term impacts, such as free basic health care, free primary education, and land reforms rather than income redistribution mechanisms like fuel or food subsidies, were used to buy the support of the non-elites.[59] These measures equipped the population with assets that empowered them to contribute to the growth process and benefit from it in the long-term. More importantly, this growth-share mechanism convinced the non-elites that they would benefit from the nation's economic growth and hence gained their support for the process.

The Malaysian leadership made a solid commitment to the shared growth of the people and enterprises and delivered on this promise.

Invested in rural areas

As seen earlier, interventions that drive sustainable and inclusive development are those that involve most citizens of the country. Such interventions should give the people a chance to both support the growth of the economy and to benefit from it. Malaysia adopted 'a strongly pro-rural, pro-poor development strategy ... a stated and actual emphasis on rural development, or development largely for the uplift of the Malays in the traditional sector'.[60] While Malaysia has on average consistently spent about a quarter of its public budget on agriculture since independence, Kenya's investment dropped from about half (48 per cent) of GDP just after independence to nearly 20 per cent in the 1970s and further to about 10 per cent in the 1980s.[61]

Kenya's hefty investment in agriculture just after independence was partly due to the colonial government's agenda for resettlement in the 'whites' highlands and not purely because of pro-poor rural investments.[62] However, Kenya's level of expenditure on agriculture remained significantly higher than Malaysia's up until the 1970s. Kenya's public spending on agriculture declined from 8.4 per cent (1980) to 6.0 per cent (1992) then 4.6 per cent in 2002, a far cry given that 70 per cent of Kenyans depend on this sector.[63] By ignoring agriculture without providing an alternative source of livelihood, Kenya's national leadership has in the past three decades ignored most of its citizenry and demonstrated a lack of commitment to realising sustainable and inclusive development. It has continued to pay lip-service to its own development plans.

Also, noteworthy is the fact that Malaysia's level of investment in agriculture later reduced as the economy transitioned from agriculture to manufacturing and services, which is typical of highly developed economies.

Figures 4.9 – 4.12 show this transition in terms of the value (as a percentage of GDP) generated by the various sectors of the economy over time.

Figure 4.9: Value added in agriculture as a percentage of GDP

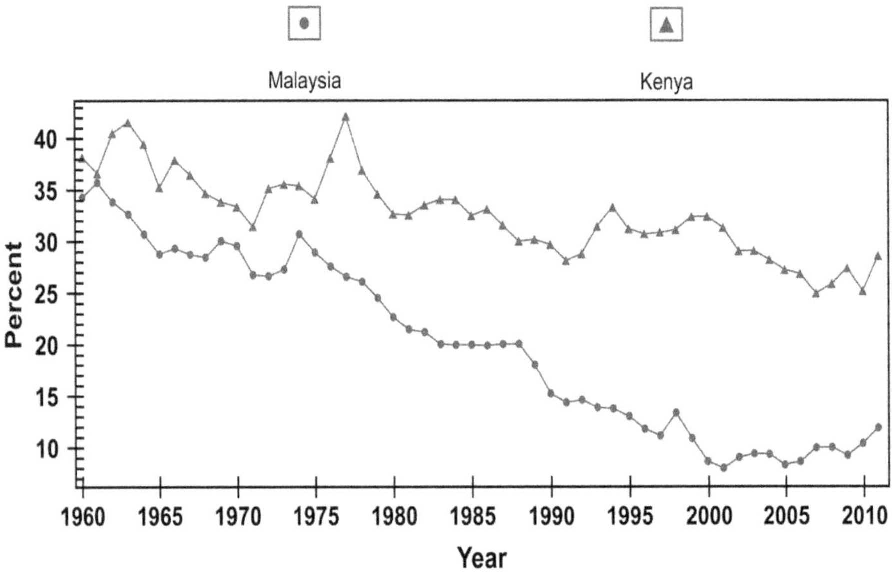

Source: Generated from International Futures Model [Computer Software, Version 7.00], 2017. Retrieved from http://www.ifs.du.edu/

As shown in figure 4.9 above, Malaysia's value added in the agricultural sector as a percentage of GDP has substantially decreased since the 1960s and continues to decrease, justifying the government's divestiture of investment into other more value adding economic sectors. On the contrary, Kenya's value added in the agricultural sector has remained relatively constant at 30 per cent to 40 per cent, despite the significant decline in public expenditure on agriculture. This implies that the value addition by the sector can be enhanced through a higher level of investment in the agricultural sector.

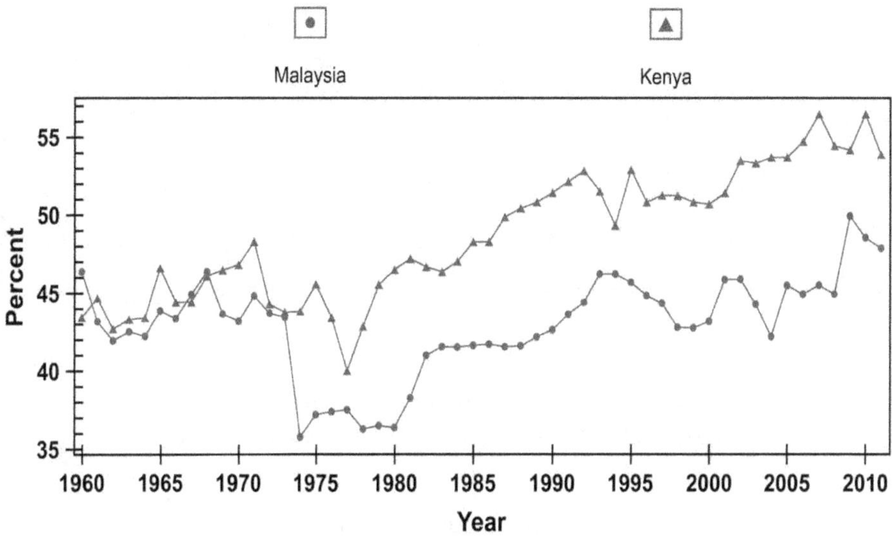

Figure 4.10: Value added in services
as a percentage of GDP over time

Source: Generated from International Futures Model [Computer Software, Version 7.00], 2017. Retrieved from http://www.ifs.du.edu/

On the other hand, figure 4.10 above shows that the value added in Kenya's services sector as a percentage of GDP has continually increased over time, almost a mirror image of the trend in the value added in agriculture. It is also significantly higher than Malaysia's. As noted earlier, right from independence, Kenya has been a service-driven economy and this requires good quality human capital or skilled labour for optimal results. On the contrary, little change has been witnessed in the contributions by industry and manufacturing sectors in Kenya while Malaysia has experienced marked growth in these sectors as illustrated in figures 4.11 and 4.12 below.

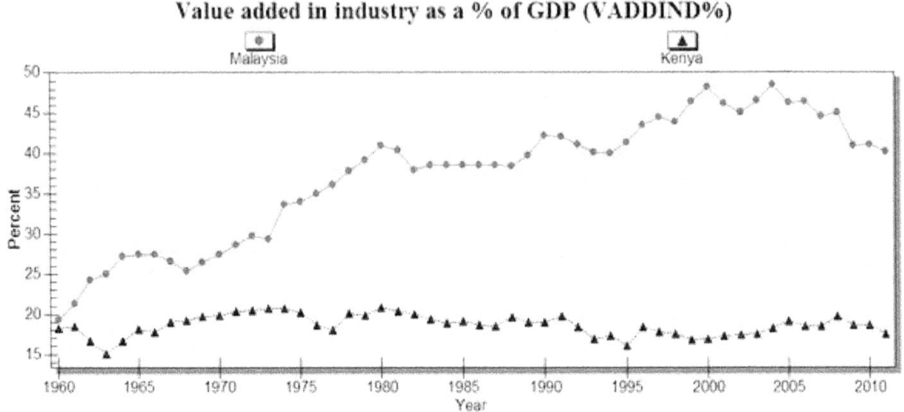

Figure 4.11: Value added in industry as a percentage of GDP over time

Source: Generated from International Futures Model [Computer Software, Version 7.00], 2017. Retrieved from http://www.ifs.du.edu/

Figure 4.12: Value added in manufacturing as a percentage of GDP over time

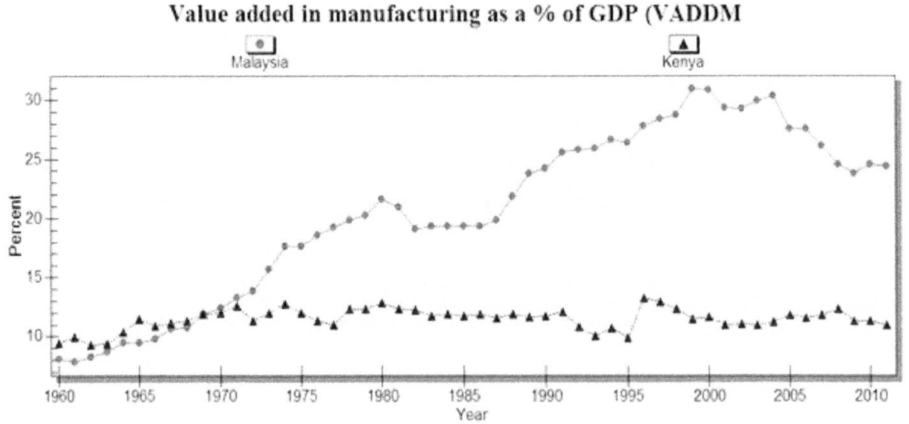

Source: Generated from International Futures Model [Computer Software, Version 7.00], 2017. Retrieved from http://www.ifs.du.edu/

These shifts in the value addition in the various sectors as a percentage of GDP explain the shift in Malaysia's investment prioritisation, a situation that required active and effective monitoring for success, which the leadership was able to do.

Governed markets for development

The fact that markets work and can deliver sustainable development is undisputed.[64] All prosperous societies have tended to be capitalistic—organised around private property and allowing markets to play a significant role in the allocation of resources and determination of economic rewards.[65] Dan Rodrik in Harf's and Lombardi's book *Taking Sides on Global Issues* says, 'capitalism has no equal when it comes to unleashing the collective economic energies of human societies'.[66] The Malaysian private sector has played a crucial role in drawing and implementing the country's development roadmaps, particularly the Vision 2020.

Furthermore, the Malaysian government played a strong catalytic role in the proper functioning of markets by aptly governing the market players.[67] Malaysia was able to fuse private sector and government interests through a clear alignment of incentives to benefit its citizenry.[68] The policy framework behind its Vision 2020 for instance guaranteed that although foreign investors were incentivised to do business in Malaysia, Malaysians retained a key stake in these firms and were charged with the responsibility of ensuring that the businesses served the interests of the country.[69] Aligning the incentives of the market players with those of the government is crucial for nations that choose to use the capitalist approach to sustainable and inclusive development.[70]

Without enforceable laws and regulatory guidelines, markets flounder.[71] Thus, markets need social institutions to govern them and ensure that they function well.[72] In sum, capitalism is not 'self-creating, self-sustaining, self-regulating or self-stabilising'.[73] Although markets work for development, they do not always work, and they never work perfectly.[74]

Furthermore, while self-interest is an important economic motivation, it is not exclusive.[75] Governments cannot, therefore, be mere bystanders, relegating the process of development to businesses, but should be an active agent and ingredient to the process without seeking to control it through instruments such as price ceilings.[76] They need to direct the activities of households and businesses to make sustainable and inclusive development happen.

The Malaysian past and present governments have had a clear sense of the role the private sector should play in driving the nation's development and have understood their part in making this happen, as exemplified in the Prime Minister's Vision 2020 foreword:

> *For the foreseeable future, Malaysia will continue to drive the private sector, to rely on it as the primary engine of growth... The State, cannot of course, retreat totally from the economic life of Malaysia. It will not abdicate its responsibility for overseeing and providing the legal and regulatory framework for rapid economic and social development.*[77]

Malaysia has over the decades done a good job in governing markets for the long-term benefit of its citizens.

Invested in its people

The government of Malaysia, like other high performing East Asian (HPEAs) governments, prioritised the development of the capacity of its citizens by investing heavily in primary and secondary education.[78] The leadership believed that each of the ethnic groups had a role to play and contributions to make to the growth process. The government envisaged human capital development as the way to attaining equality, rather than the redistribution of national resources.

The HPEAs economies experienced a dramatic increase in both the quantity and quality of education in the 1960s to 1990s and this continues.[79] With significant drops in population growth rates and a remarkable increase in the economic growth rate, these nations provided sufficient quantity and good quality education to their children—secondary school graduates had cognitive skills comparable to those of tertiary graduates in higher income economies.[80] The nations achieved near universal primary education in the late 1960s and quickly closed the gap between male and female education.

Conclusion

There is a lot that Kenya can draw from Malaysia's development success story, particularly given the parallels between the two countries outlined in this chapter. One could almost write Kenya's development history by flipping over Malaysia's. Malaysia's key success factors have distinct opposites in Kenya's challenges to attaining sustainable and inclusive growth. Yet, the development policy guidelines that have delivered success for Malaysia were also available to Kenya. This calls for a return to the basics. This chapter has laid the grounds for Kenya's emulation of Malaysia and pointed out some of the policy interventions that were core to its development success. These policy interventions will be revisited in the next chapter in developing a model for sustainable and inclusive development.

References

1   Fourie, E. (2014). 'Model students: Policy emulation, modernization, and Kenya's Vision 2030'. *African Affairs (London). 2014, Vol. 113 Issue 453*, p540-562.

2   Ibid

3   Sessional Paper No.10 (1965). 'African Socialism and its Application to Planning in Kenya'. The World Bank, Washington, DC., p. 8.

4   Fourie, E. (2014). 'Model students: Policy emulation, modernization, and Kenya's Vision 2030'. *African Affairs (London). 2014, Vol. 113 Issue 453*, p540-562.

5   Kimenyi, M., Mwega, F. & Ndung'u, N. (2016). 'The African Lions: Kenya country case study'. Brookings Institute; Donge, J., Henley, D. & Lewis, P. (2012). 'Tracking development in South-East Asia and sub-Saharan Africa: The primacy of policy'. *Development Policy Review. February 2012, Vol. 30 Issue 1*, p5–24; Nyanjom, O. & Ong'olo, D. (2012). 'Erratic development in Kenya: Questions from the East Asian miracle'. *Development Policy Review, 2012, Vol. 30 Issue 1*, p73-99.

6   World Bank (1993). *The East Asian Miracle. Economic Growth and Public Policy*. A World Bank Policy Research Report. The World Bank, Washington, DC.

7   Donge, J., Henley, D. & Lewis, P. (2012). 'Tracking development in South-East Asia and sub-Saharan Africa: The primacy of policy'. *Development Policy Review. February 2012, Vol. 30 Issue 1*, p5–24.

8   Nyanjom, O. & Ong'olo, D. (2012). 'Erratic development in Kenya: Questions from the East Asian miracle'. *Development Policy Review, 2012, Vol. 30 Issue 1*, p73-99.

9   Fourie, E. (2014). 'Model students: Policy emulation, modernization, and Kenya's Vision 2030'. *African Affairs (London). 2014, Vol. 113 Issue 453*, p540-562.

10 Kimenyi, M., Mwega, F. & Ndung'u, N. (2016). 'The African Lions: Kenya country case study'. Brookings Institute.

11 Nyanjom, O. & Ong'olo, D. (2012). 'Erratic development in Kenya: Questions from the East Asian miracle'. *Development Policy Review, 2012, Vol. 30 Issue 1*, p73-99.

12 Fourie, E. (2014). 'Model students: Policy emulation, modernization, and Kenya's Vision 2030'. *African Affairs (London). 2014, Vol. 113 Issue 453*, p540-562.

13 World Bank (1993). *The East Asian Miracle. Economic Growth and Public Policy*. A World Bank Policy Research Report. The World Bank, Washington, DC., p. vi.

14 Campos, J. E. & Root, H. L. (1996). *The Key to the Asian Miracle: Making Shared Growth Credible*. The Brookings Institution, Washington, D.C.

15 Ibid

16 Henley, D. (2012). 'The Agrarian roots of industrial growth: Rural development in South-East Asia and sub-Saharan Africa'. *Development Policy Review. Feb2012 Supplement, Vol. 30*, s25-s47.

17 Juakatiba (n.d.). 'The constitution of Kenya, 2010: The people's power'. The Citizen Handbook.

18 Donge, J., Henley, D. & Lewis, P. (2012). 'Tracking development in South-East Asia and sub-Saharan Africa: The primacy of policy'. *Development Policy Review. February 2012, Vol. 30 Issue 1*, p5–24; World Bank (1993). *The East Asian Miracle. Economic Growth and Public Policy*. A World Bank Policy Research Report. The World Bank, Washington, DC; Vlasblom, D. (2013). 'The richer harvest: Economic development in Africa and Southeast Asia compared'. African Studies Centre, Leiden.

19 Donge, J., Henley, D. & Lewis, P. (2012). 'Tracking development in South-East Asia and sub-Saharan Africa: The primacy of policy'. *Development Policy Review. February 2012, Vol. 30 Issue 1*, p5–24; Vlasblom, D. (2013). 'The richer harvest: Economic development in Africa and Southeast Asia compared'. African Studies Centre, Leiden.

20 Hammond, A. (2013). *Which World? Scenarios for 21st Century*. Earthscan Publications Ltd. Kindle Edition.

21 WTO (2010). *Global Problems, Global Solutions: Towards Better Global Governance.* World Trade Organisation, Geneva.

22 Donge, J. (2012). 'Governance and access to finance for development: An explanation of divergent development trajectories in Kenya and Malaysia'. *Commonwealth and Comparative Politics. Feb 2012, Vol. 50 Issue 1*, p53-74; Chilungu, S. (1985, Sep). 'Kenya: Recent developments and challenges'. Cultural Survival Quarterly Magazine.

23 Vlasblom, D. (2013). 'The richer harvest: Economic development in Africa and Southeast Asia compared'. African Studies Centre, Leiden; Nyanjom, O. & Ong'olo, D. (2012). 'Erratic development in Kenya: Questions from the East Asian miracle'. *Development Policy Review, 2012, Vol. 30 Issue 1*, p73-99; Fourie, E. (2014). 'Model students: Policy emulation, modernization, and Kenya's Vision 2030'. *African Affairs (London). 2014, Vol. 113 Issue 453*, p540-562; International Futures Model [Computer Software, Version 7.00], 2017. Retrieved from http://www.ifs.du.edu/.

24 International Futures Model [Computer Software, Version 7.00], 2017. Retrieved from http://www.ifs.du.edu/.

25 Fourie, E. (2014). 'Model students: Policy emulation, modernization, and Kenya's Vision 2030'. *African Affairs (London). 2014, Vol. 113 Issue 453*, p540-562; Vision 2030 (2007). Vision 2030 Brochure. Republic of Kenya.

26 Vision 2030 (2007). Vision 2030 Brochure. Republic of Kenya, p. 3.

27 Fourie, E. (2014). 'Model students: Policy emulation, modernization, and Kenya's Vision 2030'. *African Affairs (London). 2014, Vol. 113 Issue 453*, p540-562.

28 Ibid

29 Vlasblom, D. (2013). 'The richer harvest: Economic development in Africa and Southeast Asia compared'. African Studies Centre, Leiden; Donge, J., Henley, D. & Lewis, P. (2012). 'Tracking development in South-East Asia and sub-Saharan Africa: The primacy of policy'. *Development Policy Review. February 2012, Vol. 30 Issue 1*, p5–24; International Futures Model [Computer Software, Version 7.00], 2017. Retrieved from http://www.ifs.du.edu/.

30 Donge, J. (2012). 'Governance and access to finance for development: An explanation of divergent development trajectories in Kenya and Malaysia'. *Commonwealth and Comparative Politics. Feb 2012, Vol. 50 Issue 1*, p53-74; Nyanjom, O. & Ong'olo, D. (2012). 'Erratic development in Kenya: Questions from the East Asian miracle'. *Development Policy Review, 2012, Vol. 30 Issue 1*, p73-99.

31 Donge, J. (2012). 'Governance and access to finance for development: An explanation of divergent development trajectories in Kenya and Malaysia'. *Commonwealth and Comparative Politics. Feb 2012, Vol. 50 Issue 1*, p53-74 (p. 54).

32 Transparency International (n.d.). 'Corruption perceptions index 2016'. Transparency International.

33   Nyanjom, O. & Ong'olo, D. (2012). 'Erratic development in Kenya: Questions from the East Asian miracle'. *Development Policy Review, 2012, Vol. 30 Issue 1*, p73-99.

34   Campos, J. E. & Root, H. L. (1996). *The Key to the Asian Miracle: Making Shared Growth Credible*. The Brookings Institution, Washington, DC.

35   Kimenyi, M., Mwega, F. & Ndung'u, N. (2016). 'The African lions: Kenya country case study'. Brookings Institute.

36   Nyanjom, O. & Ong'olo, D. (2012). 'Erratic development in Kenya: Questions from the East Asian miracle'. *Development Policy Review, 2012, Vol. 30 Issue 1*, p73-99.

37   Donge, J. (2012). 'Governance and access to finance for development: An explanation of divergent development trajectories in Kenya and Malaysia'. *Commonwealth and Comparative Politics. Feb 2012, Vol. 50 Issue 1*, p53-74.

38   Ibid

39   Ibid

40   Kimenyi, M., Mwega, F. & Ndung'u, N. (2016). The African Lions: Kenya country case study. Brookings Institute.

41   Ibid

42   Campos, J. E. & Root, H. L. (1996). *The Key to the Asian Miracle: Making Shared Growth Credible*. The Brookings Institution, Washington, DC; World Bank (1993). *The East Asian Miracle. Economic Growth and Public Policy*. A World Bank Policy Research Report. The World Bank, Washington, DC.

43   Campos, J. E. & Root, H. L. (1996). *The Key to the Asian Miracle: Making Shared Growth Credible*. The Brookings Institution, Washington, DC.

44   Nyanjom, O. & Ong'olo, D. (2012). 'Erratic development in Kenya: Questions from the East Asian miracle'. *Development Policy Review, 2012, Vol. 30 Issue 1*, p73-99 (p. 73).

45   Abdi, A. (2016). 'Determinants of foreign policy formulation in developing countries: A case of Kenya'. *International Academic Journal of Arts and Humanities, Vol. 1 Issue 1*, p1-53.

46   Eshiwani, G. (1990). 'Implementing educational policies in Kenya'. World Bank Discussion Papers Africa Technical Department Series. The World Bank, Washington, DC.

47   Nyanjom, O. & Ong'olo, D. (2012). 'Erratic development in Kenya: Questions from the East Asian miracle'. *Development Policy Review, 2012, Vol. 30 Issue 1*, p73-99; International Futures Model [Computer Software, Version 7.00], 2017. Retrieved from http://www.ifs.du.edu/.

48   Nyanjom, O. & Ong'olo, D. (2012). 'Erratic development in Kenya: Questions from the East Asian miracle'. *Development Policy Review, 2012, Vol. 30 Issue 1*, p73-99.

49   Ibid; Donge, J., Henley, D. & Lewis, P. (2012). 'Tracking development in South-East Asia and sub-Saharan Africa: The primacy of policy'. *Development Policy Review. February 2012, Vol. 30 Issue 1*, p5–24.

50   Vision 2020 (n.d.). 'Malaysian: The way forward (Vision2020)'. United Nations Publications.

51   World Bank (1993). *The East Asian Miracle. Economic Growth and Public Policy*. A World Bank Policy Research Report. The World Bank, Washington, DC.

52   Campos, J. E. & Root, H. L. (1996). *The Key to the Asian Miracle: Making Shared Growth Credible*. The Brookings Institution, Washington, DC.

53   World Bank (1993). *The East Asian Miracle. Economic Growth and Public Policy*. A World Bank Policy Research Report. The World Bank, Washington, DC.

54   Campos, J. E. & Root, H. L. (1996). *The Key to the Asian Miracle: Making Shared Growth Credible*. The Brookings Institution, Washington, DC.

55   Ibid

56   Ibid

57   Ibid

58   Ibid

59   Ibid

60   Henley, D. (2012). 'The Agrarian roots of industrial growth: Rural development in South-East Asia and sub-Saharan Africa'. *Development Policy Review. Feb2012 Supplement, Vol. 30*, s25-s47.

61   Ibid

62   Ibid

63   Akroyd, S. & Smith, L. (2007). 'Review of public spending to agriculture'. World Bank-DFID.

64   Kay, J. (2003). 'The truth about markets'. *Progressive Politics. Vol 2. Issue 2*, p44-48; Hammond, A. (2013). *Which World? Scenarios for 21st Century*. Earthscan Publications Ltd. Kindle Edition.

65   Harf, J. E. & Lombardi, M. O. (2013). *Taking Sides: Clashing Views on Global Issues*. McGraw-Hill Create.

66   Ibid, p. 193

67   Fourie, E. (2014). 'Model students: Policy emulation, modernization, and Kenya's Vision 2030'. *African Affairs (London). 2014, Vol. 113 Issue 453*, p540-562; Nyanjom, O. & Ong'olo, D. (2012). 'Erratic development in Kenya: Questions from the East Asian miracle'. *Development Policy Review, 2012, Vol. 30 Issue 1*, p73-99; World Bank (1993). *The East Asian Miracle. Economic Growth and Public Policy*. A World Bank Policy Research Report. The World Bank, Washington, DC; Campos, J. E. & Root, H. L. (1996). *The Key to the Asian Miracle: Making Shared Growth Credible*. The Brookings Institution, Washington, DC.

68   Fourie, E. (2014). 'Model students: Policy emulation, modernization, and Kenya's Vision 2030'. *African Affairs (London). 2014, Vol. 113 Issue 453*, p540-562. World Bank (1993). *The East Asian Miracle. Economic Growth and Public Policy*. A World Bank Policy Research Report. The World Bank, Washington, DC; Campos, J. E. & Root, H. L. (1996). *The Key to the Asian Miracle: Making Shared Growth Credible*. The Brookings Institution, Washington, DC.

69   Vision 2020 (n.d.). 'Malaysian: The way forward (Vision2020)'. United Nations Publications.

70   Nyanjom, O. & Ong'olo, D. (2012). 'Erratic development in Kenya: Questions from the East Asian miracle'. *Development Policy Review, 2012, Vol. 30 Issue 1*, p73-99; Kay, J. (2003). 'The truth about markets'. *Progressive Politics. Vol 2. Issue 2*, p44-48.

71   Hammond, A. (2013). *Which World? Scenarios for 21st Century*. Earthscan Publications Ltd. Kindle Edition.

72   Harf, J. E. & Lombardi, M. O. (2013). *Taking Sides: Clashing Views on Global Issues*. McGraw-Hill Create.

73   Ibid, p. 193

74   Kay, J. (2003). 'The truth about markets'. *Progressive Politics. Vol 2. Issue 2*, p44-48.

75   Ibid

76   Ibid

77   Vision 2020 (n.d.). 'Malaysian: The way forward (Vision2020)'. United Nations Publications, p. 5.

78   Campos, J. E. & Root, H. L. (1996). *The Key to the Asian Miracle: Making Shared Growth Credible*. The Brookings Institution, Washington, DC; World Bank (1993). *The East Asian Miracle. Economic Growth and Public Policy*. A World Bank Policy Research Report. The World Bank, Washington, DC.

79   World Bank (1993). *The East Asian Miracle. Economic Growth and Public Policy*. A World Bank Policy Research Report. The World Bank, Washington, DC.

80   Ibid

CHAPTER 5

Building human capital for sustainable development

There is no wealth like knowledge,
and no poverty like ignorance. —Buddha

This chapter provides an understanding of how human capital development can be used to realise lasting and inclusive growth and identifies where Kenya's opportunity for sustainable development lies.

Defining human capital

Until the time of Adam Smith, economists believed in four factors of production: land, labour, capital (money), and the enterprise, that is, the spirit or initiative to turn an idea into an output.[1] Labour was thought of as the collective mass of people who contributed to the production process. The concept of human capital has its origin in Smith, who firmly believed that economic activity is not driven by this collective mass of people but by the nature of human capital which he described as 'the acquired and useful abilities of all the inhabitants or members of the society'.[2] These abilities are acquired through education, study, or apprenticeship. Human capital has also been defined as the knowledge, skills or value of people.[3]

The term human capital was later popularised by Jacob Mincer in the post-Second World War years, in the 1950s.[4] The OECD defines human capital as 'knowledge, skills, competencies, and attributes embodied in individuals that facilitate the creation of personal, social and economic well-being'.[5] Human capital development entails interventions that make workers more productive such as efforts to improve physical health, education, and training.[6] Although health is an equally important determinant of human capital, the discussion in this chapter and the rest of this book is focused on the acquisition of knowledge and skills to enhance human capital.

Human capital and sustainable growth

The fact that human capital is a crucial factor in economic development is undisputed.[7] Even at that early stage in the quest for an understanding of human capital, Mincer, in his work in the 1950s, considered investing in human capital a powerful force in promoting an individual's economic growth by making him or her more productive.[8] Mincer's argument can validly be extended to the society which is an aggregation of individuals. According to Adam Smith, human capital is as much the individual's fortune as it is that of the society.[9] Unlike traditional neoclassical economic models that were more focused on the accumulation of physical capital (equipment and structures), recent models have attributed greater importance to the accumulation of human capital and productive knowledge, and the interaction between these two factors in achieving growth.[10]

In 1909, Peter Drucker strongly argued that 'the basic economic resource—the means of production—is no longer capital, nor natural resources, nor labour. It is and will be knowledge'. This view holds as true today as it did a century ago. Human capital forms a major portion of multifactor productivity (MFP)—also referred to as the total productivity—which determines the level of economic growth.[11] Other contributors to MFP are research and development, and the existing economic policies. Although labour— the proportion of the population that is of working age—and physical capital are necessary for economic development, high growth in labour and physical capital alone have been demonstrated to have minimal impact on economic growth.[12]

Furthermore, as seen in Chapter 2, policy interventions that promote sustainable and inclusive development are those that enable the citizens of a nation to contribute to as well as benefit from its economic growth. Such policies are based on human capital. They entail investing in people by ensuring equal access to health and education for the majority. To Mincer, this investment in people in the form of education and training, that is, human capital, is a major principle of explaining the existing distribution of income in societies.[13] Furthermore, the non-economic returns of education such as improved personal well-being and more social cohesion are as important as economic growth.[14]

Even though human capital has been proven to be a key contributor to economic development, the exact level of this contribution varies across countries.[15] There are many factors that contribute to this variation, including the type of education provided in schools. As a result, comparing the quality of human capital development across countries is difficult.[16] The same increase in the years of education attained in two countries is likely to have different results. However, 'expenditure per student' is now globally used as a proxy for education quality to standardise measurement.[17]

While the accumulation of human capital is proportionate to the total factor of productivity (TFP) or multifactor productivity (MFP) in the IFs model *lingua,* the cost of education compared with the returns from it seem less proportionate.[18] This lack of proportionality accounts for low schooling quality and quantity in developing countries where returns on investments in education are perceived to be lower than those from other investment options.

This is because the causality chain between the investment and return on education is longer. The returns are usually not immediate and at times not obvious or directly associated with education, and determining the returns is much more complex than for other investments. Regrettably, the opportunity cost of not investing in education has been high in developing countries. Additionally, human capital further contributes to variances between country incomes because low human capital stock hinders physical capital accumulation.[19]

Theoretically, human capital, which is the knowledge and skills embodied in people, directly raises productivity through the ability to develop and adopt new technologies and hence economic growth.[20] A country's level of human capital is, therefore, indicative of its ability to generate and apply knowledge from research and development, and to make use of emerging technology for economic growth.[21]

Evidence shows that human capital also influences the level of diffusion of technology and innovation in a country.[22] Countries with low human capital thus lag in innovation and miss opportunities to benefit from emerging global technologies for economic development. As societies shift from agriculture into industrialisation (manufacturing), and eventually services, which Noble[23] sees as an inevitable aspect of the social change process, the economic success of nations and individual citizens within them becomes more reliant on the quantity and quality of human capital and less on the other factors of production.[24]

Investment in human capital in the form of expenditure on education and training, therefore, has a more sustained impact on economic growth when the acquisition of skills and training are accompanied by intensive research and development and faster technological progress through development, or adoption of new technologies.[25] Technological change only happens where the necessary human capital exists to make it happen.[26]

Education, in terms of the average number of years spent in school and the aggregate amount of education attained by the population, is a key driver of human capital and in turn the multifactor productivity rate of a nation. This means that a policy intervention that promotes education for the majority would have a positive effect on human capital, multifactor productivity, economic growth, and eventually equality.

Research undertaken by Bassanini and Scarpetta using OECD data for the period 1971 to 1998 showed that increasing schooling by one year resulted in a 6 per cent increase in GDP per capita.[27] The level of expenditure on education is dependent on both the cost of education and the public expenditure subsidy, that is, the proportion of GDP a country spends on education.

A country's stock of human capital is measured by the average years of schooling among the working-age population (15 and 65 years), average years of schooling of the population, and the composition of the population by level of education (primary school, secondary school or tertiary).[28] The IFs model looks at human capital in terms of years of education attained or schooling, life expectancy, expenditure on education, and spending on health, as a proxy for quality of health.

The implication is that growth in any of these factors would lead to an improvement in human capital and ultimately economic growth.[29] Changing a country's expenditure on education and health would thus increase its MFP, leading to economic growth. However, as mentioned above these indicators are crude proxies which do not necessarily reflect the quality aspects of education or other dimensions of human capital.[30] Following are brief descriptions of these indicators:

i) *Average years of schooling among the working population*: The IFs model defines the productive working age as between 15 and 65 years and uses the parameter of education, that is the average years of schooling for those 15 years and above (EDYearsAge15Total), to measure it.

ii) *Education expenditure*: This refers to the proportion of GDP that is spent on education. The higher the expenditure, the greater the expected level of education attained—holding all other things constant. Education expenditure can also be looked at per capita or per student and includes spending by both government and households.

   iii) Life expectancy: Life expectancy is the number of years one is expected to live at the point of birth.[31] The longer the average life expectancy in a nation, the greater the human capital stock and the contribution to economic growth by extension. In his cross-sectional analysis, Soares[32] found out that 10 years of additional life expectancy added 0.7 years to the average years of education attained by the population. Similar results were found by Ashraf, Lester, and Weil in their study of seven Sub-Saharan African countries—that a 20-year increase in life expectancy added on average 0.386 years of education to the population.[33] The IFs model attributes each additional year of life expectancy to 0.035 years of education to those 15 years old and above.

Some other factors that affect human capital are stunting, due to undernutrition of children, and disability due to morbidity. Stunting affects human capital development and hence people's capacity to contribute to MFP especially in the later years of adulthood. In extreme cases, stunting could cost as much as one percent of economic growth.[34]

The youth (aged 15 to 29 years) form a significant proportion of the populations of most developing nations. Human capital development in these nations, therefore, implies making a substantive investment in the youth. Education as a key component of human capital development has a long payback period—lessons taught in a primary school class today do not lead to an improvement in economic growth tomorrow. Yet, lessons learnt early in life are much harder to master when people are adults (World Bank, 2007). Thus, making the right decisions concerning the children today can have significant payoffs in the future and for generations to come as the youth transition into the labour market and become heads of households and decision-makers themselves.[35]

Most nations have now attained universal primary education as promoted by the United Nations' Millennium Development Goals (MDGs). However, a lot more than just primary school education is required as shown in the World Bank's 2007 *Development and Next Generation* survey. The growing wave of technologically driven globalisation is asking for more from workers than the core competencies acquired in primary school.[36] Consequently, a well-functioning society today is also likely to require higher skills than primary school education.

Yet, overarching these education attainment arguments is the need for quality—this cannot be substituted by a higher level of education or by spending more years in school. As evidenced in the massive education drives of the 1980s and 1990s, rapid expansion, and high enrolment into schools can significantly cost quality.[37] Both the quantity and quality of human capital stock are important.

Kenya's youth bulge: A demographic dividend or bomb?

Kenya has many opportunities for economic growth. This includes its coastal location, which serves as a gateway to the landlocked countries in the region, its market orientation for development, the ever-increasing globalisation, and its youth population—a source of and hence comparatively cheap labour.[38] Out of all of these, the youth population are Kenya's greatest opportunity for sustainable and inclusive development today.

At about 2.5 per cent, Kenya's current annual population growth rate is one of the highest globally, even higher than the Sub-Saharan Africa average, as shown in figure 5.1 below. While the population growth rate is forecasted to reduce significantly to nearly 2.0 per cent by 2030 based on the current trajectory, this will still be higher than most other nations.

Figure 5.1: Population growth rates

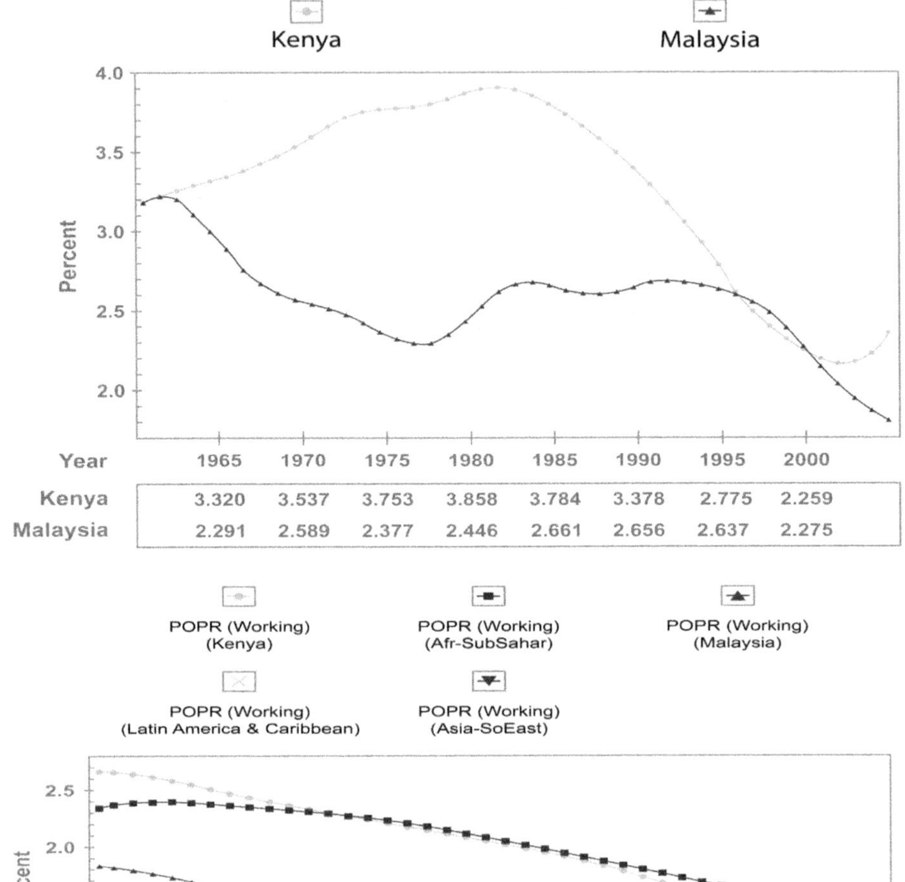

Source: Generated from International Futures Model [Computer Software, Version 7.00], 2017. Retrieved from http://www.ifs.du.edu/

As shown in figure 5.2 below, Kenya has a young population with a median age of 19.5 years.[39]

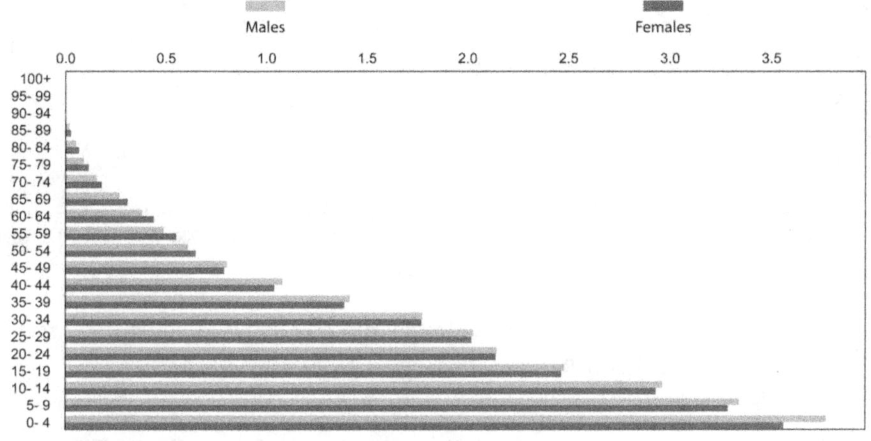

Source: Generated from International Futures Model [Computer Software, Version 7.00], 2017. Retrieved from http://www.ifs.du.edu/

As seen earlier, the biggest asset of a nation is its human capital. The youth (aged 15 to 29 years) form a significant part of Kenya's population (estimated at 48 per cent in 2016). While we cannot predict the future, we can forecast some future events with a degree of certainty.[40] Based on the prevailing demographic trend, the youth will become either a blessing (demographic dividend) or a curse (demographic bomb) to Kenya depending on the nation's development policy interventions.[41] The youth are a mixed bag of resources for the nation, laden with huge opportunities for development, which if not harnessed, can pose considerable economic risks.[42] The proportion of youth in the Kenyan population is expected to gradually decrease with the current drop in the population growth rate which is mainly driven by a decline in total fertility rates (TFR) as shown in figure 5.3 below.

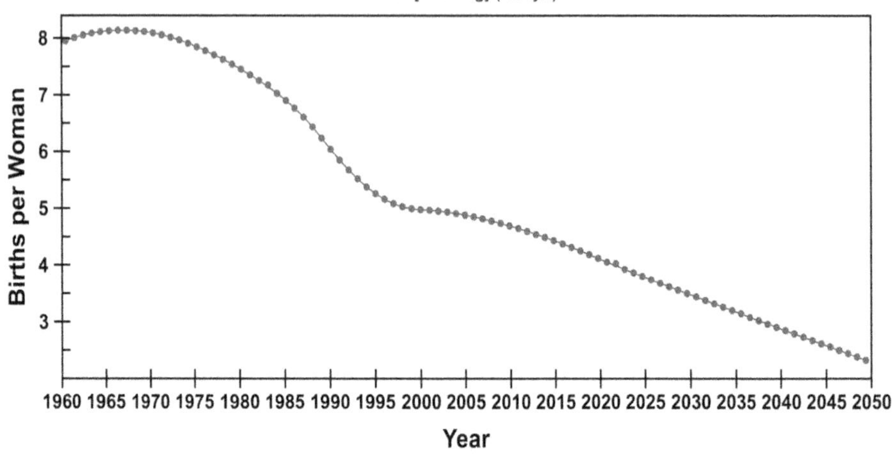

Figure 5.3: Kenya's total fertility rate (TFR)

Source: International Futures Model [Computer Software, Version 7.00], 2017. Retrieved from http://www.ifs.du.edu/

Kenya is presently experiencing a youth bulge, with a high proportion of its population (48 per cent) in the age bracket 15 to 29 years. This situation is expected to continue up to the year 2050 when the youth will be a third of the population as shown in figure 5.4 below.

Figure 5.4: Kenya's youth bulge over time

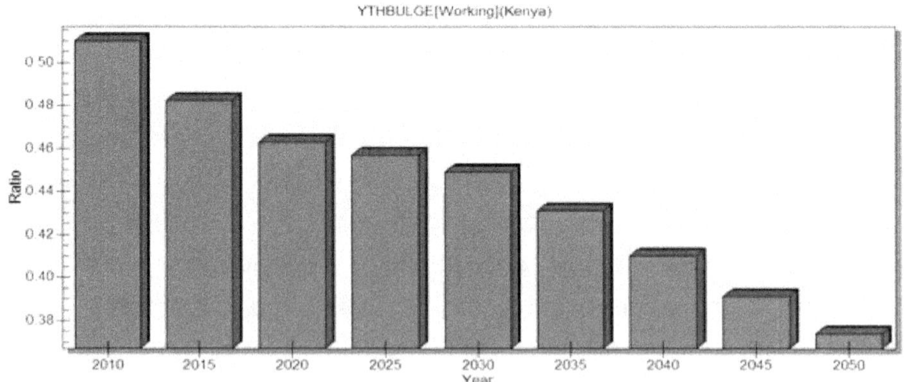

Source: Generated from International Futures Model [Computer Software, Version 7.00], 2017. Retrieved from http://www.ifs.du.edu/

Moreover, the nation's proportion of working age population (15 to 65 years) is high and forecasted to increase consistently in the foreseeable future. The percentage of youth compared to the total working population grew steadily from 1950 to a peak of 67.7 per cent in 2002 and is projected to decline to 59 per cent by 2030.[43] The youth bulge presents a significant opportunity for Kenya's economic growth and points to where Kenya's development efforts should be focused for sustainability and inclusion. Contrary to the ageing economies, Kenya stands to optimally benefit from any investments made in its youth as they form a significant part of the population and are to be productive for a long time.

Another aspect of the Kenya demographic profile worth attention is the dependency ratio, which is defined as 'the number of children and older persons per 100 persons of working age'.[44] The dependency ratio represents the proportion of the working population (15 to 65 years) to those not working, that is, the dependent population (ages 0 to 14 years and above 65 years). Since the 1960s, Kenya's labour force has been growing faster than the dependent population and is estimated to have reached 56 per cent in 2016 and 60 per cent in 2030.[45] This trend is projected to continue as shown in figure 5.5 below.

Figure 5.5: Kenya's population segments profiles – dependence

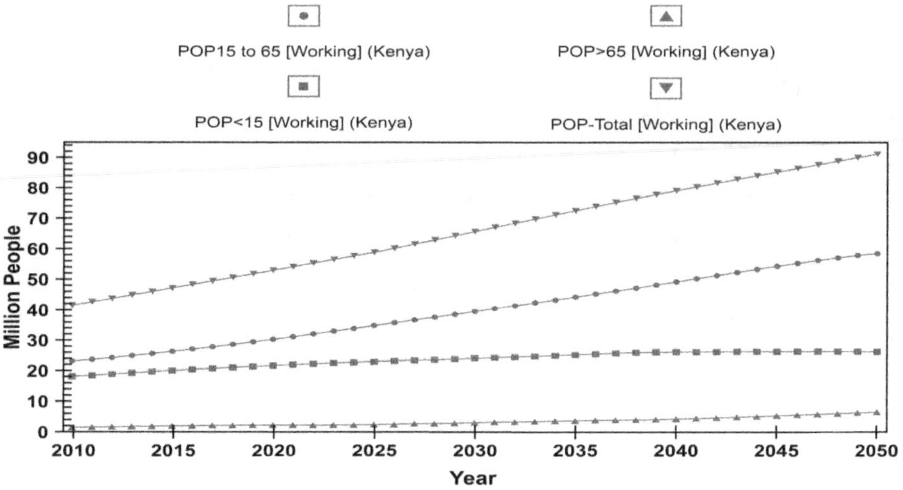

Source: Generated from International Futures Model [Computer Software, Version 7.00], 2017. Retrieved from http://www.ifs.du.edu/

A sustained drop in the dependency ratio has been shown to create a demographic dividend or bonus, that is, a window of opportunity for faster economic growth and poverty reduction.[46]

Changes in the demographic profile resulting from the declining fertility rates are, for a defined period, beneficial for economic growth. With a decline in fertility, the proportion of children (0 to 14 years) in the population falls, and the percentage of those of working age grows, leading to a lower dependency ratio (United Nation, n.d.(a)). A country can reap the benefits of increased productivity and lower the costs related to the decreasing proportion of dependants, provided there are sufficient job opportunities for this growing working age population.[47] A sustained fertility decline in the long-term however, reverses the scenario, naturally shutting the demographic dividend window.

As more and more of the working population transition to retirement (above 65 years) and become dependants themselves with fewer entrants into the labour market due to the low fertility rates, dependency ratios start to rise again. This is currently the situation in several countries in Europe where fertility rates have fallen below replacement levels—generations are not having enough children to replace themselves, which eventually leads to a real reduction in the population size.[48] Such ageing populations are anticipated to have adverse impacts on sustainable growth in the long run, which paradoxically is a consequence of development since 'people are living longer because of better nutrition, sanitation, health care, education and economic well-being'.[49]

What does this mean for Kenya? Like most other nations in Africa, Kenya is poised for a demographic dividend in the future. That is, going by the consistently declining average total fertility rate and dependency ratio as shown in figure 5.6,[50] most of Kenya's population will be in the working age bracket by 2030.

Figure 5.6: Trends for working age population in six regions

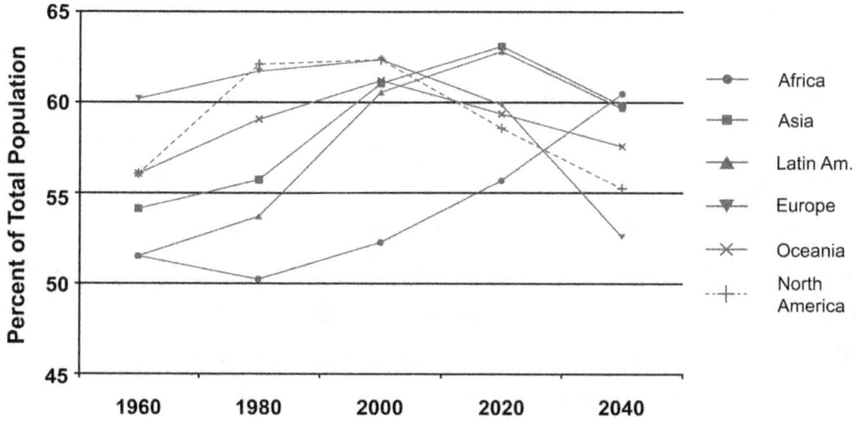

Note: Reprinted from 'Understanding the demographic dividend' (p. 5) by J. Ross, 2004, *Policy Project*.

However, this demographic dividend will only be realised if the right socio-economic policies are developed and implemented. For instance, having an enormous working age population that is unemployed will not translate into an advantage. Rather, it is the ability of Kenya's youth to find gainful employment that will yield a demographic dividend. Otherwise, the youth will grow frustrated and become a source of social conflict and instability in the nation, a demographic bomb.[51] Moreover, unemployment will be a waste of the country's investment in human capital and could lead to frustrations due to unmet expectations and unrest, further dampening the investment climate.[52]

Whether Kenya will reap from its youth bulge or suffer from it will, therefore, depend on its ability to develop its human capital and create opportunities for employment. Like many other developing countries, Kenya's problem is not unemployment but rather underemployment, a situation where people work for fewer hours than they want to or do jobs that do not utilise all the skills and knowledge that they have.[53] Over 80 per cent of Kenya's labour force is employed in the informal sector, whose contribution to employment has continued to grow as the formal sector's share has shrunk.[54]

Many young people are entering self-employment, either out of necessity or because of the opportunities the sector provides.[55] Kenya needs to continually increase opportunities for both wage employment and self-employment, the latter by facilitating access to factors of production such as financial capital, and linkage to business networks.[56] While there have been several attempts by the Kenyan government to provide the youth access to seed capital through revolving funds such the *Youth Enterprise Fund* and the *Uwezo Fund*, these have done little to improve the situation. However, partnerships with development organisations agencies such as the World Bank, U.S. Agency for International Development (USAID) could yield the right results. Kenya is one of the focus countries for Mastercard Foundation's 2018-2030 *Young Africa Works Strategy* whose mission is '*Finding solutions to youth unemployment in Africa*'.[57]

The volume of these funds has been minimal and even worse, contrary to expectations, they have failed because those accessing them consider the cash a political reward or 'nobody's money'. Market-oriented approaches to this financing problem would be more impactful and sustainable. Instead of participating directly in financial markets, the government should incentivise the financial services sector to innovatively serve this market segment by de-risking their exploration of suitable solutions. As argued earlier, the government should seek to catalyse and effectively govern markets to bridge this financing gap.

Due to the falling birth rates and the resultant population structure, a decreasing level of investment will be needed to meet the needs of those aged 0 to 14 years, such as education and health care, which will free up resources for investment in other development initiatives.[58] Mobilising considerable domestic savings has been a struggle for Kenya as seen in Chapter 3, due to the high dependency ratios. Nevertheless, the future presents an opportunity for growth in this area.

Based on the current trajectory, Kenya's demographic dividend is projected to happen between 2050 and 2060 as per figure 5.7 below, and USAID's demographic's dividend model (DEMDIV).[59] A faster decline in the total fertility rate through family planning and education would make this happen sooner. For instance, halving current total fertility rates (TFRM halved) would bring forward the demographic dividend to around 2030 as shown in figure 5.7 below.[60]

Figure 5.7: Kenya's population distribution scenarios

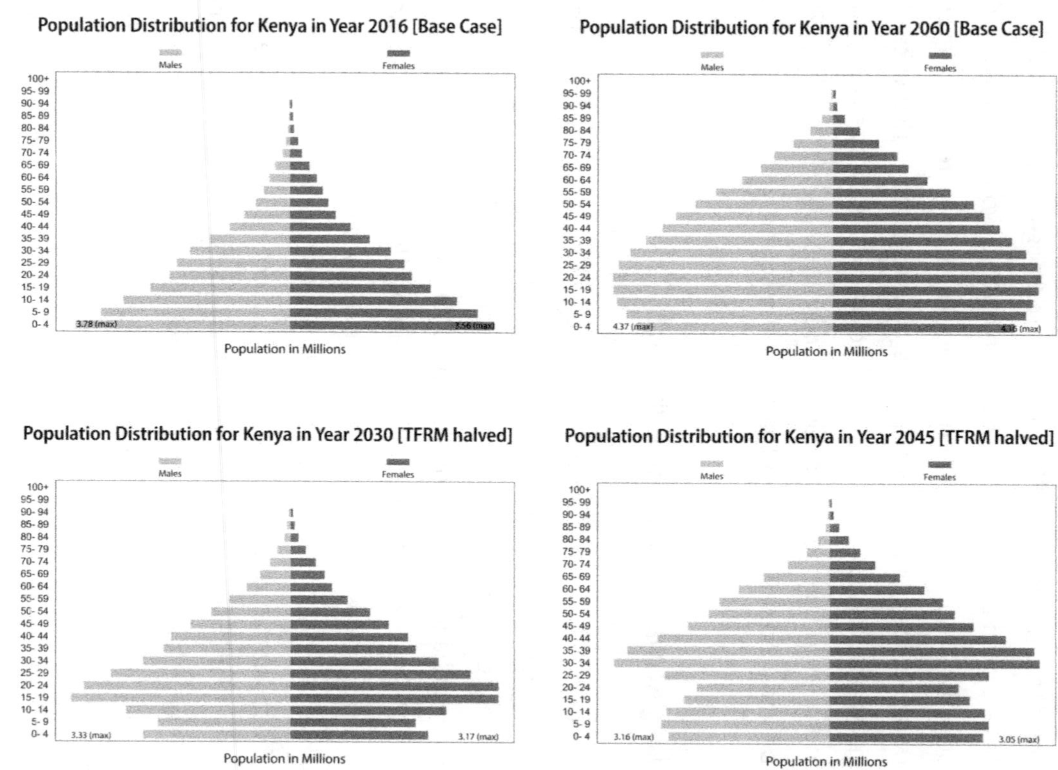

Source: Generated from International Futures Model [Computer Software, Version 7.00], 2017. Retrieved from http://www.ifs.du.edu/

In conclusion, Kenya needs to get future ready. To borrow the words of Werner Erhard, the American critical thinker and transformational leadership author, Kenya needs to create its future from the future, not its past. The leadership needs to become aware of this imminent window of economic opportunity and prepare itself to take maximum advantage of it before it closes. As shown under the halving of TFR scenario, the demographic dividend window would have closed by 2045 as the bulge shifts to beyond 29 years, which is less productive, and the dependency ratio starts to increase again due to the growing number of older dependants. As illustrated in figure 5.5 above, the demographic dividend window would close with finality as happened in many countries in Europe at the turn of the century.[61] Missing this window would be a lost economic opportunity for the country.

Actualising Kenya's demographic dividend

A demographic dividend does not just happen.[62] Only those nations that can see and understand the signs of a looming demographic dividend and act appropriately can reap rewards from it. Realising a demographic dividend requires the enhancement of the working population's productivity.[63]

The HPEAs turned their youth bulge into a demographic dividend. It is estimated that almost a third of the growth realised by the HPEAs was from this source.[64] Part of the reason for the dramatic growth in these economies was the substantive reduction in unemployment—some to single digits.[65] This meant that their youth, whose capacity was being developed through their robust education systems (discussed in Chapter 4), readily found employment and were able to contribute to their economies and to benefit from them.[66]

Drawing from the experience of these successful East Asia nations, the *International Family Planning Conference* held in Ethiopia in November 2013 identified the following as critical strategic investment areas to realise a demographic dividend: changing the population age structure; improving people's health; investing in education; and tailored economic and governance policies.[67] Gribble and Bremner[68] illustrate the interconnection between these strategic policy interventions in figure 5.8 below.

Figure 5.8: Policy interventions for
facilitating a demographic dividend

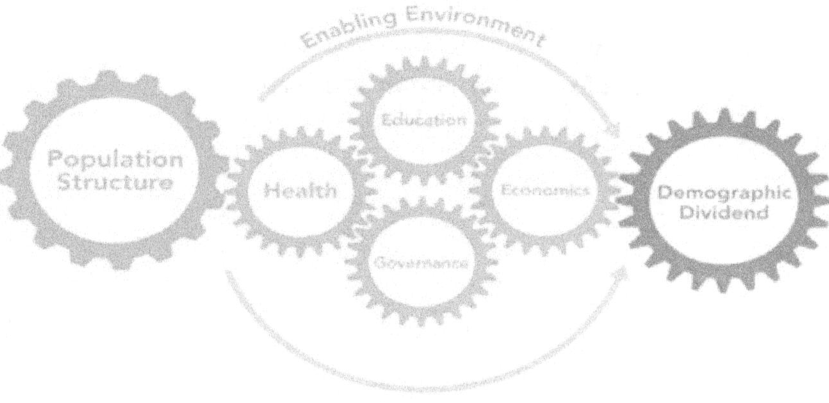

Note: Reprinted from 'Achieving a demographic dividend' (p. 3), by J. Gribble and J. Bremner, 2012, *Population Reference Bureau, Policy Brief, Vol. 67 Issue 2.*

The causal pathways of each these interventions to a demographic dividend are described below.

(a) *Changing the population age structure*: Achieving a rapid drop in fertility rates is a first and crucial step in realising a demographic dividend. This can be attained by educating girls and meeting the family planning needs of the reproductive population through provision of knowledge and contraceptives. A lower fertility rate leads to fewer children and hence a lower dependency ratio.

(b) *Improving people's health*: Good health creates a conducive environment for learning, leading to better-skilled labour. Additionally, health care is one of the key inputs to human capital development, which is crucial in improving multifactor productivity (MFP). A healthy workforce is a more productive workforce. Health programmes also contribute to increasing the life expectancy of people and ensuring optimal productivity by working age.

As shown in figure 5.9 below, the average life expectancy in Kenya is currently about 69 years (2020), higher than the working age upper limit (retirement age) of 65 years, and it is projected to increase to 77 years by 2050.

Figure 5.9: Kenya's life expectancy

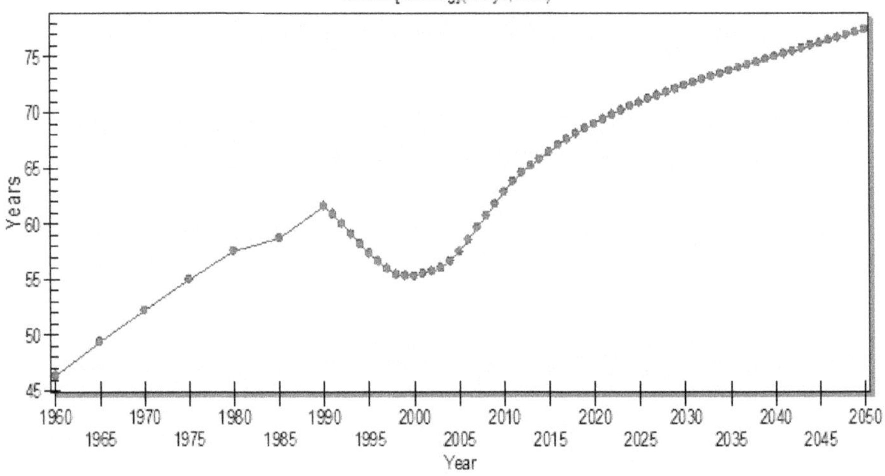

Source: Generated from International Futures Model [Computer Software, Version 7.00], 2017. Retrieved from http://www.ifs.du.edu/

(c) *Investing in education*: Education systems should focus on the youth, the key driver of the demographic dividend, to equip them with skills and knowledge to become a highly productive labour supply.

(d) *Tailored economic and governance policies*: Developing and implementing development policies that foster labour-intensive sectors and create an attractive environment for foreign investment to drive growth is crucial. There is need to ensure that the human capital created is employed for economic growth.

Ross,[69] on the other hand, sees the antecedents to attaining a demographic dividend as savings, labour supply, and human capital. A growing labour supply through an increase in population is necessary, he argues. As the young transition from dependency to active productivity, they form part of the labour supply of the economy (15 to 65 years). As illustrated in figure 5.10 below, Kenya's working population is relatively high—58 per cent of the population in 2020—and is projected to increase to 68 per cent by 2050.

Figure 5.10: Kenya's working population

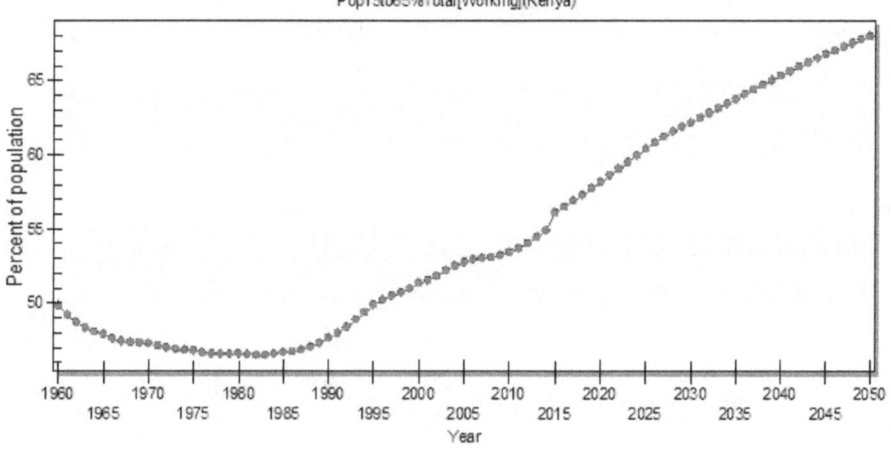

Source: Generated from International Futures Model [Computer Software, Version 7.00], 2017. Retrieved from http://www.ifs.du.edu/

The 15 to 29 years' bracket is considered the most economically productive. The young who are the future labour supply should be prepared through quality education to achieve optimal productivity. The time to prepare them is now, not after they have entered the labour market. Alongside the development of labour, opportunities for employment need to be expanded to ensure that the youth are economically engaged.

With improved dependency ratios, the working population can save more, which can be invested into the nation's economic activities to fuel economic growth, while at the same time providing an incentive to people to accumulate assets for old age.[70] A lower dependency ratio leads to accumulation of savings for investment.[71] In tandem, the right economic environment would also attract foreign investments for economic growth.

In the run-up to a demographic dividend, nations experience lower total fertility rates, which implies that there are fewer dependants, especially those under 14 years. Holding all things constant, this means that households have more resources to invest in developing the capacity of their children through better education. Consequently, the amount of GDP per capita per student increases. As population growth rates drop, the growing economic gains are distributed among fewer people, increasing the GDP per capita. This leads to better services such as education and health care to the population and enhances the nation's stock of human capital.

The World Bank's *World Development Report of 2007: Development and the Next Generation,* identifies broadening the opportunities for developing human capital through increasing access to and improving the quality of education and health care to youth, as one of the three key interventions to development in future. Secondary education provides the needed skills and knowledge for growth. The aim should be, therefore, to consistently increase the proportion of those attaining secondary education—the dark grey area—among the youth (age 15 to 29 years) in figure 5.11 below, and to minimise the mid grey—those with no education and hence less productive in the economy.

Figure 5.11: Kenya's forecasted
education profiles at current trajectory

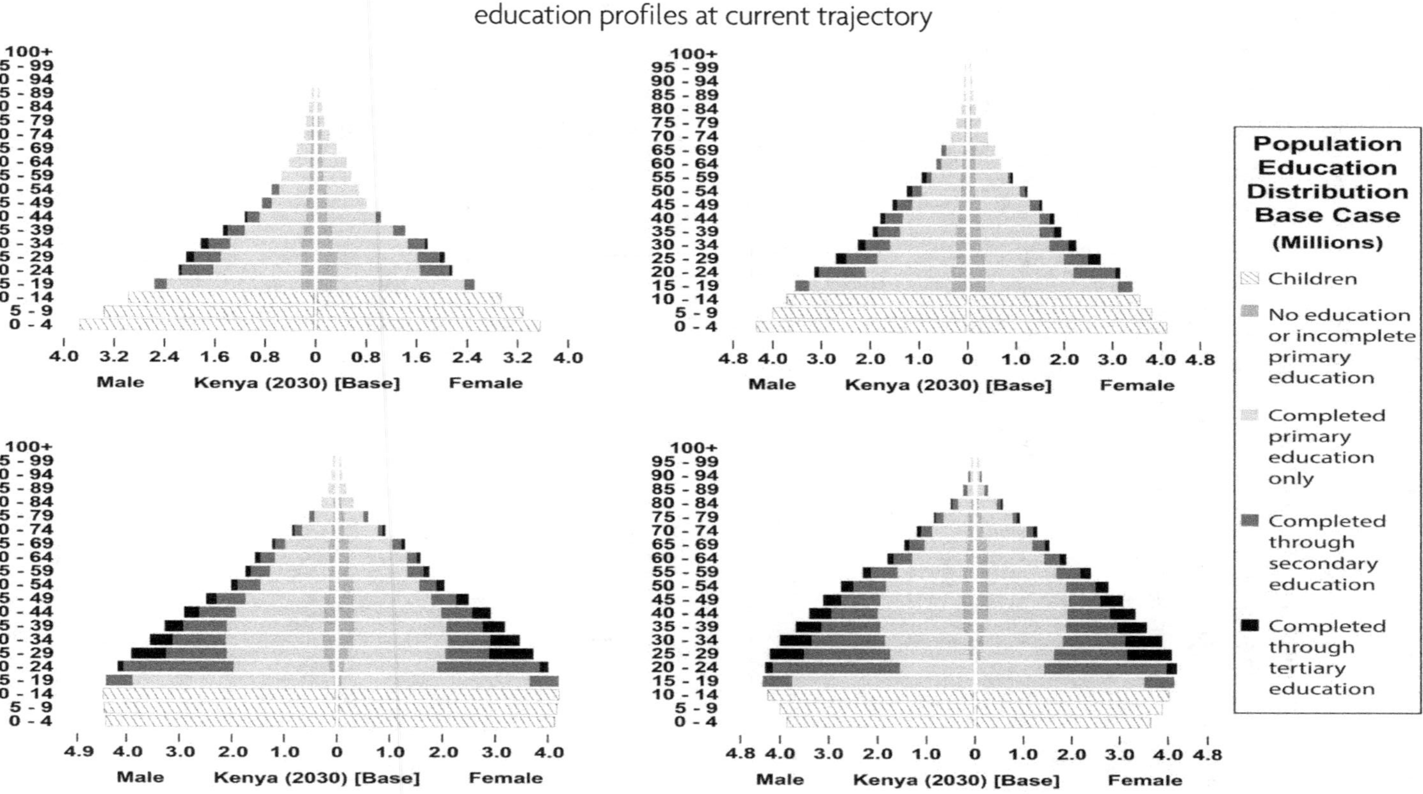

Source: Generated from International Futures Model [Computer Software, Version 7.00], 2017. Retrieved from http://www.ifs.du.edu/

A model for sustainable and inclusive development

This section builds a human capital approach to sustainable and inclusive development using the International Futures (IFs) model. IFs is an integrated and interconnected model featuring six issue modules, namely: demographic, agricultural, energy, environmental, technological, and socio-political. These six modules are connected through the economics module, as illustrated in figure 5.12 below.

Figure 5.12: Components of the IFs model

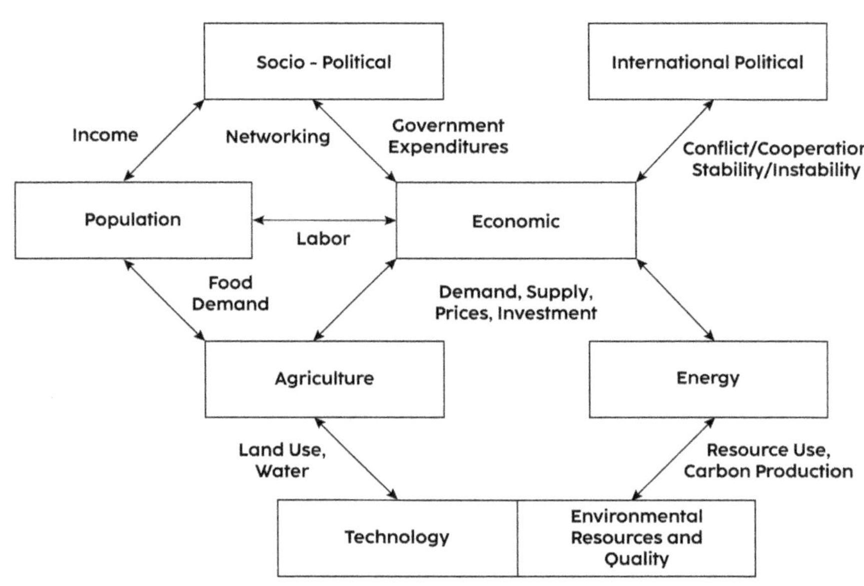

Source: Reprinted from International Futures Model [Computer Software, 7.00], 2017. Retrieved from www.ifs.du.edu/ifs/

The IFs model enables the user to make forecasts up to the year 2100 using over eight hundred variables that are built into the model. The model is global and systemic, that is, it factors in the global implications of interventions that happen in each one of these six modules in any of the 186 countries whose data is in the database. It also accounts for the knock-on effects these are likely to have on other issues both locally and globally. It is a long-term horizon forecasting model and not a projecting one. This means that it does not merely predict what might happen in the future by extrapolating the past, but rather makes use of the mathematical relationships between the variables and parameters based on the available historical evidence to forecast general trends. This entails neither a linear nor non-linear extrapolation but rather a dynamic, interactive analysis.

By means of the IFs model, one can use scenario analysis to compare the base case scenario (a trajectory of current circumstances into the future), with scenarios generated using interventions on the various variables to see if the interventions would yield a preferable future. The IFs model presents a safe way of policy development and testing, as ineffective or unfavourable policy interventions can be identified and abandoned in the 'lab', as it were, before actual implementation.

Linking human capital to economic growth

As seen in Chapter 3, human capital plays a vital role in sustainable and inclusive development. An increase in human capital has a twofold return: an economic return by increasing human capital, and hence the total factor productivity (TFR)—also referred to as multifactor productivity (MFP), and a wide range of social returns.[72] Any kind of education or training adds to the stock of human capital in the nation, with varying degrees of returns.

Primary education has been demonstrated to have significantly higher social returns than higher level education because it forms the basis for subsequent education as well as enhancing labour.[73] Government interventions targeted at the tertiary or university level, on the other hand, have little impact because they do not directly benefit the poor and are neither financially sustainable nor scalable.[74] Very few poor students seek entry into tertiary institutions.

Better educated people make better decisions—including those concerning their health, such as making better choices concerning reproduction, which has a direct impact on a nation's population size. Higher levels of education normally reflect in lower total fertility rates, reducing population growth. Extensive primary education has wider spill-over effects, thus, a greater impact in generating inclusive growth compared to higher level education.[75] Similarly, secondary education would have greater and more spread impact than tertiary education.

As noted earlier in this chapter, human capital development is a key input to economic development. Human capital development entails interventions that make the labour supply more productive, such as improvements in physical health, education, and training.[76] Based on the IFs model, at a rate of +1.093 per cent currently, Kenya is one of the countries in which human capital has a significant contribution to multifactor productivity, and hence to economic growth (compared to Malaysia at +0.3012 per cent and Singapore at -0.767 per cent, and its neighbours Tanzania and Uganda at +0.8734 per cent and +0.2968 per cent, respectively).

Kenya's human capital contribution to economic growth is expected to remain relatively high in the foreseeable future as shown in figure 5.13 below. The main driver of Kenya's high human capital contribution to multifactor productivity (MFP) is the current youth bulge, which is anticipated to continue past 2060 when the nation is likely to realise a demographic dividend as per the current trajectory.

Figure 5.13: Kenya's multifactor productivity contribution from human capital

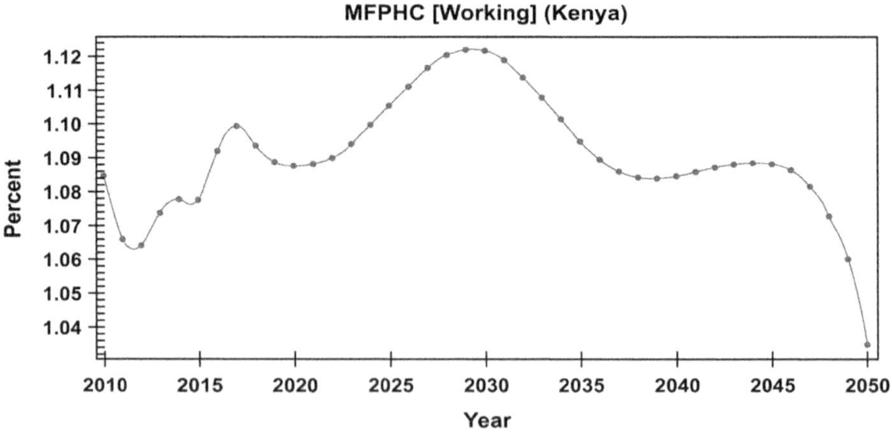

Source: Generated from International Futures Model [Computer Software, Version 7.00], 2017. Retrieved from http://www.ifs.du.edu/

Education, in terms of the average number of years spent in school and the collective amount of education attained by the population, is an important contributor of human capital and in turn the multifactor productivity rate (MFPRATE) of a nation. Figure 5.14 below illustrates the key variables in the relationship between human capital and economic development.

Figure 5.14: Human capital - economic growth flow chart

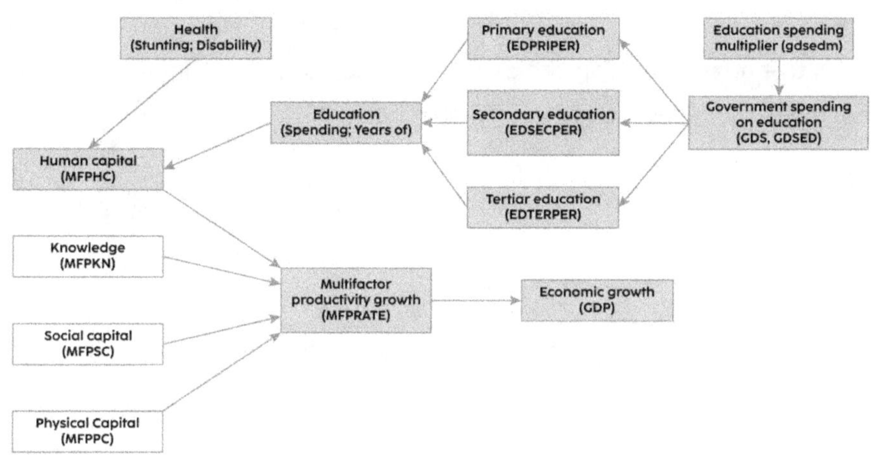

Source: Adapted from International Futures Model [Computer Software, Version 7.00], 2017. Retrieved from www.ifs.du.edu/ifs/

This implies that a policy intervention that promotes education for the majority would have a positive effect on human capital, the multifactor productivity from human capital, economic growth, and eventually equality. This can be summed up by Benjamin Franklin, one of the United States of America's founding fathers, who said that 'an investment in knowledge always pays the best interest'.

Human capital impact pathways

The causal loop diagram in figure 5.15 below outlines the key variables that relate to human capital development (accumulation), their interconnected causality, and the envisaged impact pathways to sustainable and inclusive growth. The diagram illustrates the complex relationships between the variables that are involved in human capital development and how they are likely to evolve in the future to bring about rapid economic growth and reduce inequality. The arrows indicate the direction of the relationships between the dependent and independent variables, with the arrows pointing towards the dependent variables. The causal relationships are either positive (+) or negative (-) as indicated, where a positive relationship means that an increase in the independent variable leads to an increase in the dependent variable.[77] A negative relationship on the other hand means that the independent and dependent variables are negatively correlated.

Figure 5.15: Human capital-economic growth causal loop diagram

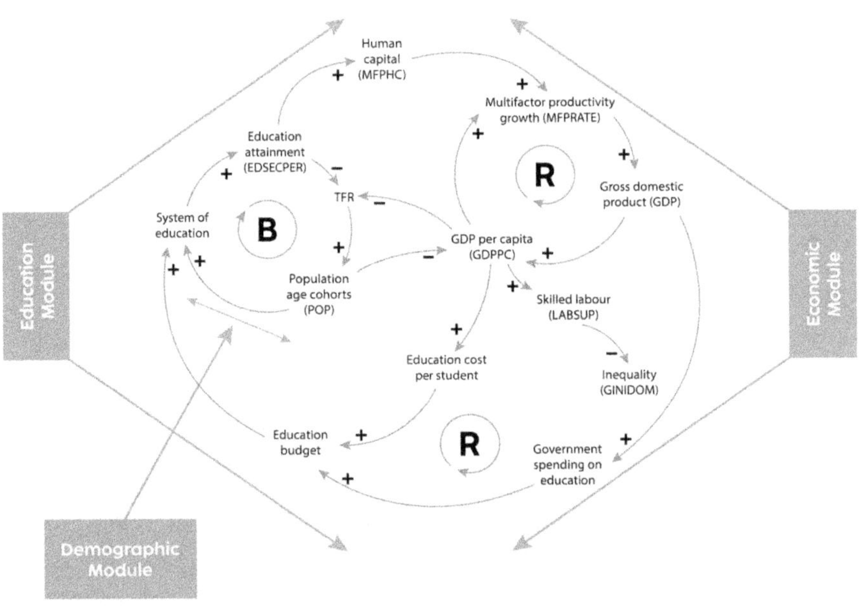

Source: Adapted from International Futures Model [Computer Software, Version 7.00], 2017. Retrieved from www.ifs.du.edu/ifs/

As per this causal loop diagram, increasing the government expenditure on education would lead to an increase in the overall education budget. This would in turn result in an increase in the system of education (described as the intake, survival, completion, and transition by the IFs model). A surge in the system of education would increase the country's education attainment (the average years of education attained by a certain segment of the population, for example, those 15 years and above).

A growth in education attainment would then lead to increased human capital, which embodies workers' productivity. Higher human capital raises the multifactor productivity rate by increasing the multifactor productivity contribution by human capital (the skill level and labour supply), and in turn intensifies economic growth (GDP). An increase in GDP would lead to a larger government budget and hence a surge in its expenditure on education, completing this reinforcing or positive feedback loop, 'R', between education and economic growth.

On the other hand, increasing the level of education attained would lead to a decline in the total fertility rate (TFR), that is the average number of live births per woman, which would subsequently result in a lower population growth rate and, eventually, a decrease in the population. This is because attaining education entails spending longer periods in school, delaying marriage and hence childbearing for females. Furthermore, education creates understanding and empowers young women with the knowledge to make important life choices such as when to marry and the number of children to have.[78]

Research has shown that extending the time spent in school could reduce population growth significantly. Delaying marriage and the time before having the first child through schooling by five years, could slow population growth in Sub-Saharan Africa by as much as 15 to 20 percent.[79] An increase in the population would, however, result in an increase in the education system in the form of higher enrolment into institutions of learning, survival, completion, and transitioning from one level of education to another. This would again in general increase the education attainment in the country, which would then lead to a further decline in TFR forming a balancing or negative feedback loop ('B', in figure 5.15 above).

Evidence from Africa, and Kenya specifically, support this causality between female education and total fertility decline. For instance, the switch to the 8-4-4 education system in Kenya, which increased the length of primary school education by one year, resulted in higher female education attainment and delayed marriage and childbearing.[80] A similar study carried out in Nigeria showed that increasing female education by one year reduced childbearing before 20 years by 0.26 births.[81] Moreover, research has shown that although a general increase in education (for both males and females) leads to a decline in fertility rates, female education has a larger impact on delayed fertility and the age of marriage than male education.[82] Educating girls would thus considerably enhance the prospects for economic and shared growth.

The population size determines the GDP per capita budget that is available for each student, and hence the total years of education that can be attained. A growth in the population would, therefore, result in a lower GDP per capita (GDPPC) while an increase in GDP per capita would result in a lower total fertility rate, as those of a reproductive age could more readily afford and use contraceptives. For instance, according to a study undertaken in Karatina in central Kenya in 2008, nearly thirteen hundred women aged between 20 and 49 years showed a highly significant association between fertility rate and the woman's level of education attainment, age at first marriage, and wealth index.[83]

On the other hand, a growth in GDP per capita would mean that households would have more to spend on education, leading to a higher education cost per student, which would increase the total education budget and boost both the quantity and quality of education attained. The formal education of adults determines the proportion of the labour supply that is skilled (LABSUP). An increase in GDP per capita thus leads to more skilled labour supply (LABSUP), and eventually decreases the level of inequality, as most of the country's population gains education.

The next chapter uses the International Futures (IFs) model with the understanding developed in this chapter to explore the effect of increased upper secondary education on sustainable and inclusive growth, by looking at various scenarios.

Conclusion

Kenya has an opportunity to realise accelerated growth in the next couple of decades with a demographic dividend. However, this is not guaranteed. Its current youth bulge will either be a blessing or a curse. This chapter has outlined the link between human capital and inclusive growth and presented a model that will be used to explore the options for tapping into this opportunity for shared growth.

References

[1] Keeley, B. (2007). *Human Capital: How What You Know Shapes Your Life*, OECD Publishing, Paris.

[2] Ibid (p. 28); Goldin, C. (2014). *Human Capital. Handbook of Cliometrics*. Harvard.

[3] Pelinescu, E. (2015). 'The impact of human capital on economic growth'. *ScienceDirect, Procedia Economics and Finance. 2015, Vol.22*, p184 – 190.

[4] Teixeira, P. (2007). 'Jacob Mincer and the centrality of human capital for contemporary labour economics'. History of Recent Economics.

[5] Keeley, B. (2007). *Human Capital: How What You Know Shapes Your Life*, OECD Publishing, Paris (p. 29).

[6] Hughes, B. B. & Hillebrand, E. E. (2016). *Exploring and Shaping International Futures*. Routledge Taylor and Francis Group, NY. Kindle Edition.

[7] Ibid; Pelinescu, E. (2015). 'The impact of human capital on economic growth'. *ScienceDirect, Procedia Economics and Finance. 2015, Vol.22*, p184 – 190; World Bank (2016). *Kenya Country Economic Memorandum: From Economic Growth to Jobs and Shared Prosperity*. The World Bank, Washington, DC; Fuente, A. (2011). 'Human capital and productivity'. *Barcelona Economics Working Paper Series, Working Paper Nº 530*.

[8] Teixeira, P. (2007). 'Jacob Mincer and the centrality of human capital for contemporary labour economics'. History of Recent Economics.

[9] Keeley, B. (2007). *Human Capital: How What You Know Shapes Your Life*, OECD Publishing, Paris.

[10] Fuente, A. (2011). 'Human capital and productivity'. *Barcelona Economics Working Paper Series, Working Paper Nº 530*.

[11] Hughes, B. B. & Hillebrand, E. E. (2016). *Exploring and Shaping International Futures*. Routledge Taylor and Francis Group, NY. Kindle Edition.

[12] Ibid

[13]   Teixeira, P. (2007). 'Jacob Mincer and the centrality of human capital for contemporary labour economics'. History of Recent Economics.

[14]   Keeley, B. (2007). *Human Capital: How What You Know Shapes Your Life*, OECD Publishing, Paris.

[15]   Pelinescu, E. (2015). 'The impact of human capital on economic growth'. *ScienceDirect, Procedia Economics and Finance. 2015, Vol.22*, p184 – 190; Hughes, B. B. & Hillebrand, E. E. (2016). *Exploring and Shaping International Futures*. Routledge Taylor and Francis Group, NY. Kindle Edition; Erosa, A., Koreshkova, T. & Restuccia, D. (2010). 'How important is human capital? A quantitative theory assessment of world income inequality'. *Review of Economic Studies. 2010, Vol. 01*, p1–32; International Futures Model [Computer Software, Version 7.00], 2017. Retrieved from http://www.ifs.du.edu/.

[16]   Erosa, A., Koreshkova, T. & Restuccia, D. (2010). 'How important is human capital? A quantitative theory assessment of world income inequality'. *Review of Economic Studies. 2010, Vol. 01*, p1–32.

[17]   World Bank (1993). *The East Asian Miracle. Economic Growth and Public Policy*. A World Bank Policy Research Report. The World Bank, Washington, DC.

[18]   Erosa, A., Koreshkova, T. & Restuccia, D. (2010). 'How important is human capital? A quantitative theory assessment of world income inequality'. *Review of Economic Studies. 2010, Vol. 01*, p1–32.

[19]   Ibid

[20]   Hughes, B. B. & Hillebrand, E. E. (2016). *Exploring and Shaping International Futures*. Routledge Taylor and Francis Group, NY. Kindle Edition; Fuente, A. (2011). 'Human capital and productivity'. *Barcelona Economics Working Paper Series, Working Paper Nº 530*.

[21]   Ibid; Pelinescu, E. (2015). 'The impact of human capital on economic growth'. *ScienceDirect, Procedia Economics and Finance. 2015, Vol.22*, p184 – 190.

[22]   Pelinescu, E. (2015). 'The impact of human capital on economic growth'. *ScienceDirect, Procedia Economics and Finance. 2015, Vol.22*, p184 – 190.

[23]   Noble, T. (2000). *Social Theory and Social Change*. Palgrave, NY.

[24]   Keeley, B. (2007). *Human Capital: How What You Know Shapes Your Life*, OECD Publishing, Paris.

[25]   Bassanini, A. & Scarpetta, S. (2001). 'The driving forces of economic growth: Panel data evidence for the OECD countries'. *OECD Economic Studies No. 33, 2001/II*.

[26]   Goldin, C. (2014). *Human Capital. Handbook of Cliometrics*. Harvard.

[27]   Pelinescu, E. (2015). 'The impact of human capital on economic growth'. *ScienceDirect, Procedia Economics and Finance. 2015, Vol.22*, p184 – 190.

[28]   Hughes, B. B. & Hillebrand, E. E. (2016). *Exploring and Shaping International Futures*. Routledge Taylor and Francis Group, NY. Kindle Edition; Fuente, A. (2011). 'Human capital

and productivity'. *Barcelona Economics Working Paper Series, Working Paper Nº 530*; Erosa, A., Koreshkova, T. & Restuccia, D. (2010). 'How important is human capital? A quantitative theory assessment of world income inequality'. *Review of Economic Studies. 2010, Vol. 01*, p1–32.

29 Hughes, B. B. & Hillebrand, E. E. (2016). *Exploring and Shaping International Futures*. Routledge Taylor and Francis Group, NY. Kindle Edition.

30 Bassanini, A. & Scarpetta, S. (2001). 'The driving forces of economic growth: Panel data evidence for the OECD countries'. OECD Economic Studies No. 33, 2001/II.

31 Hughes, B. B. & Hillebrand, E. E. (2016). *Exploring and Shaping International Futures*. Routledge Taylor and Francis Group, NY. Kindle Edition.

32 Soares, R. (2007). 'On the determinants of mortality reductions in the developing world'. *Nber Working Paper Series. Working Paper 12837*.

33 International Futures Model [Computer Software, Version 7.00], 2017. Retrieved from http://www.ifs.du.edu/.

34 Ibid

35 World Bank (2007). 'World development report 2007: Development and the next generation'. World Bank, Washington, DC.

36 Ibid

37 Ibid; Eshiwani, G. (1990). 'Implementing educational policies in Kenya'. *World Bank Discussion Papers Africa Technical Department Series*. The World Bank, Washington, DC.

38 Kimenyi, M., Mwega, F. & Ndung'u, N. (2016). 'The African ions: Kenya country case study'. Brookings Institute.

39 World Factbook (2017, Jan 12). Kenya. Central Intelligence Agency.

40 Cornish, E. (2004). *Futuring: The Exploration of the Future*. World Future Society. Kindle Edition.

41 Lin, J. (2012, Jan 5). 'Youth bulge: A demographic dividend or a demographic bomb in developing countries?' The world Bank, Washington, DC.

42 World Bank (2007). 'World development report 2007: Development and the next generation'. World Bank, Washington, DC.

43 Kimenyi, M., Mwega, F. & Ndung'u, N. (2016). 'The African lions: Kenya country case study'. Brookings Institute.

44 United Nations (n.d.(a)). 'Sustainable development indicators: Total fertility rate'. United Nations.

45 International Futures Model [Computer Software, Version 7.00], 2017. Retrieved from http://www.ifs.du.edu/.

46   United Nations (n.d.(a)). 'Sustainable development indicators: Total fertility rate'. United Nations; Kimenyi, M., Mwega, F. & Ndung'u, N. (2016). 'The African lions: Kenya country case study'. Brookings Institute; World Bank (2007). 'World development report 2007: Development and the next generation'. World Bank, Washington, DC; Ross, J. (2004). 'Understanding the demographic dividend'. Policy Project.

47   United Nations (n.d.(a)). 'Sustainable development indicators: Total fertility rate'. United Nations.

48   Ibid

49   UNFPA (2015, Oct 13). 'Ageing'. United nations Population Fund.

50   Kimenyi, M., Mwega, F. & Ndung'u, N. (2016). 'The African lions: Kenya country case study'. Brookings Institute; World Bank (2007). 'World development report 2007: Development and the next generation'. World Bank, Washington, DC.

51   Lin, J. (2012, Jan 5). 'Youth bulge: A demographic dividend or a demographic bomb in developing countries?' The world Bank, Washington, DC.

52   World Bank (2007). 'World development report 2007: Development and the next generation'. World Bank, Washington, DC.

53   World Bank (2009, Feb 10). 'What is inclusive development?' World Bank, Washington, DC.

54   Kimenyi, M., Mwega, F. & Ndung'u, N. (2016). 'The African lions: Kenya country case study'. Brookings Institute; World Bank (2007). 'World development report 2007: Development and the next generation'. World Bank, Washington, DC.

55   World Bank (2007). 'World development report 2007: Development and the next generation'. World Bank, Washington, DC.

56   Ibid

57   Mastercard Foundation (n.d.). 'Young Africa works strategy'. Retrieved (Nov 2020) from https://mastercardfdn.org/our-strategy/young-africa-works/

58   Ross, J. (2004). 'Understanding the demographic dividend'. Policy Project.

59   Ibid; Kimenyi, M., Mwega, F. & Ndung'u, N. (2016). 'The African lions: Kenya country case study'. Brookings Institute; World Bank (2007). 'World development report 2007: Development and the next generation'. World Bank, Washington, DC; International Futures Model [Computer Software, Version 7.00], 2017. Retrieved from http://www.ifs.du.edu/.

60   International Futures Model [Computer Software, Version 7.00], 2017. Retrieved from http://www.ifs.du.edu/; Kimenyi, M., Mwega, F. & Ndung'u, N. (2016). 'The African lions: Kenya country case study'. Brookings Institute.

61   Ross, J. (2004). 'Understanding the demographic dividend'. Policy Project.

62   Ibid; Kimenyi, M., Mwega, F. & Ndung'u, N. (2016). 'The African lions: Kenya country case study'. Brookings Institute.id; Kimenyi, M., Mwega, F. & Ndung'u, N. (2016). The African Lions: Kenya country case study. Brookings Institute.

63   Ibid

64   Ross, J. (2004). 'Understanding the demographic dividend'. Policy Project; Lin, J. (2012, Jan 5). 'Youth bulge: A demographic dividend or a demographic bomb in developing countries?' The world Bank, Washington, DC.

65   Lin, J. (2012, Jan 5). 'Youth bulge: A demographic dividend or a demographic bomb in developing countries?' The world Bank, Washington, DC.

66   Ibid

67   USAID (n.d.). 'The challenge ahead: Initiating a demographic dividend'. International Conference on Family Planning.

68   Gribble J. & Bremner, J. (2012). 'Achieving a demographic dividend'. *Population Reference Bureau, Policy Brief, Vol. 67 Issue 2*, p. 1-12.

69   Ross, J. (2004). 'Understanding the demographic dividend'. Policy Project.

70   Ibid; United Nations (2015, Oct 21). 'Inequality measurement'. *Department of Economic and Social Affairs. Development Issues No. 2*. United Nations; The Economist (2012, Aug 2). 'Fertility decline, the demographic dividend, poverty, and inequality'. The Economist.

71   Kimenyi, M., Mwega, F. & Ndung'u, N. (2016). 'The African lions: Kenya country case study'. Brookings Institute.

72   Campos, J. E. & Root, H. L. (1996). *The Key to the Asian Miracle: Making Shared Growth Credible*. The Brookings Institution, Washington, DC.

73   Ibid

74   World Bank (2007). 'World development report 2007: Development and the next generation'. World Bank, Washington, DC.

75   Ibid

76   Hughes, B. B. & Hillebrand, E. E. (2016). *Exploring and Shaping International Futures*. Routledge Taylor and Francis Group, NY. Kindle Edition.

77   Ibid

78   World Bank (2007). 'World development report 2007: Development and the next generation'. World Bank, Washington, DC; Gribble J. & Bremner, J. (2012). 'Achieving a demographic dividend'. *Population Reference Bureau, Policy Brief, Vol. 67 Issue 2*, p. 1-12.

79   Gribble J. & Bremner, J. (2012). 'Achieving a demographic dividend'. *Population Reference Bureau, Policy Brief, Vol. 67 Issue 2*, p. 1-12; Pradhan, E. (2015). 'Female education and childbearing: A closer look at the data'. The world Bank, Washington, DC.

80   Pradhan, E. (2015). 'Female education and childbearing: A closer look at the data'. The world Bank, Washington, DC.

81   Ibid

82   Ibid

83   Mathenge, G. (n.d.). 'The role of education in influencing fertility levels of women in Central Province, Kenya'. The Organization for Economic Cooperation and Development (OECD).

CHAPTER 6

Identifying high leverage points

Give me a place to stand, and I will move the earth.
—Archimedes of Syracuse

Using the International Futures forecasting model and the human capital model developed in Chapter 5, this chapter identifies high leverage points and makes practical recommendations on policy interventions that will help Kenya get onto the path of sustainable and inclusive development.

The context

To recap, right after independence, Kenya identified poverty, illiteracy, and disease as the three key constraints to development and has been working to eliminate this. The 1965 Sessional Paper No. 10 aptly laid the foundation and set the goal for Kenya's future, the quest for sustainable and inclusive development. Kenya has been pursuing this goal until now. A lot of effort and resources have been applied to this endeavour, but the results have been less than proportionate. At times, the various policy interventions have yielded negative outcomes, as was the case in the 1980s and 1990s, taking the nation further away from this goal. The challenges are many and the destination still far, but we cannot stop before reaching the desired destination—that is not an option.

Despite the sub-optimal economic performance since independence, Kenya's opportunities for attaining sustainable and inclusive development abound. The biggest of these opportunities is its youth—about 50 per cent of the country's population are youth, aged 15 to 29 years as shown in Figure 6.1 below. This highly youthful demographic profile is projected to last into the foreseeable future. Accompanying this youth bulge is a sustained decline in the dependency ratios, that is, the ratio of the working population (15 to 65 years) to the dependent population (0 to 14 years and over 65 years). This is underpinned by the sustained decline in fertility rates—the number of live births per woman.

With a youth bulge and a sustained decline in fertility rates and dependency ratios, Kenya is poised for a demographic dividend, that is, a window of opportunity for accelerated economic growth and poverty reduction, between 2040 and 2060. However, the youth could become a demographic bomb if not well managed. To ready itself to benefit from this demographic dividend, Kenya needs to prepare its youth for the labour market and to expand the opportunities for employment—both formal and informal.

Figure 6.1: Kenya's youth bulge

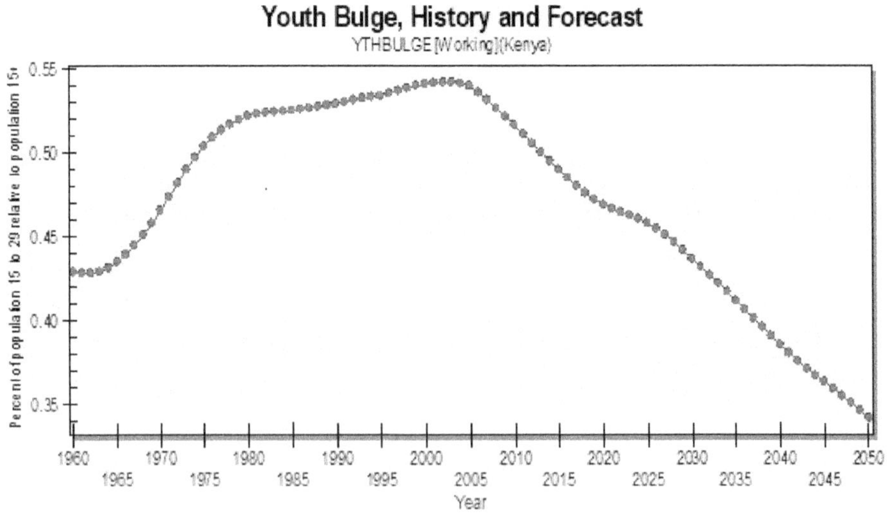

Source: Generated from International Futures Model [Computer Software, Version 7.00], 2017. Retrieved from http://www.ifs.du.edu/

The way to sustainable and inclusive development is undisputedly through developing a nation's human capital, as outlined in Chapters 2 and 5. Effective policy interventions need to be broad-based, benefitting most of the population. Kenya's highest leverage point is, therefore, developing the capacity of its youth. Evidence also shows that human capital development interventions that are undertaken earlier in life yield far higher returns to growth than those involving adults. Moreover, the spill over effects of lower levels of education have been shown to significantly outweigh those of higher education attainment—for example, benefits of primary education compared with tertiary (university and other college) education.

As illustrated in the human capital development for sustainable and inclusive growth causal loop diagram in the previous chapter, one of the spill over effects of education attainment is reduced fertility rates. One extra year of girls' schooling has been demonstrated to have a significant impact on the number of births per woman due to delayed marriage and the bearing of the first child. Again, this impact is higher if education is provided earlier in life than in adulthood. Based on this understanding, the way to realise a significant and sustained decline in Kenya's fertility rate, and hence actualise the looming demographic dividend, is through educating the youth, and girls in particular.

A Kenyan model for sustainable development

Through the NARC government's initiated free primary education programme, Kenya has attained almost universal primary school education. Yet, as shown under the review of Vision 2030, this will not deliver the desired average 10 per cent per annum of economic growth, let alone a reduction in inequality in the foreseeable future. Moreover, given the rate of technologically driven globalisation, the marketplace is demanding a lot more than a primary school level of knowledge and skills. This situation is not unique to the workplace but cuts across the whole society. Skills and knowledge that were in past decades sufficient for personal life and societal decisions are no longer adequate.

As illustrated in figure 6.2 below, there is a marked gender bias regarding education in Kenya. While the estimated proportion of pupils finishing primary school (education, primary survival rate, EDPRISUR) was roughly the same for both girls and boys at about 75 per cent in 2016, the number that transitioned into secondary education as reflected by the enrolment rate is noticeably lower at 63 per cent. This means that just about 50 per cent of the population that is of secondary school age get enrolled for secondary education. The likelihood of a girl joining secondary school in 2017 was even lower at 60 per cent compared to that of a boy at 66 per cent.

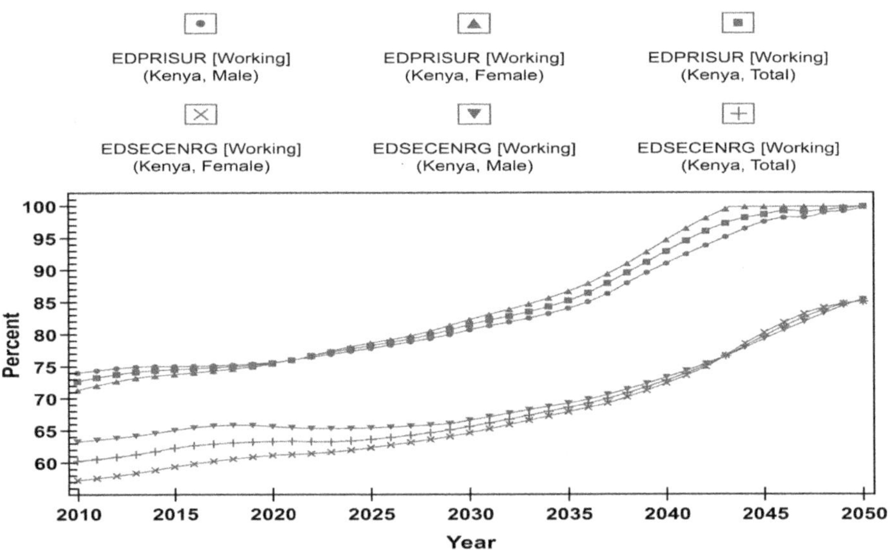

Figure 6.2: Education in Kenya - primary survival and secondary school enrolment and rates

Source: Generated from International Futures Model [Computer Software, Version 7.00], 2017. Retrieved from http://www.ifs.du.edu/

Girls have a much lower chance of attaining secondary education, yet they hold a greater promise to realising the demographic dividend because a higher level of education attainment by women (years of schooling) would drive down the total fertility rate and contribute to labour productivity by adding to the country's stock of human capital. Contrary to past cultural practices when women were confined to the home as caregivers, Kenyan women are increasingly able to work away from their homes.

Figure 6.3 below shows the status of girls' education in Kenya. The survival rates are relatively the same for both primary and secondary school levels at about 74 per cent and 73 per cent, respectively. This means that a girl enrolled in primary school has a similar chance of completing this level of education as one enrolled in secondary school has in completing form four. However, a clear divergence in favour of primary education survival rate is starting to emerge.

Figure 6.3: Girl primary and secondary
school enrolment and survival rates in Kenya.

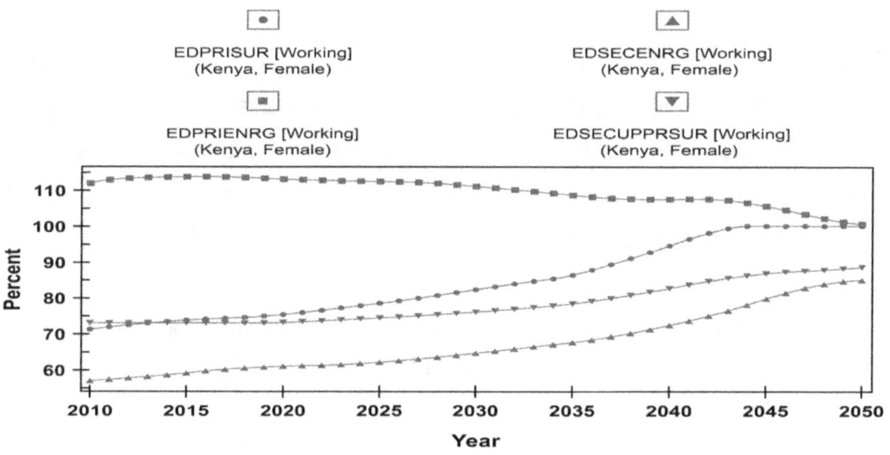

Source: Generated from International Futures Model [Computer Software, Version 7.00], 2017. Retrieved from http://www.ifs.du.edu/

The real challenge relates to the ability to join secondary education as shown in figure 6.4. Although the proportion of those who miss opportunities for enrolment into secondary school is almost the same for both boys and girls, the situation is slightly swayed in favour of boys. Limited places in secondary schools and the initial costs have denied many girls an opportunity to access secondary education. This has had a direct knock-on effect on increased fertility rates as the primary school graduates enter marriage early and this increases the likelihood of having many children.

Figure 6.4: Percent of primary school graduates
not enrolled in secondary school

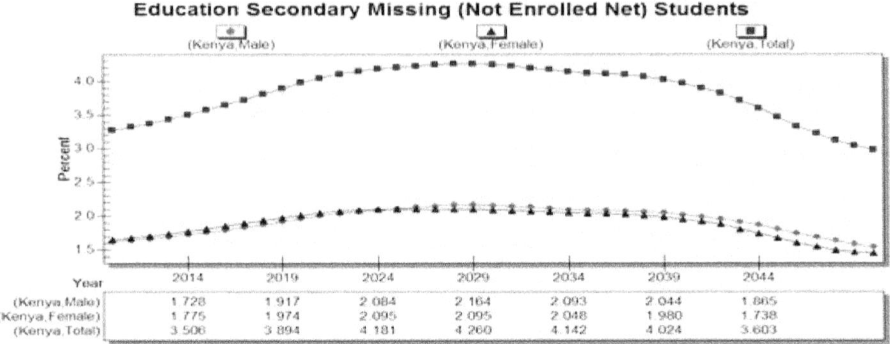

Source: Generated from International Futures Model [Computer Software,
Version 7.00], 2017. Retrieved from http://www.ifs.du.edu/

Consequently, girls miss an opportunity to enhance their capacity to generate
more income to support themselves and their families. Simultaneously, the
economy loses an opportunity for growth, while at the same time creating
more dependents for society. The same bias for males is reflected in the
overall population education levels, as shown in figure 6.5 below.

Figure 6.5: Education, years obtained by population 15+

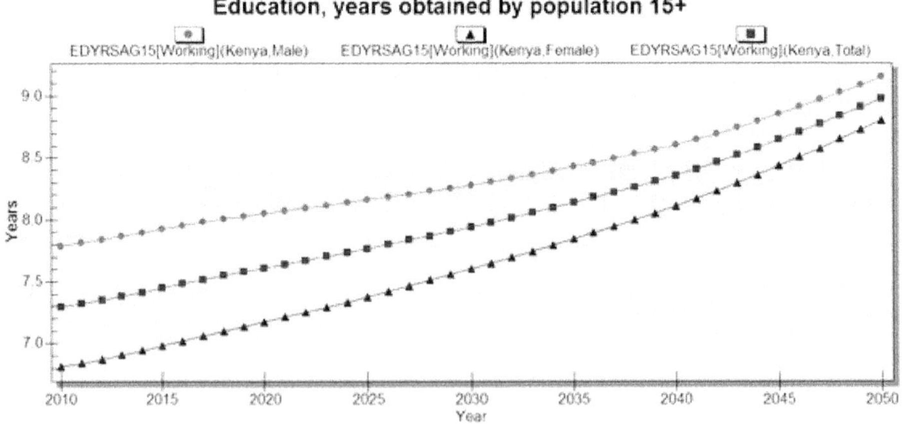

Source: Generated from International Futures Model [Computer Software,
Version 7.00], 2017. Retrieved from http://www.ifs.du.edu/

The difference in education attained between men and women in the Kenyan population is currently estimated at one year in favour of men. While this might have been perpetuated by certain cultural practices, it demonstrates whose education gets sacrificed when resources are limited. The common practice throughout the generations is that girls drop out of education first when households lack enough resources to keep all their children in school. Although good quality education would have a bigger economic impact, merely keeping girls in school, thus delaying early marriage and the age of childbearing, assuming there are no in-school pregnancies, would reduce their total fertility rate and lead to significant benefits.[1] A higher education attainment would enable girls to make better life decisions, including how many children to have and when to have them.[2]

Kenya's expenditure on secondary school education has been shrinking over time, as shown in figure 6.6, and is projected to continue to decrease at the current trajectory up to around 2020.

Figure 6.6: GDP per capita expenditure on secondary education

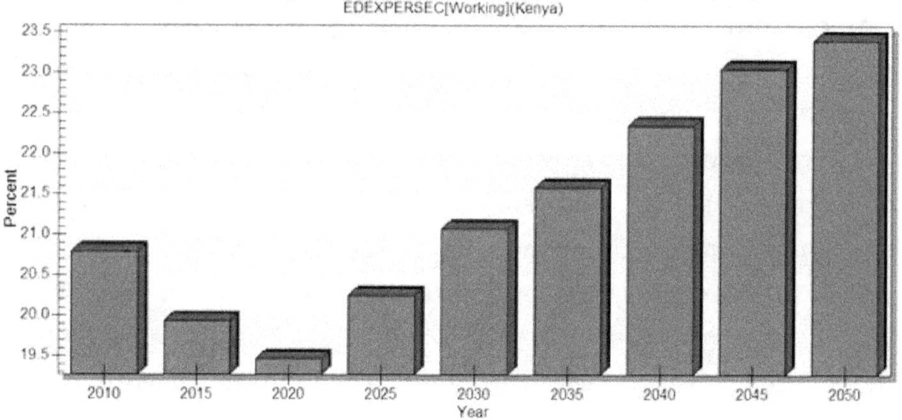

Source: Generated from International Futures Model [Computer Software, Version 7.00], 2017. Retrieved from http://www.ifs.du.edu/

In conclusion, the time to start to build human capital is now—not in the future when it is required. The effort should be broad-based to ensure that most of the population benefits. It should be targeted at the young, whose absorptive capacity is higher and the spill over effects bigger. Although education for all is important, ensuring that girls stay in school presents a greater opportunity for realising the imminent demographic dividend as it would eventually lower the total fertility rate.

Scenario analysis and results

This section presents the results of a scenario building exercise I have undertaken using the International Futures (IFs) model, based on the human capital model for sustainable and inclusive growth developed in Chapter 5.

The International Futures (IFs) model

The International Futures (IFs) model is a tool that is designed to help people explore what the future might look like and to start to think critically about it.[3] The model involves discovering past trends of key human systems such as health, economy, agriculture, and demographics, and demonstrates how they interact to shape the future.[4] IFs entails getting answers to four core questions: 'Where have we been? Where do we seem to be going? Where do we want to be? And how do we get there?'.[5]

IFs is built on an economic theory, that is, the various sub-systems or modules, namely: demographic, agricultural, energy, environmental, technological, and socio-political. These connect through the economic module. The IFs model is grounded in sound data for 186 countries in these main human systems, from credible sources such as the World Bank and the United Nations, which enables one to generate a realistic picture of the future rather than merely speculating, and to come up with viable policies to actualise it.[6] It provides a one-stop shop for credible global information on the main human systems for forecasting. IFs enables users to easily experiment with the approximately eight hundred variables and the parameters in the model to create and analyse global futures.[7]

The model helps organisations, businesses, and governments understand the world around them and the future it portends, and to explore how they can shape that future or at least be ready for it.[8] By asking where we have been, IFs helps us to explore historical trends and the relationships between variables by gathering and analysing data across proximate variables and time.[9] It enables us to understand the interconnectedness of variables in the global system and how these are changing over time, that is, where the trends are going.[10]

Through trend analysis, we can comprehend where current policies and interventions are likely to lead us in the future, and so the base case or *Working* scenario. While the future cannot be predicted, it can be forecasted.[11] Informed by the base case, the IFs model then helps us to frame uncertainties about the future and to explore what trends we need to create today to frame the future we want. Using IFs, we can develop scenarios about what the future is likely to look like and through simulation, come up with interventions to shape the future we desire.

In exploring the future, the aims are to understand the core changes that are taking place currently, where these changes seem to be leading (trend analysis), what future might be preferable to the country, and how much leverage exists to bring that preferred future into being.[12]

Scenario analysis

Based on the information and arguments presented here and in previous chapters, I explore the hypothesis that an increase in upper secondary education is the foundation for Kenya's path to sustainable and inclusive development. The variables selected for this are the gross domestic product (GDP) and GDP growth rate (GDPR) for economic growth and the poverty gap based on $1.25/day income (POVGAP index) for inequality. Alongside these two, I also look at societal well-being using GDP per capita (GDPPC), life expectancy (LIFEXP), education attainment in the population 15 years and above (EDYRSAG15), and access to electricity (INFRAELECACC). I also examine other intermediate variables in the impact pathway as outlined in the causal loop diagram in figure 5.15 in Chapter 5, such as population and multifactor productivity from human capital contribution. This will provide an indication of whether Kenya is making progress towards attaining sustainable and inclusive development, which is the ultimate goal.

The IFs model for global forecasting groups secondary education into lower and upper. In Kenya, the 8-4-4 system, however, does not have lower and upper classifications. The upper secondary education attainment is used here to represent full secondary education. In this scenario analysis, I explore whether improving secondary school graduation rates and hence the level of education attained by the population aged 15 years and above would enable Kenya to realise the demographic dividend and hence achieve sustainable and inclusive development. I will consider the following key drivers of upper secondary education: (a) survival rate in upper secondary school, that is, the percentage of students entering upper secondary school who reach the last grade; (b) the government's expenditure on education; (c) the total fertility rate (TFR); and (d) elasticity of multifactor productivity to education spending.

I have used government expenditure as a proxy for both the quantity and quality of secondary education. A high government expenditure on secondary school education would mean more and better learning facilities and an improved teacher-student ratio in public schools, which most children attend. In addition to driving up the enrolment rate, this would ensure that more students are kept in secondary school until graduation (an improvement in survival rate). Halving of the total fertility rate would mean a targeted intervention at driving down the fertility rate in addition to keeping girls in school. This would decrease the number of children of school-going age and hence enhance the survival rates in upper secondary school leading to more upper secondary education graduates.

Additionally, I will examine the elasticity of multifactor productivity to education spending since it has a direct effect on whether increased expenditure on education would lead to a higher multifactor productivity (MFP), and hence better economic growth. This factor is not restricted solely to government expenditure on education but covers all other types of expenditure on education, including that by households. Generally, it is estimated that a 1.5 per cent increase in government spending on education leads to about a 0.3 per cent increase in annual economic growth.[13] The selected IFs parameters related to these key drivers and the adjustments that are made to these parameters to generate the various scenarios are shown below.

Table 3: Selected parameters and resultant scenarios

Variable	Parameter	Definition	Intervention	Scenario/effect
Upper secondary education survival rate (EDUSECUPPRSUR)	edsecupprsurm	Education, upper secondary, survival rate multiplier - percentage of entering students who reach the last grade	Value increased three times	Tripling the upper secondary survival rate (Upsecsurv)
Spending on secondary education	Gsedm – education	Government expenditure on education by level multiplier	Value increased from Base to High	Maximising government expenditure on education (High Govspd)
Total fertility rate	tfrm	Total fertility rate multiplier	Value reduced by half	Reducing total fertility rate by half (TFR halved)
Education spending	mfpedspn	Elasticity of multifactor productivity to education spending – No of units	Value increased from Base to High	Maximizing the elasticity of expenditure on education (High mfpedsp)

Note: Adapted from International Futures Model [Computer Software, Version 7.00], 2017. http://www.ifs.du.edu/

As indicated in table 3 above, five scenarios will be considered—the fifth is the *Base Case* or '*Working*' scenario which assumes a continuation of the current trajectory (no change in current policy interventions). We will look at the forecasted scenarios under each of these interventions related to economic growth (GDP and GDP growth rate,) and income inequality (the poverty gap––POVGAP). Opportunity inequality has been left out because it is too complex to measure within the scope of this chapter. In addition, some measures of societal well-being (quality of life), such as GDP per capita, life expectancy, education attainment, and access to electricity will also be considered since this is of direct interest to Kenya as spelled out in Vision 2030.

It is important, again, to draw your attention to the interconnectedness of the IFs model before getting into the scenario analysis. This will enhance your understanding of the various scenario outcomes. The outcome of each of the four interventions means that if the current policy state were maintained and only this intervention was undertaken, the resultant impacts would be as forecasted. The earlier categorisation in looking at sustainable and inclusive development, i.e. economic growth, inequality, and societal well-being or quality of life, will be maintained.

Economic growth scenarios results

In this part of the analysis I explore the effect of each of the four policy interventions proposed here on economic growth, as measured by the gross domestic income (GDP) and the GDP annual growth rate.

Gross domestic product

The gross domestic product (GDP) is the total production of goods and services for a country, region or the world. A country's GDP is used to gauge the economic health of the nation.

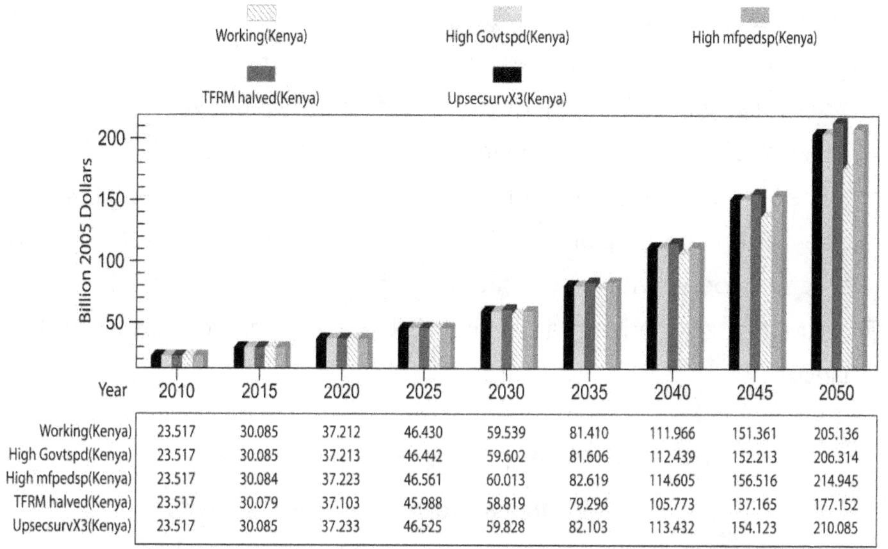

Year	2010	2015	2020	2025	2030	2035	2040	2045	2050
Working(Kenya)	23.517	30.085	37.212	46.430	59.539	81.410	111.966	151.361	205.136
High Govtspd(Kenya)	23.517	30.085	37.213	46.442	59.602	81.606	112.439	152.213	206.314
High mfpedsp(Kenya)	23.517	30.084	37.223	46.561	60.013	82.619	114.605	156.516	214.945
TFRM halved(Kenya)	23.517	30.079	37.103	45.988	58.819	79.296	105.773	137.165	177.152
UpsecsurvX3(Kenya)	23.517	30.085	37.233	46.525	59.828	82.103	113.432	154.123	210.085

Source: Generated from International Futures Model [Computer Software, Version 7.00], 2017. Retrieved from http://www.ifs.du.edu/

As per figure 6.7 above, three of the four policy interventions under exploration would make little difference to Kenya's gross domestic product by 2030, compared to the *Working* (base case) scenario. However, at $60.013 billion, maximising the elasticity of multifactor productivity to education spending (*High mfpedsp*) would lead to a much wider positive margin compared to the current policy interventions, which are projected to get the nation to an income of $59.539 billion. Noteworthy is that halving the total fertility rate (TFRM halved) would consistently lead to a lower gross domestic product than the *Working* scenario up to the year 2050. A look at 2050 shows that optimising the elasticity of spending on education on MFP would still give the best results, followed by tripling the survival rate in upper secondary education.

GDP annual growth rate

Similar to GDP, all the scenarios, apart from halving the TFR lead would have positive impacts on the GDP annual growth rate in the foreseeable future, as shown in figure 6.8 below. By 2030, the greatest impact would result from maximising the elasticity of the multifactor productivity to education spending (at 5.76 per cent), compared with the Working scenario at 5.63 per cent. The second greatest impact would come from tripling the survival rate in upper secondary school (at 5.70 per cent). Maximising the elasticity of multifactor productivity to education spending would yield a 0.1 per cent GDP growth rate per annum, a positive differential compared to the Working scenario.

Figure 6.8: GDP annual growth rate scenarios

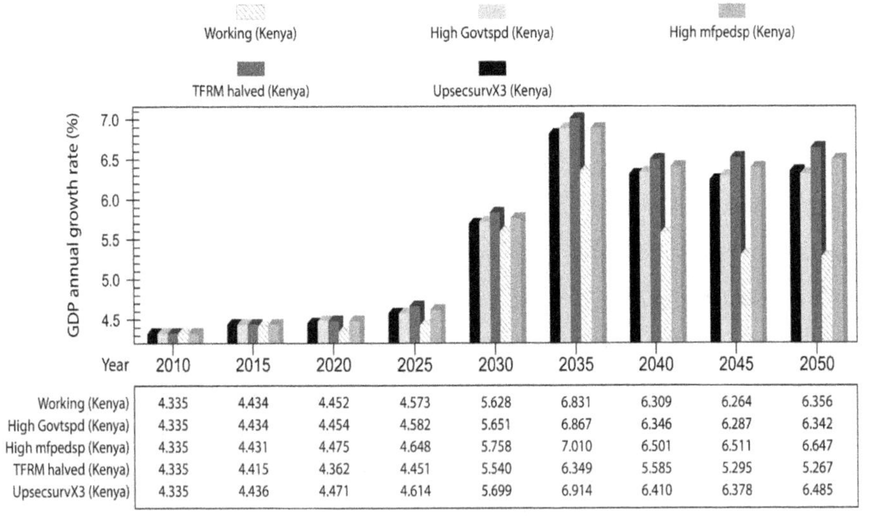

	2010	2015	2020	2025	2030	2035	2040	2045	2050
Working (Kenya)	4.335	4.434	4.452	4.573	5.628	6.831	6.309	6.264	6.356
High Govtspd (Kenya)	4.335	4.434	4.454	4.582	5.651	6.867	6.346	6.287	6.342
High mfpedsp (Kenya)	4.335	4.431	4.475	4.648	5.758	7.010	6.501	6.511	6.647
TFRM halved (Kenya)	4.335	4.415	4.362	4.451	5.540	6.349	5.585	5.295	5.267
UpsecsurvX3 (Kenya)	4.335	4.436	4.471	4.614	5.699	6.914	6.410	6.378	6.485

Source: Generated from International Futures Model [Computer Software, Version 7.00], 2017. Retrieved from http://www.ifs.du.edu/

In all scenarios, the annual GDP growth rate would peak around 2035, then start to gradually decline to a high of 6.65 per cent under the elasticity of multifactor productivity to education spending by 2050, with projections under the other scenarios being much lower. Halving TFR would have the lowest result at 5.27 per cent.

Conclusion

Based on these economic growth scenarios, increasing the elasticity of multifactor productivity to education spending would have the greatest impact on increasing economic growth. An increase in government's expenditure on upper secondary education would lead to a more than proportionate increase in the number of students finishing upper secondary education (higher survival rates). This would translate into a larger human capital stock as more of these upper secondary graduates join the labour market, leading to an increased contribution to MFP and economic growth. Increasing the elasticity of multifactor productivity to education spending would thus be the preferred policy intervention if the focus was solely rapid economic growth. More importantly, the growth would be shared because it would be spread across millions of students who would get an opportunity to complete secondary school.

Inequality scenarios results

Due to the complexity of measuring opportunity inequality mentioned earlier, the focus in this section is on income inequality. This section considers the impact of the four policy intervention proposals on inequality, as measured by the Poverty gap at $ 1.25 a day. The poverty gap is used to measure the depth of poverty. The non-poor are considered to have a zero shortfall, thus the bigger the number, the worse the poverty gap.

Poverty gap at $ 1.25 a day (POVGAP)

The results from the five scenarios on income inequality, as measured by the Poverty gap at $ 1.25 a day, are presented in figure 6.9 below. A lower

POVGAP measure means less inequality. Looking at the scenario analysis results, halving the TFR (*TFRM halved*) would clearly be the most effective intervention in reducing the poverty gap by 2030 at 13.98 per cent. While the other four scenarios would yield similar results at between 17.53 per cent (tripling upper secondary survival rate) and 17.75 per cent (*Working*), the three proposed policy interventions would be slightly better at addressing inequality than the current scenario. The declining poverty trend would be sustained under all five scenarios to 2050, with a bit of a bump around 2040. The halving of TFR scenario would yield the best results at 9.01 per cent in 2050.

Figure 6.9: Poverty gap (POVGAP) scenarios

Poverty gap (POVGAP) scenarios

Year	2014	2019	2024	2029	2034	2039	2044
Working (Kenya)	16.964	18.297	20.920	18.860	13.826	12.466	12.002
High Govtspd (Kenya)	16.963	18.292	20.888	18.797	13.746	12.363	11.908
High mfpedsp (Kenya)	16.964	18.302	20.897	18.722	13.635	12.180	11.689
TFRM halved (Kenya)	16.872	17.585	18.850	15.118	10.747	9.622	9.011
UpsecsurvX3 (Kenya)	16.948	18.239	20.804	18.657	13.598	12.175	11.674

Source: Generated from International Futures Model [Computer Software, Version 7.00], 2017. Retrieved from http://www.ifs.du.edu/

Conclusion

Based on the scenario analysis results presented here, income inequality in Kenya is escalating. There was a projected spike in equality from around 2015 to 2025 under all scenarios. However, a decline in inequality is forecasted to happen in the foreseeable future up to 2050 based on the current trajectory.

Looking at the four policy interventions under exploration, the highest decline would be realised under the halving TFR (*TFRM halved*) scenario.

A significant decrease in fertility rates, as is the case with halving the fertility rate multiplier, would translate to a marked decline in the divergence between the rich and the poor. Usually, this decline in fertility is not uniform across the economy. The rich lead the decline because they are the first to benefit from this demographic change. This results in a widening of the divergence in poverty as measured by the poverty gap in the short-term[14] which could be the spike that we see in the decade from mid 2010s. However, the poor catch up in the longer-term and the demographic benefits get to spread widely. From the scenario results presented here, it would appear that these wider societal benefits from halving the total fertility rate would only become evident from around 2025, when the drop in the poverty gap would become significant. The scenarios also project a similar but smaller wave of a further drop in fertility rates around 2040.

Well-being (quality of life) scenarios results

I have explored the following aspects of societal well-being and quality of life under this scenario analysis: GDP per capita, life expectancy, years of education attained by the proportion of the population that is 15 years and above, and access to power. Given that the focus of this scenario analysis is the impact of upper secondary education on sustainable and inclusive development, I will also look at upper secondary education graduation rates.

GDP per capita

Contrary to the GDP and GDP annual growth rate variables, halving the total fertility rate would have the most favourable impact on GDP per capita in the next three decades, as shown in figure 6.10 below. By 2030, the GDP per capita under the *TFRM halved* scenario would be $2,451, followed by that under *High mfpedsp* at $2,195, and tripling upper secondary education survival rates at $2,193, compared with the lowest under the *Working* scenario at $ 2,183.

Figure 6.10: GDP per capita scenarios

GDP per capita scenarios

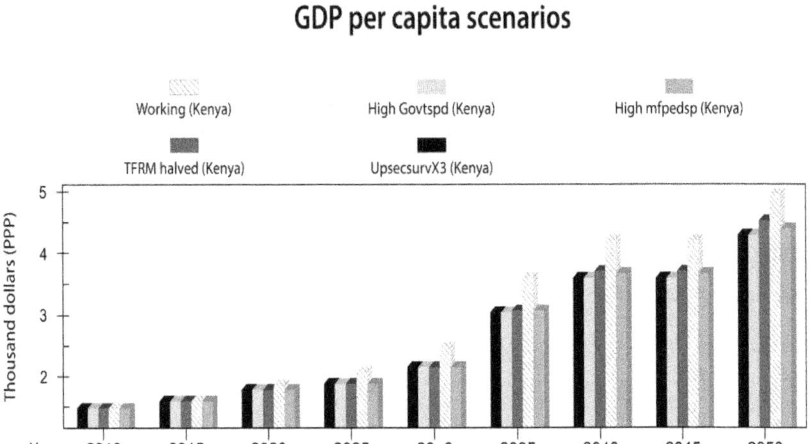

Year	2010	2015	2020	2025	20 0	2035	2040	2045	2050
Working (Kenya)	1.471	1.633	1.773	1.945	2.183	2.573	3.066	3.636	4.350
High Govtspd (Kenya)	1.471	1.633	1.773	1.945	2.185	2.579	3.078	3.654	4.371
High mfpedsp (Kenya)	1.471	1.633	1.773	1.949	2.195	2.600	3.116	3.721	4.492
TFRM halved (Kenya)	1.471	1.642	1.839	2.103	2.451	2.954	3.540	4.187	4.968
UpsecsurvX3 (Kenya)	1.471	1.633	1.773	1.949	2.193	2.592	3.100	3.692	4.438

Source: Generated from International Futures Model [Computer Software, Version 7.00], 2017. Retrieved from http://www.ifs.du.edu/

Based on these results, Kenya stands to gain more from any one of these four policy interventions in increasing its GDP per capita than in the current scenario. The relative impact of each of these scenarios is projected to be sustained up to 2050, with halving TFR giving the most favourable result at $4,968 compared to the lowest at $4,350 as per the *Working* scenario.

In real life, the birth of every additional child effectively reduces the living standards of other family members at the family level.[15] At the economy level, the share of GDP per each member of the population (GDP per capita) increases more rapidly when the number of working-age adults (15 to 65 years) is growing faster than the number of children under 15 years.[16] In other words, GDP per capita grows more rapidly under decreasing dependency ratios.

Life expectancy

Figure 6.11 below shows that Kenya's life expectancy is forecasted to increase under all the five scenarios from the current 61 years to about 64 years in 2030, and further to about 70 years by 2050.

Figure 6.11: Life expectancy over time

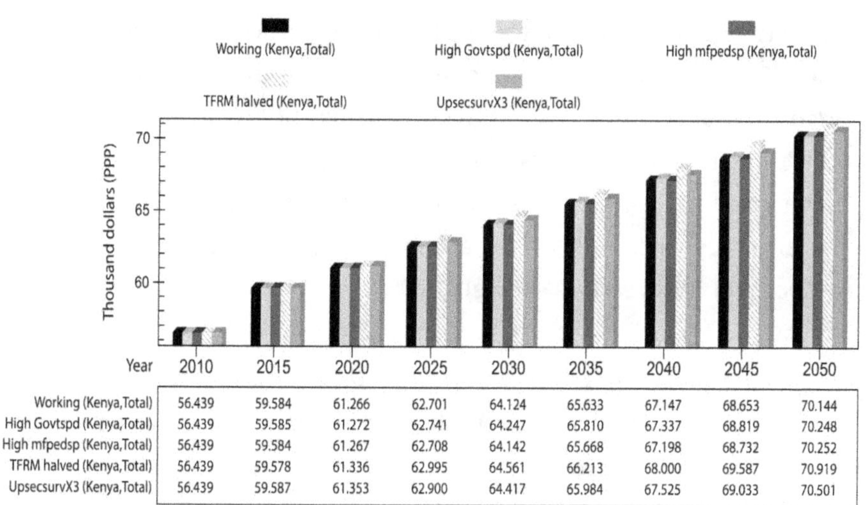

Year	2010	2015	2020	2025	2030	2035	2040	2045	2050
Working (Kenya,Total)	56.439	59.584	61.266	62.701	64.124	65.633	67.147	68.653	70.144
High Govtspd (Kenya,Total)	56.439	59.585	61.272	62.741	64.247	65.810	67.337	68.819	70.248
High mfpedsp (Kenya,Total)	56.439	59.584	61.267	62.708	64.142	65.668	67.198	68.732	70.252
TFRM halved (Kenya,Total)	56.439	59.578	61.336	62.995	64.561	66.213	68.000	69.587	70.919
UpsecsurvX3 (Kenya,Total)	56.439	59.587	61.353	62.900	64.417	65.984	67.525	69.033	70.501

Source: Generated from International Futures Model [Computer Software, Version 7.00], 2017. Retrieved from http://www.ifs.du.edu/

This trend will be sustained under all the scenarios. The halving of TFR scenario is forecasted to yield the most favourable results at 64.6 years by 2030, followed by the tripling of upper secondary education survival rate at 64.4 years, with the *Working* scenario's outcome being the poorest at 64.1 years. The scenario ranking for this parameter will be sustained until 2050 when halving TFR will lead to 70.9 years, compared with the base case (*Working*) scenario at 70.1 years.

To extend the same explanation offered above, a better living standard would lead to a longer life and, therefore, a significant reduction in TFR would yield both a higher life expectancy and economic growth—through higher levels of productivity and for longer. The tripling of survival in upper secondary school has good prospects of reducing the TFR and enhancing the quality and longevity of life. It is intervening just a step lower in terms of fertility rates by keeping girls in school longer to delay marriage and first births. Additionally, more education means higher human capital, higher MFP, and eventually higher economic growth, and hence a better quality of life.

Years of education attained by population 15 years plus

The average number of years attained by the proportion of Kenya's population that are 15 years and above is forecasted to remain the same under both the *Working* (current) scenario and the maximising the elasticity of multifactor productivity to education spending (*High mfpedsp*) scenario until 2030—approximated at 7.94 years, as shown in figure 6.12 below. The outcomes under both scenarios will then start to increase, to reach 8.99 years (*High mfpespd*) and 8.98 years (*Working*) in 2050.

Figure 6.12: Education, years obtained by population 15+ scenarios

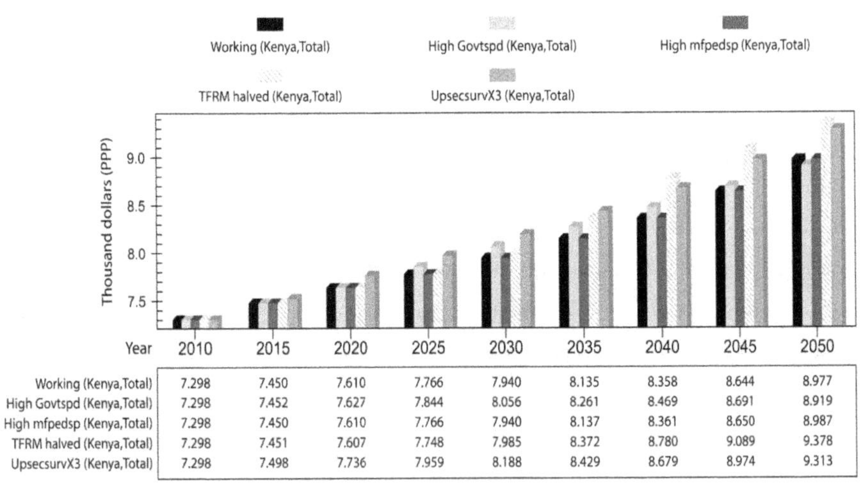

	2010	2015	2020	2025	2030	2035	2040	2045	2050
Working (Kenya,Total)	7.298	7.450	7.610	7.766	7.940	8.135	8.358	8.644	8.977
High Govtspd (Kenya,Total)	7.298	7.452	7.627	7.844	8.056	8.261	8.469	8.691	8.919
High mfpedsp (Kenya,Total)	7.298	7.450	7.610	7.766	7.940	8.137	8.361	8.650	8.987
TFRM halved (Kenya,Total)	7.298	7.451	7.607	7.748	7.985	8.372	8.780	9.089	9.378
UpsecsurvX3 (Kenya,Total)	7.298	7.498	7.736	7.959	8.188	8.429	8.679	8.974	9.313

Source: Generated from International Futures Model [Computer Software, Version 7.00], 2017. Retrieved from http://www.ifs.du.edu/

The more impactful intervention in this variable would be to triple the upper secondary education survival rate, which would lead to an average of 8.19 years of education attainment by 2030, compared with the Working scenario at 7.94 years, which offers the lowest outcome. The second-best intervention would be maximising the government's spending on education which would result in an average attainment of 8.06 years of education. Halving the TFR is forecasted to have the best outcome in this variable by 2050 at 9.38 years, overtaking that of the tripling upper secondary education survival rate. The *Working* scenario's outcome would remain the lowest.

Ensuring enrolment in upper secondary education immediately leads to a higher level of education attainment. In the long run, an improvement in average education attainment could be realised by decreasing the TFR which would translate to higher government spending on education per student and also higher GDP per capita, a significant portion of which goes to education as a basic service. Improved enrolment for upper secondary education and GDP per capita would be intermediate outcomes, which would eventually lead to a higher average education attainment by the population and hence a better-skilled labour supply.

Access to electricity

As shown in figure 6.13 below, improved and sustained access to electricity is forecasted in all the scenarios in the future with the impact being greatest under the halving of TFR scenario.

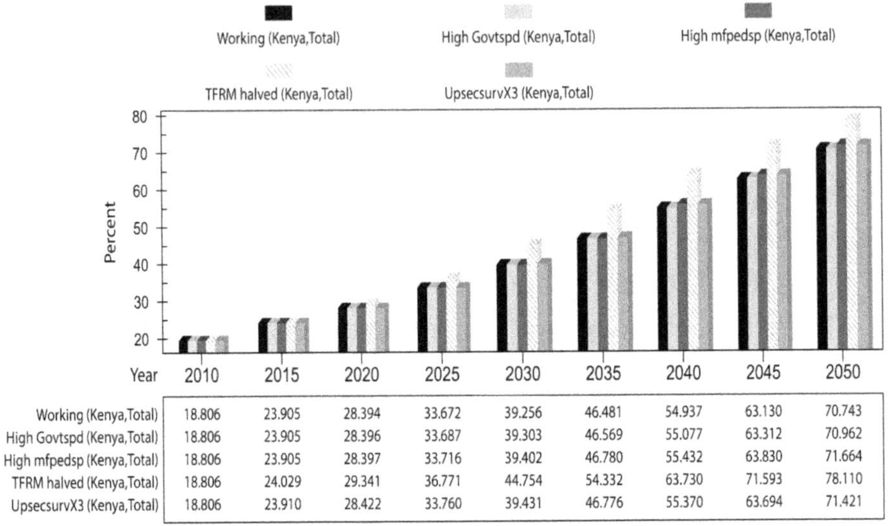

Figure 6.13: Access to electricity

Year	2010	2015	2020	2025	2030	2035	2040	2045	2050
Working (Kenya,Total)	18.806	23.905	28.394	33.672	39.256	46.481	54.937	63.130	70.743
High Govtspd (Kenya,Total)	18.806	23.905	28.396	33.687	39.303	46.569	55.077	63.312	70.962
High mfpedsp (Kenya,Total)	18.806	23.905	28.397	33.716	39.402	46.780	55.432	63.830	71.664
TFRM halved (Kenya,Total)	18.806	24.029	29.341	36.771	44.754	54.332	63.730	71.593	78.110
UpsecsurvX3 (Kenya,Total)	18.806	23.910	28.422	33.760	39.431	46.776	55.370	63.694	71.421

Source: Generated from International Futures Model [Computer Software, Version 7.00], 2017. Retrieved from http://www.ifs.du.edu/

Expectedly, as the population growth rate decreases due to a lower fertility rate, the current level of effort at building an infrastructure for electricity would need to cover a much lower proportion of the population (holding all other factors constant). An estimated 45 per cent and 78 per cent of Kenyans would have power by 2030 and 2050, respectively, under the halving TFR multiplier scenario. Throughout this forecasting period, the lowest outcome would be under the *Working* scenario, with the *High mfpedsp* scenarios coming second best.

Conclusion

While all four policy interventions would lead to a better quality of life, the most immediate results would be realised by halving the total fertility rate. Halving TFR would reduce the number of additional children and hence improve the effective standard of living at both the household and national levels as reflected in these four measures: GDP per capita, life expectancy, years of education, and access to electricity.

The high leverage points

Table 4 below presents a summary of the scenario analysis results. It is important to note that all the identified interventions would have a positive impact on upper secondary education graduation rates and, by extension, on the nation's stock of human capital, human capital contributions to MFP rates, and eventually on economic growth and inequality. The aim here is to identify the high leverage points based on their likely impact on sustainable and inclusive growth, regardless of where they are positioned in the system, and their implied distance to the ultimate outcome, as illustrated in the causal loop diagram on development earlier. As seen in Chapter 2, the most direct intervention is not necessarily the most effective.

The results have been grouped into two-time horizons: 2030 and 2050. Although a longer-term perspective is useful when the demographic dividend is anticipated (refer to Chapter 5 discussions), the 2030 horizon is included for comparison with Vision 2030. The table shows the rankings of the policy interventions explored against each of the sustainable and inclusive development categories identified earlier, namely: economic growth, inequality, and well-being (quality of life). The interventions' rankings are in order of their impact on sustainable and inclusive growth, with the scenario with the greatest impact ranked '1' and the one with the least impact ranked '5'.

Table 4: The scenarios analysis results

Category	Variable	Scenario impact ranking (highest to least) - 2030				
		Working	High Govtspd	High mfpedsp	TFRM halved	UpSecSurvX3
Economic growth	GDP	4	3	1	5	2
	GDP growth rate	4	3	1	5	2
Inequality	Poverty gap	4	3	5	1	2
Well-being	GDP per capita	5	4	2	1	3
	Life expectancy	5	3	4	1	2
	Education attainment	4	2	4	3	1
	Access to electricity	5	4	3	1	2
Category	Variable	Scenario impact ranking (highest to least) - 2050				
		Working	High Govtspd	High mfpedsp	TFRM halved	UpSecSurvX3
Economic growth	GDP	4	3	1	5	2
	GDP growth rate	3	4	1	5	2
Inequality	Poverty gap	3	4	5	1	2
Well-being	GDP per capita	5	4	2	1	3
	Life expectancy	5	4	3	1	2
	Education attainment	4	5	3	1	2
	Access to electricity	5	4	2	1	3

Note: Adapted from International Futures Model [Computer Software, Version 7.00], 2017. http://www.ifs.du.edu/

The results are largely consistent across all the sustainable and inclusive growth variables identified in the model, with the economic growth variables being the only exception and for only two interventions—halving of TFR and changing the elasticity of multifactor productivity to education spending from the base to high (maximising). Based on these results, halving the total fertility rate (TFRM halved) as shown in the dotted circle would be the highest leverage point in the identified system (education-population-economic) for realising sustainable and inclusive development in Kenya. Second would be tripling the upper secondary education survival rate (UpSecSurvX3) as shown in the dot-dash circle. This would be the case for both time horizons, 2030 and 2050. The impacts of the other two interventions are not as clear-cut.

Figure 6.14 below illustrates this leverage, with the intervention farthest from the pivot point being the most impactful.

Figure 6.14: High leverage points for sustainable and inclusive development

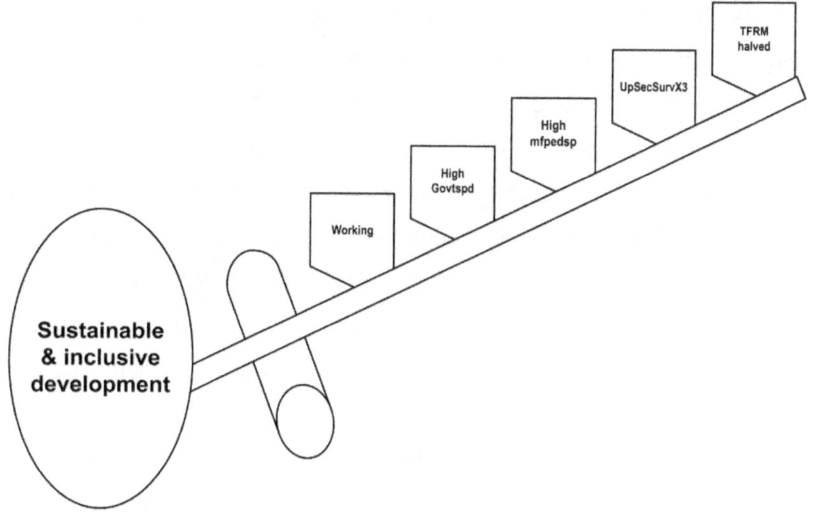

Source: Author's own illustration

Noteworthy, however, is the fact that increasing the proportion of government expenditure on upper secondary education from its current level to 'high' would not be the highest leverage point in the system, although it is an important driver for the other variables such as the upper secondary education survival rate and TFR. Without the subsidy the government provides in secondary education in form of tuition (employment of teachers), and other aspects outside the school such as regulation (quality control through examinations), most Kenyans would not be able to access education. Even the private sector needs the government to do that which only a government can do.

Another fact to point out is that all the interventions under exploration show better results in about half of the parameters compared with the current policy interventions that are represented by the *Working* scenario. This is particularly the case when the *Working* scenario is compared with the halving of TFR and tripling of upper secondary education scenarios.

This means that the current policy interventions are not optimal and can be improved on.

As highlighted in these results—the dashed circle in table 4 above—the most effective intervention for driving economic growth would be optimising the elasticity of multifactor productivity to education spending (the *High mfpedsp* scenario). An increase in expenditure on education would lead to more than a proportionate increase in the MFP rate. As seen in Chapter 2, Kenya has one of the highest rates of human capital contribution to MFP rates (MFPHC)—higher than its East African peers and even Malaysia and Singapore. This could be explained by the fact that it is largely a service sector driven economy as seen in figure 4.9 (b). This implies that an input to human capital development yields comparably huge returns in form of MFP and economic growth. Kenya's MFPHC is forecasted to remain high for the foreseeable future (beyond 2050).

The scenario analysis results show that halving the total fertility rates would produce the most significant positive outcomes relating to both inequality and societal well-being (quality of life). While halving TFR would still lead to a growth in GDP, this would be at a lower rate than under the current (*Working*) scenario—see the ranking of '5' within the dashed circle compared with a ranking of '4' for the *Working* scenario. What this might mean in real terms is that as per the current circumstances, the economic growth is neither sustainable nor inclusive.

Fast growth is not necessarily good, especially if it is not inclusive. As seen in Chapter 5, given its youth bulge, Kenya will encounter either a demographic dividend or demographic bomb in the future and the time for action to realise the desired future is now. A slower growth rate of about 5.5 per cent and 5 per cent by 2030 and 2050, respectively, as shown in figure 6.7 under the halving the TFR scenario, is what would likely be sustainable for Kenya in the long run.

Although directly halving the TFR would yield the quickest results, it is not the only way to sustainable and inclusive growth, especially when there is a need to boost opportunities for employment in readiness for the potential demographic dividend. An intervention like increasing the government's expenditure on upper secondary education that appears oblique, ends up hitting all of these key variables eventually. The variables are highly connected and interdependent, like in every other system, and one only needs to know where to intervene to have the largest impact on the system. These results provide useful guidance in relation to increasing upper secondary education attainment as a driver of sustainable and inclusive development.

Sense-making of the proposed interventions

Some important questions to answer before we conclude this chapter are: what do these policy interventions mean in practical terms? Are they feasible? This section seeks to answer these pertinent questions before moving on to policy recommendations.

Halving TFR: Kenya's current total fertility rate (the base) stands at 4.4 live births per woman and has been on a downward trend since 1960 when it was nearly 8 live births per woman (IFs model, 2017). The TFR is projected to drop to 3.6 by 2030 and to 2.4 by 2050 under the current trajectory, as shown in figure 6.15 below. Therefore, halving the current TFR is feasible with targeted interventions such as increased use of contraceptives and other family planning measures, since use of contraceptives in Kenya has been consistently and significantly increasing.

Figure 6.15: Kenya's projected TFR and contraceptives usage rates

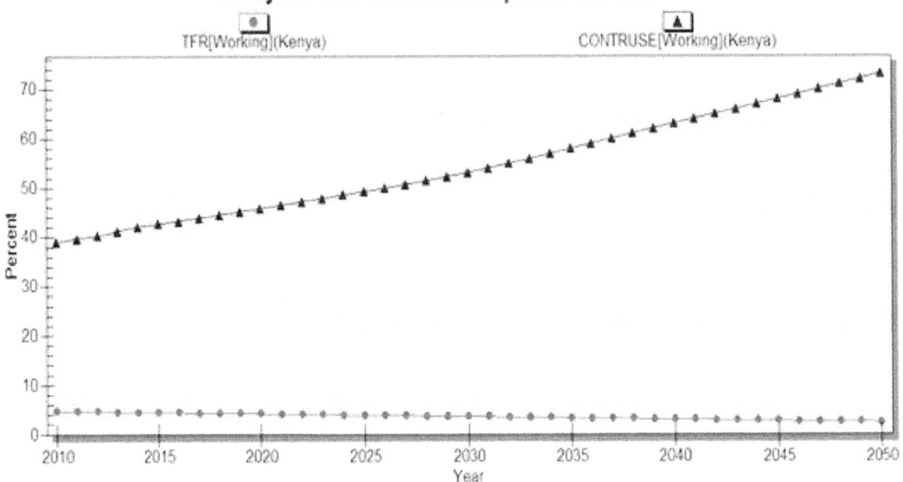

Source: Generated from International Futures Model [Computer Software, Version 7.00], 2017. Retrieved from http://www.ifs.du.edu/

Furthermore, reducing fertility rates is inevitable if Kenya is to realise the imminent demographic dividend. By attaining a TFR rate of 2.2, Kenya would still be above the self-replacement threshold. The success of the East Asian role models that Kenya is looking towards was largely driven by their ability to significant drive down their fertility rates—Malaysia's from 6.3 in 1960 to 2.4 by 2016 (IFs model, 2017). In Kenya, there has also been a de-prioritisation of family planning over other social services. Reprioritising this would yield the expected results.

Increasing elasticity of multifactor productivity to education spending from base to high: This means that an increase in government spending on upper secondary education would lead to a more than proportionate change in the number of students attaining upper secondary school. This is feasible considering the change in enrolment experienced with the free primary education programme. Based on the education attainment figures presented in figure 6.11, the current average education level of Kenyans is 7.45 years which is below the primary graduate level under the 8-4-4 system of education.

Further, subsidising the cost of secondary education beyond the current tuition levels and improving the quality of the education offered through better teacher-student ratios would lead to a higher education attainment in the nation. As discussed in Chapter 5, an increase in the quality and years of education would be a direct input to human capital, and in turn a contribution of human capital to the multifactor productivity rate (MFPRATE) and economic growth. A higher GDP would mean a larger budget to spend on education, reinforcing the initial investment.

Increasing government expenditure on secondary education from base to high: Currently, there is an active effort by the Kenyan government to drive reforms in the education sector which have had the most tangible impact on secondary education thus far. The effort is particularly focused on driving the quality of education but at the expense of increasing the numbers of those attending secondary school. This was necessitated by the marked deterioration in the quality of education since the 1980s as seen earlier. There is need to improve the equity of government spending on secondary education for greater developmental impact.[17]

Most of the government's current efforts are focused on free primary education, which rightly forms the basis for secondary education. Expenditure on upper secondary education has been on a steep decline, as shown in figure 6.16 below, and is projected to continue. This trend should be reversed.

Figure 6.16: Kenya's government expenditure
on upper secondary education

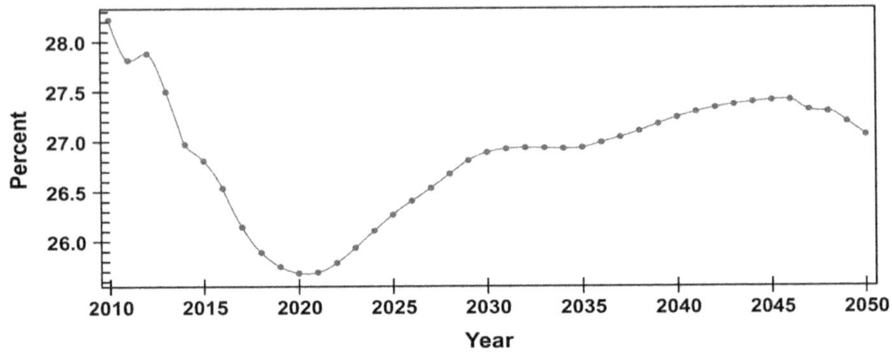

Source: Generated from International Futures Model [Computer Software, Version 7.00], 2017. Retrieved from http://www.ifs.du.edu/

Despite the competing government priorities, the demonstration of upper secondary education as a high leverage point for sustainable and inclusive development should enable prioritisation of this intervention, availing the resources that would be required to implement it. In addition to drawing from the public budget, the government can form both public and private partnerships to foster investment in secondary education. There has been a notable growth in the private education sector since 2003 when universal primary education was introduced, and subsequently a spill-over into the secondary school level to meet the increasing demand.

The Bridge International Academies, which has reached nearly 100,000 students since its launch in 2008, presents good prospects of how private investment in education could be attained at scale.[18] In sum, although a significant portion of the investment necessary for a near universal secondary education will come from private sources such as households and the market, the government needs to have the capacity to match this in form of its own budgetary commitment. It must also attract and facilitate the market players to partner in this endeavour with supportive policies and governance. The effective solution would, therefore, be a combination of regulation, public financing, and private market-based financing.

Tripling upper secondary school survival rate, that is, the ability to remain in this level of education from the first grade to the last. In the current system of education, there is only one level of secondary school. However, the IFs system categorises secondary education into lower and upper. This parameter has been selected to reflect the need for full secondary education as opposed to lower grades only. Even without establishing what the current level of survival in secondary school is, the aim should be to attain universal secondary education (14 years of education).

Most secondary school students drop out due to lack of tuition fees and other related expenses. The so-called 'school development costs' in public schools have turned out to be markedly heftier than tuition fees and a deterrent to many students in their pursuit of secondary education. Increased government expenditure coupled with an increase in household incomes, which is premised on the increasing GDP per capita rates, is likely to lead to a growing household expenditure on education.

In sum, Vision 2030 emphasises the need for high, and by implication, sustained economic growth until the year 2030. These identified interventions provide a demonstration of how Kenya could improve its prospects of attaining the average 10 per cent per annum economic growth goal. More importantly, the interventions would enable Kenya to sustain this growth in the long-term in a manner that benefits most Kenyans and the private sector, which has been the engine of Kenya's development. The hope is that these IFs generated interventions provide this demonstration.

Limitations of the approach

This section highlights some of the limitations of the IFs model's scenario analysis approach in exploring policy interventions for sustainable and inclusive development in Kenya. The first limitation is that although very robust and comprehensive, like other forecasting models, IFs is only as good as the data that goes into it. The generated forecasts are therefore only as credible as the historical evidence (data) upon which they are built. Like most other developing countries, Kenya's historical data has some gaps.

However, IFs' team does not collect its own data but uses country data that is as credible as possible by relying on renowned sources such as the World Bank and the United Nations. The IFs model uses multiple data sources which enables triangulation of evidence, and hence it is much more reliable compared with other models. Nevertheless, this does not surmount the data challenges because these sources are themselves limited. Both the World Bank and the United Nations identify massive country data gaps as the biggest challenge that many developing countries must contend with in formulation of policy interventions.[19] Nonetheless, the IFs database is constantly updated with the most recent country data and the model regularly revised to make it more robust.

Secondly, the further one forecasts into the future, the less reliable the forecast is. This limitation needs to be taken into consideration when looking at policy proposals, especially given the long-term horizon of the forecasts. There is no knowing what might happen in other parts of the globe during this timeline that could affect economic performance and inequality in Kenya. However, as said earlier, IFs is not a prediction model but a forecasting model. The future is unpredictable, but people can make informed guesses about what it might look like and based on these, work to create the future they desire.

Furthermore, there are likely to be other variables that affect the quality and quantity of upper secondary education in Kenya besides the ones considered here which have not been explored, such as health. An exploration of a wider range of policy interventions encompassing these would inform a better judgement of which ones to prioritise. This search for sustainable and inclusive development solutions does not consider other government priorities, such as security, which has in recent years become an important factor to Kenya with growing incidents of terrorism.

Finally, it is important to note that the data within the IFs model is based on available country data and changes frequently. For instance, these scenarios do not take into consideration the impact of the COVID-19 pandemic which is anticipated to push more people into poverty and to shift government expenditure priorities.

References

1   Mathenge, G. (n.d.). 'The role of education in influencing fertility Levels, of women in Central Province, Kenya'. *The Organization for Economic Cooperation and Development (OECD)*.

2   Teixeira, P. (2007). 'Jacob Mincer and the centrality of human capital for contemporary labour economics'. History of Recent Economics.

3   Firnhaber, E. (n.d.). 'Introduction to international futures'; Hughes, B. B. & Hillebrand, E. E. (2016). *Exploring and Shaping International Futures*. Routledge Taylor and Francis Group, NY. Kindle Edition.

4   Hughes, B. B. & Hillebrand, E. E. (2016). *Exploring and Shaping International Futures*. Routledge Taylor and Francis Group, NY. Kindle Edition; Echoledge (2014, Mar 6). International futures model infographic.

5   Hughes, B., Irfan, M., Margolese-Malin, E., Moyer, J., Neill, C. & Solorzano, J. (n.d.). 'International Futures Training Manual'.

6   Firnhaber, E. (n.d.). 'Introduction to international futures'.

7   Pearson, R. (2011). 'Using the International Futures global modeling system (IFs) for alternative scenarios by the numbers'. Foresight Insight, Summer 2011, p.13-19.

8   Echoledge (2014, Mar 6). 'International futures model infographic'.

9   Firnhaber, E. (n.d.). 'Introduction to international futures'.

10 Echoledge (2014, Mar 6). 'International futures model infographic'.

11 Hughes, B. B. & Hillebrand, E. E. (2016). *Exploring and Shaping International Futures*. Routledge Taylor and Francis Group, NY. Kindle Edition.

12 Ibid

13 International Futures Model [Computer Software, Version 7.00], 2017. Retrieved from http://www.ifs.du.edu/.

14 The Economist (2012, Aug 2). 'Fertility decline, the demographic dividend, poverty, and inequality'. The Economist.

15 Mason, A. & Lee, S. (2004). 'The demographic dividend and poverty reduction'. United Nations

16 Ibid

17 Lin, J. (2008). 'New structural economics. A framework for rethinking development and policy'. The World Bank, Washington, DC.

18 The Economist (2017, Jan 28). 'Bridge International Academies gets high marks for ambition but its business model is still unproven'. The Economist.

19 World Bank & UNDP (2016). 'Transitioning from the MDGs to the SDGs'. United Nations Development Programme.

CHAPTER 7

Stepping stones to a sustainable and inclusive future

Create your future from your future, not your past.
— Werner Erhard

This chapter uses the model developed in Chapter 5 and the policy interventions that emerged from the scenario analysis in Chapter 6 to determine if Kenya is on the right path to sustainable and inclusive development. It also makes recommendations on practical policy interventions for attaining this goal..

Vision 2030's prospects of realising sustainable development

The model for sustainable and inclusive development presented here entails building Kenya's stock of human capital to drive and sustain its development. The natural starting point is to explore where the country stands in terms of these policy interventions by looking at Vision 2030, its present roadmap. Table 5 below summarises Vision 2030's education and training goals and the relevant strategies to human capital development based on the model developed in Chapter 5.

Table 5: Vision 2031 human capital development goals and strategies

Education: Overall goal for 2012 is to reduce illiteracy	
Goals	Strategies
i) improving the transition rate from primary to secondary schools, ii) raising the quality and relevance of education, iii) integrating all special needs education into learning and training institutions, iv) achieving an 80 per cent adult literacy rate, v) increasing the net enrolment rate to 95 per cent, vi) increasing the transition rates to technical institutions and universities from 3 per cent to 8 per cent, and vii) expanding access to university education from 4.6 per cent to 20 per cent, with an emphasis on science and technology courses.	i) integrating early childhood into primary education, ii) reforming secondary curricula, iii) modernising teacher training, and iv) strengthening partnerships with the private sector.
Health: Overall goal is to provide an efficient and high-quality health care system with the best standards	
Strategies i) provision of a robust health infrastructure network; and ii) improving the quality of health service delivery to the highest standards and promotion of partnerships with the private sector.	

Note: Adapted from Vision 2030 Brochure. Republic of Kenya, 2007, p11-12.

Based on the evidence presented in the earlier chapters, Chapter 5 in particular, guaranteeing secondary education attainment is what would make a notable difference in improving Kenya's stock of human capital. It would also ensure that there are sufficient spill-over effects to bring about sustainable and inclusive development. While Vision 2030 hopes to attain this objective, the strategies to implement it are not concrete. For instance, as seen in Chapter 6 (figure 6.1), transitioning from primary education into secondary education is a key challenge in attaining secondary education. This has been correctly identified in the vision as a goal. However, the strategies listed in table 5 above do not show how this will happen.

As a result of the free primary education programme, there are now many primary education graduates who do not get enrolled in secondary education. Consequently, the government's plan to improve enrolment in secondary education by building 560 new secondary schools to accommodate the growing number of primary education graduates is a good one. However, supporting the transition from primary to secondary school is just the initial step in secondary education. More important is the ability for these students to stay in secondary school until they graduate (survival). This has a dual benefit; equipping them with knowledge and skills and delaying early marriage and childbearing for the girls.

Equally important are the strategies to improve the quality of secondary education through improving the curriculum and increasing teacher recruitment programmes, as outlined in the vision. Both these strategies would go a long way in enhancing Kenya's human capital, but there is need for more specific thinking about how this is to happen. Otherwise, they remain merely aspirational and hard to implement. Increasing the transition from secondary to tertiary education is a positive intervention. However, as earlier pointed out in Chapter 5, it will not benefit most poor households who mainly strive for basic education. Tertiary education has minimal spill-over effects—its benefits end up being confined to the immediate beneficiary. Focusing on tertiary education will thus only widen the inequality divergence between the poor and the rich—the dual economy—a situation that cannot be sustained in the long-run.

None of the Vision 2030 education strategies are specifically targeted at the secondary education graduation rate. Based on the arguments presented in Chapter 5, this would be most important for sustainable and inclusive development and is a prerequisite for Kenya to realise her demographic dividend. Ensuring completion of secondary education would require having enough affordable schools. This would necessitate increased government subsidies in the form of government spending on education to ease-off the burden on households.

However, the government expenditure on education would gradually decline as higher GDP per capita is realised, which would effectively mean an increase in households' expenditure on their children's education. Increasing the literacy rate as identified in the vision would be a bare minimum of what the country could do through formal education to develop its human capital. This would prepare the youth for the labour market whose current demand is much more than primary education.

The top priority policy intervention based on the human capital model for sustainable and inclusive development, and the scenario analysis results presented in this book, are to reduce the total fertility rate. This falls squarely within the health sector policy area, yet it is conspicuously missing from all the health policy interventions and strategies. Additionally, the health strategies do not say much about how high quality health is to be attained besides merely mentioning that private sector partnerships will be established. Realising the anticipated demographic dividend will mean actively working to significantly reduce fertility rates beyond the current trajectory. Given the demonstrated impact of this intervention, the government will need to deliberately drive down the fertility rates through promotion and use of contraceptives and create awareness of the benefits of having fewer children, especially for poorer households.

As alluded to under both education and health strategies, private partnerships will be used to realise the identified goals. This is in line with how the government should work together with markets to realise sustainable and inclusive development. Doing this would be of mutual benefit to both the government and markets. This is inevitable given the task but there is need for clarity and concreteness on what these partnerships will entail or look like.

Policy recommendations

As shown in Chapter 6, all four human capital policy interventions explored, that is; (a) maximising government's expenditure on education (*High Govtspd*); (b) optimising the elasticity of multifactor productivity to education spending (*High mfpedspd*); (c) halving total fertility rates (*TFRM halved*); and (d) tripling the upper secondary education survival rate (*UpSecSurvX3*), would have much higher impact on sustainable and inclusive growth than the Vision 2030 ones (*Working* scenario). However, some of these proposed interventions show better promise for lasting growth than others.

Based on the scenario analysis, the two highest leverage points would be halving the total fertility rate (*TFRM halved*) and tripling the upper secondary education survival rate (*UpSecSurvX3*), in that order. What this means is that Kenya can realise sustainable and inclusive development by ensuring that its youth attain upper secondary education through halving the total fertility rate and tripling the survival rate of students in secondary education. Based on this understanding, the policy interventions outlined below are recommended.

Halve total fertility rates

To recap, total fertility rate is a key variable in the sustainable and inclusive growth equation. Lowering fertility rates is crucial if Kenya is to reduce inequality and realise the looming demographic dividend. As seen in Chapter 5, although keeping girls in school longer would translate to delayed marriage and delay having the first child, a more active and immediate effort is required if the significant reduction in fertility rate is to be realised.

Contraception usage in Kenya continues to increase, as illustrated in figure 7.1 below, but the rate of usage is far below what is required to attain sustainable growth by halving the TFR.

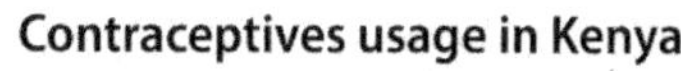

Figure 7.1: Contraceptives usage in Kenya future scenarios

Contraceptives usage in Kenya

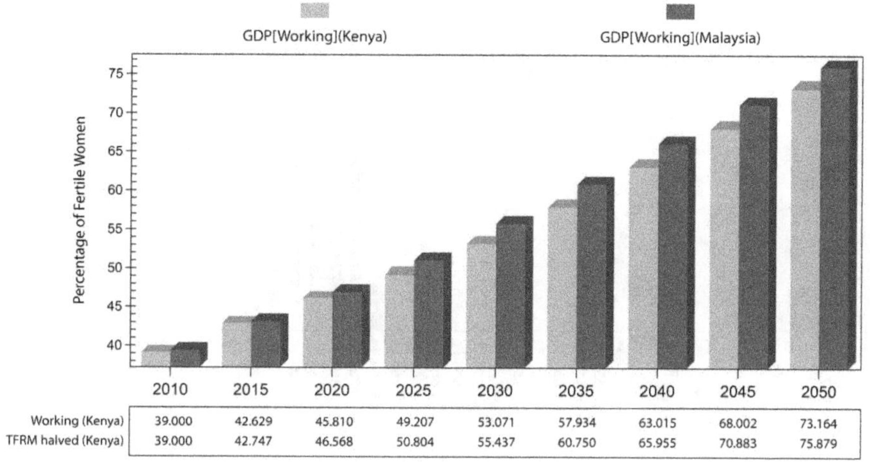

	2010	2015	2020	2025	2030	2035	2040	2045	2050
Working (Kenya)	39.000	42.629	45.810	49.207	53.071	57.934	63.015	68.002	73.164
TFRM halved (Kenya)	39.000	42.747	46.568	50.804	55.437	60.750	65.955	70.883	75.879

Source: Generated from International Futures Model [Computer Software, Version 7.00], 2017. Retrieved from http://www.ifs.du.edu/

This usage is also likely to be more among the wealthier members of society, who can afford contraceptives. Moreover, there tends to be a lack of awareness about the benefits of family planning, especially among the poor whose household well-being is more severely affected by each additional child than it is with rich households. As shown, halving TFR will require a higher level of contraceptive usage than there is at present. The government actively needs to promote family planning with a focus on 20- to 29-year-old women who are most fertile, as shown in figure 7.2 below. This can be attained by making contraceptives and information readily available at public hospitals and health care centres, and by creating awareness about sexual health and family planning through the mass media. In addition, there are many non-governmental organisations and development organisations working in the health sector, which presents opportunities for partnership.

Figure 7.2: TFR rates scenarios in Kenya

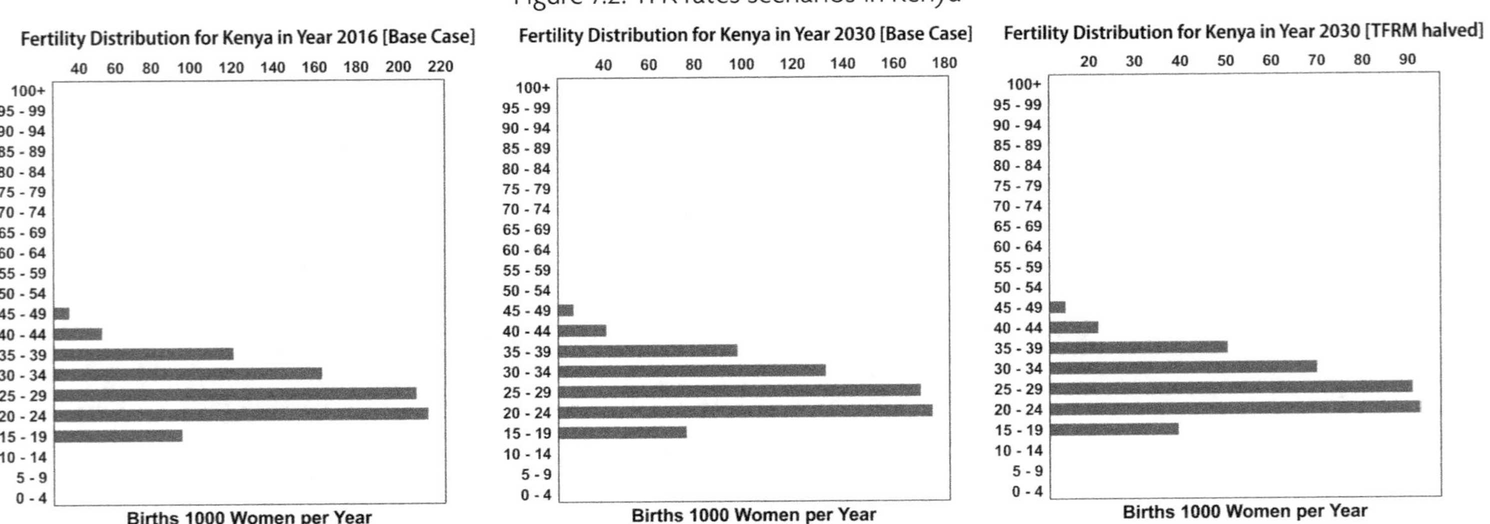

Source: Generated from International Futures Model [Computer Software, Version 7.00], 2017. Retrieved from http://www.ifs.du.edu/

Triple upper secondary education survival rate

As pointed out earlier, there is a marked difference between the number of pupils graduating from primary schools and the number being enrolled into secondary school, as reflected in transition rates of about 70 per cent (71 per cent for boys and 69 per cent for girls) in 2016 in figure 7.3 below.

Figure 7.3: Primary to secondary education transition rates

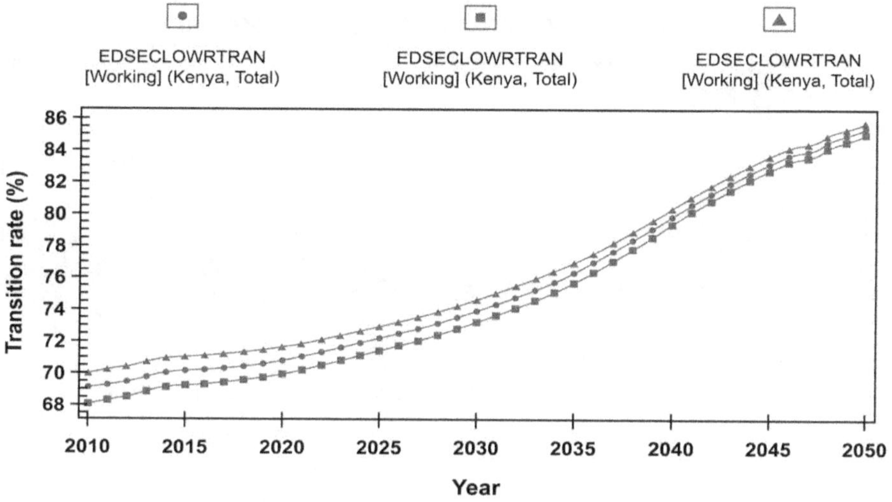

Source: Generated from International Futures Model [Computer Software, Version 7.00], 2017. Retrieved from http://www.ifs.du.edu/

However, the bigger challenge is keeping those enrolled in secondary schools in school until they graduate, that is, boosting the upper secondary education survival rate. Although many factors determine this survival rate, a key reason for dropping out of school has been due to lack of school fees and the inability to meet the myriad of other school related costs such as school infrastructure development.

The burden of infrastructure development, which is often higher than other fees paid for education in public schools, has shifted from the government to households—the government mainly subsidises tuition by paying teachers. Given the generally low GDP per capita and considering other basic demands such as food and shelter, secondary education becomes a luxury to many low-income households. Much more than just constructing the 560 extra secondary schools outlined in Vision 2030 is required. The government can ease the burden on households by increasing its expenditure on upper secondary education—reversing the current negative trend shown in figure 7.4 below.

Figure 7.4: Education expenditure per upper secondary as a percentage of GDP per capita

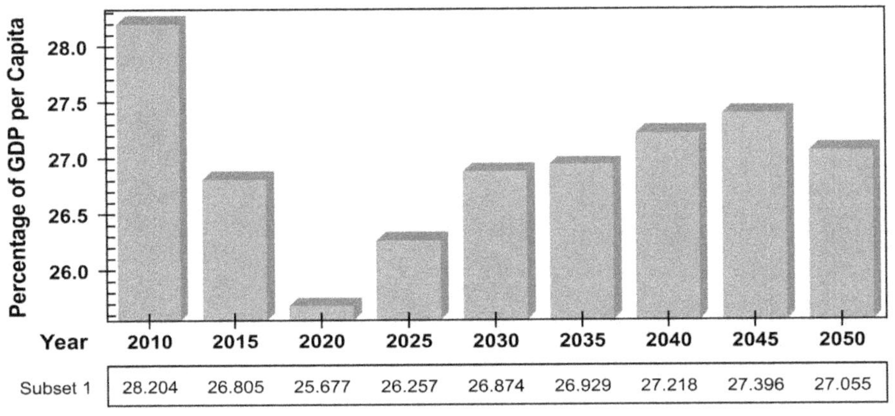

Source: Generated from International Futures Model [Computer Software, Version 7.00], 2017. Retrieved from http://www.ifs.du.edu/

The IFs model projects additional public expenditure after 2020. If some of this government budget is directed at school infrastructure development, it would enhance the secondary school survival rates and the quality of education. The latter can be improved by improving both the teacher to student ratio and using technology to deliver content. The benefit of this would be twofold; increase efficiency and prepare students for the increasingly technologically driven labour market after school.

The expectation is that as a higher education attainment is achieved in the populace, there would be an increase in the human capital stock. Subsequently, GDP and GDP per capita would grow. There would also be equality in the distribution of this growth. This means that there would be more disposable income at the household level that could be invested in education. Consequently, the proportion of government expenditure on secondary education could be reduced with time. A higher expenditure on education will lead to a more than proportionate increase in MFP rates given Kenya's relatively high human capital contribution to the MFP rate.

In the words of Charles Darwin, 'in the long history of humankind (and animal kind too) those who learned to collaborate and improvise most effectively have prevailed'. This is not to downplay what is required to accomplish the desired quantity and quality of secondary education—it will be hard for the government to realise it on its own. As seen earlier in this book, since independence, Kenya has relied on markets for development. These partnerships are alluded to in Vision 2030 by the mention of the use of private partnerships as a strategy. The government's ability to build effective and mutually beneficial partnerships with the private sector in education will be key. These partnerships will take the form of creating a conducive environment for secondary education investments in a manner that serves the interest of both the private sector and the government.

Cost effective and scalable model demonstrations already exist locally, such as the Bright International Academies that reportedly offer good quality primary school education. The government should encourage more of such private sector models that require less public investment. However, like with any other market, the government should play an active facilitation and oversight role in education. It would need to effectively govern this sector to assure the quality of the education being delivered. One way of doing this would be by certifying and regularly checking on the mode of teaching. Even more important would be having a credible method of gauging the knowledge and skills attained by the students.

Conclusion

While the Vision 2030 policy interventions and strategies show some prospects for success, as seen thus far in the *Working* scenario forecasts, these will not enable Kenya to realise sustainable and inclusive development. As illustrated in Chapter 6, all four policy proposals have better prospects of realising lasting and inclusive growth than the interventions and strategies under Vision 2030. Halving the total fertility rate and tripling the upper secondary education survival rates present the best prospects for Kenya to realise the looming demographic dividend, and to achieve sustainable and inclusive development. Noteworthy is that the economic growth goal of 10 per cent per annum remains unachievable and unsustainable even under the proposed policy interventions.

The aim in this section was to identify an intervention or a combination of interventions that would make a significant contribution towards realising sustainable and inclusive development in Kenya. While the impact of each of the two interventions proposed here might appear minimal, combining them would yield much higher impacts than forecasted. The scenario analysis results show that upper secondary education is a high leverage point for driving inclusive growth. Given the relatively long pay-back periods typical of human capital development interventions, it would take time for the results to show. However, in the long-term, the impact would be positive and significant if these policy interventions were sustained.

Furthermore, the proposed interventions, that is, halving the total fertility rate and tripling the survival rate of upper secondary education, are far from exhaustive. However, they point to where the greatest future developmental impacts are likely to come from. Obviously, these interventions will require backward and forward linkages in the form of other policy interventions to ensure effectiveness. For instance, secondary education is dependent on primary education and on health. Additionally, sustained investment in education by households, and particularly the poor, will depend on both the real and perceived future returns on education in the form of employment opportunities. To the poor, the motivation is never education for knowledge sake, but education that translates into improved incomes and a better life.

Enhancing opportunities for employment will thus be crucial for Kenya to realise its demographic dividend. The relevant interventions need to be identified and implemented in tandem with the human capital development interventions proposed here. Currently, most employment is informal. Informal employment has grown consistently over the decades since independence while formal employment has shrunk.[1] Policy interventions that foster business growth will be important, such as creating a conducive environment for doing business that accommodates both the local informal organisations and global organisations.

Access to seed capital has been shown to be the biggest limitation to starting small businesses, and hence self-employment. To address this constraint, the government needs to create and maintain an environment for innovation through appropriate and right-paced regulation that supports rather than stifles new financing ideas. It could also catalyse these innovations through tax incentives for successful innovation and aptly designed risk funds, rather than the creation of youth funds that hardly revolve. Kenya has the opportunity to work with its development partners to create employment opportunities for the youth, such as Mastercard Foundation through its Young Africa Works programme.

Furthermore, the extremely dynamic nature of the world necessitates continuous scanning of the global environment. This will enable us to spot any weak signals and make the necessary adjustments to the policies, to fine tune their implementation, or to develop new ones. This vigilance will ensure that the country remains on track to realising sustainable and inclusive development. It is important to remember that the IFs model is a systemic global economic model. None of its modules stand in isolation of the others and interventions undertaken in other parts of the globe would eventually manifest locally.

The proposed interventions thus serve as maps to guide Kenya into the future with the appreciation that one can never fully comprehend the impact of human actions.[2] National and global developments in each of these areas would need to be closely monitored as part of the day-to-day policy implementation. Issue monitoring units or departments within the relevant government ministries would need to be created to spearhead this activity.

Successful implementation of these policy interventions would demand leadership that exemplifies commitment and strategic foresight, that is, the ability to mentally step into the future and back-cast to the present.[3] This would enable the leadership to plan and act to bring about the desired future. This kind of leadership understands that the economy is comprised of interrelated, interacting, and interdependent components that form the complex and unifying whole and that every part of the system must be present for the system to function optimally.[4]

Such leaders are systemic thinkers who can strike the right balance between short-term and long-term thinking and gains. This understanding of systems and their behaviour over time helps strategic leaders to anticipate future implications or consequences of events that are happening in the present and to act now to create a desired future outcome.[5]

Strategic leaders have the capacity to anticipate where the global economy is headed and to catch weak signals of emerging change at the periphery long before it becomes a reality.[6] This ability would allow the country sufficient lead time to respond to the evolving issues before they become a reality. An example of this is the looming demographic dividend or bomb, depending on how one looks at it. Such leadership would be able to create the country's future from an understanding of the future and not its past, going by Werner Erhard's wisdom.

In the words of Buckminster Fuller, a twentieth century futurist and a comprehensive thinker, the strategic leader is an anticipatory thinker or 'trim tab'—the small rudder that is used to turn the larger rudder of giant ships (Gabel & Walker, 2006). This type of leader understands the power of leverage and can use small and strategic interventions to cause a huge and profound change in the system or economy.[7] He [or she] possesses the ability to identify the right leverage points and to intervene at these points for optimal results.[8]

As a 'trim tab,' the anticipatory leader: (a) knows what ship he is steering (understands what he wants to change); (b) knows what direction his ship is currently heading in (can see the 'big picture' and is able align the direction with the destination); (c) knows what outside winds, tides, currents, and events are affecting his ship; (d) is able to decide where his ship ought to be going (can change direction midstream if necessary); (e) is able to navigate successfully despite changing tides (is creative and innovative); (f) knows where to exert pressure for greater leverage (is an ardent issue manager); and (g) he knows how to exert the pressure for greater efficiency (envisions and plans) (Gabel & Walker, 2006, p. 41).

Strategic leaders can study the behaviour of systems by looking at trends and patterns to determine where the system could be headed, and are open to learning from their mistakes and from other players in the system (Meadows, 2002; Meadows, 2008). In the words of Winston Churchill, for great leaders 'success is not final, failure is not fatal: it is the courage to continue that counts'. Lastly, the proposed policy interventions would not work in a vacuum. As Harris Mule, who was an economist during the formulation of the Sessional Paper No. 10 in 1965 and served under its mastermind, argued, 'policies are formulated and implemented within an institutional framework'.[9] The lack of the right institutional framework has been one of Kenya's biggest struggles in implementing its development strategies. While some progress has been made in this area following the promulgation of the new constitution, a lot more needs to be done to yield the effectiveness that is needed to realise Kenya's development mission.

The development roadmap that was drawn in 1965 is as valid today as it was then. We have made some progress down this road, but we still have a long way to go before we reach our sustainable and inclusive development destination. I hope that understanding what the future might look like and knowing how to create that desired future renews the courage, determination, and enthusiasm to keep moving until we reach our destination.

As stated in the Introduction, please note that the analysis and projections presented in this book do not take into consideration the impact of the COVID-19 pandemic on the Kenyan economy, which happened subsequently.

References

[1]   Kimenyi, M., Mwega, F. & Ndung'u, N. (2016). 'The African lions: Kenya country case study'. *Brookings Institute.*

[2]   Hughes, B. B. & Hillebrand, E. E. (2016). *Exploring and Shaping International Futures.* Routledge Taylor and Francis Group, NY. Kindle Edition.

[3]   Cornish, E. (2004). *Futuring: The Exploration of the Future.* World Future Society. Kindle Edition.

[4]   Senge, P. (2014, Dec 15). 'Systems thinking for a better world'. *Aalto Systems Forum 2014.*

[5]   (Anderson & Johnson, 1997; Senge, 2014; Dean, 2014; Kauffman, 1980). *System Thinking Basics: From Concepts to Causal Loops.* Peagus Communication Inc. Waltham, MA; Senge, P. (2014, Dec 15). Systems thinking for a better world. *Aalto Systems Forum 2014;* Dean, S. (2014, Oct 31). System thinking and UX part 2: System traps and advice on how to avoid them; Kauffman, D. L. (1980). Systems One: An Introduction to Systems Thinking. *TLH Associates Inc.* St. Paul.

[6]   Schoemaker, P., Krupp, S. & Howland, S. (2013). Strategic leadership: The essential skills. *January–February 2013 Harvard Business Review;* Ashley, W. & Morrison, J. (1995). *Anticipatory Management: 10 Power Tools for Achieving Excellence into the 21st Century.* Leesburg, VA: Issue Action Publishing; Gabel, M. & Walker, J. (2006). The anticipatory leader: Buckminster Fuller's principles for making the world work. *Futurist. Sep/Oct2006, Vol. 40 Issue 5,* p39-44.

[7]   Gabel, M. & Walker, J. (2006). 'The anticipatory leader: Buckminster Fuller's principles for making the world work'. *Futurist. Sep/Oct2006, Vol. 40 Issue 5,* p39-44; Meadows, D. (1997). Places to intervene in a system. *Whole Earth, Winter 1997.*

[8]   Meadows, D. (1997). Places to intervene in a system. *Whole Earth, Winter 1997.*

[9]   Mule, H. (2004). Mboya as a Minister. *Tom Mboya Foundation.*